SASKATCHEWAN ROUGHRIDERS

The Players, the History & the Fans

Graham Kelly

OVER
TIME
BOOKS

The Publisher: OverTime Books is an imprint of Éditions de la Montagne Verte

Library and Archives Canada Cataloguing in Publication

Kelly, Graham, 1942–
     Saskatchewan Roughriders: the players, the history, & the fans /
     Graham Kelly.

Includes bibliographical references.
ISBN 978-1-897277-23-2

     1. Saskatchewan Roughriders (Football team)–History. I. Title.

GV948.3.S37K45 2012   796.335'6409712445   C2012-901085-5

Project Director: Deanna Howell
Editor: Kathy van Denderen
Photo Credits: City of Regina Archives
Front Cover Background: © iStockphoto
Front Cover Football: © (2008) Chris Hart / iStockphoto

We acknowledge the financial support of the Government of Canada through the Canada Book Fund (CBF) for our publishing activities.

 Canadian   Patrimoine
Heritage   canadien

PC: 1

Contents

Dedication

To my wonderful grandchildren,
Zaria and Zephran

Acknowledgements

I want to thank all past and present players, coaches and officials of the Saskatchewan Roughriders who have been so helpful to me over the years.

I would like to thank former sports editor Phil Johnson and managing editor Pete Mossey and present publisher Mike Hertz of the *Medicine Hat News* for giving me the opportunity to write a weekly column on the Canadian Football League for the last 40 years.

I would like to thank the late Dennis Johnson for believing in me and publishing my books, *Grey Cup: A History* (1999), *Grey Cup Glory* (2003) and *Go Stamps Go* (2010).

I am deeply indebted to Stan Schwartz, the executive vice-president of the Calgary Stampeders for his constant friendship and support.

I want to thank Lorne Dunsmore, the greatest Roughrider fan of them all, for his insights and advice.

I especially wish to thank my publisher, OverTime Books, and my editor, Kathy van Denderen.

And finally, from the bottom of my heart, I wish to express my love and gratitude to my dear wife of 49 years, Lorena, my sons Robert and David, daughters-in-law Stacy and Janice, granddaughters Kassidy and Kaitlind and grandson Russell.

Introduction

If there is such a thing as "Canada's" team, it would be the Saskatchewan Roughriders. Formed in 1910, the Roughriders have survived two world wars, the Great Depression and the longest playoff drought in league history. They have won only three Grey Cups and have lost a few under the most bizarre circumstances, such as the 13th man in 2009. Although the team mascot is Gainer the Gopher, it should be a cat. This is an organization with nine lives.

Roughrider fans are the best in the country. Despite only one first-place finish since 1976, the team drew an average of 25,000 fans, while at the same time the population of the province was showing only marginal growth and the farm economy was always in crisis.

About eight percent of the population of Regina attends Roughrider home games. About 20 percent of those gracing the stands at Mosaic Stadium come from the rest of the province. If Calgary and Edmonton did as well, their stadiums would have to be expanded to accommodate more than 80,000 fans!

Impressive as the Riders' home fan base may be, more fans live beyond the province's borders than within. When the Roughies play in Calgary and Edmonton, they do so before a sea of green. General managers of the two Alberta teams have always tried to get the Riders scheduled late in the season, knowing those who wear the green will always come out no matter the circumstances or the weather.

Said Stampeders GM Rogers Lehew in 1965, "What irritated me was there were so many Rider fans in Calgary. You'd think if you lived here 40 years, you could at least be a Stampeder fan."

My family in Airdrie is typical. My son Rob, his wife Stacy and their children Kassidy and Russell are Calgary Stampeder season-ticket holders and wear red-and-white for all the games except when the Roughriders are in town, at which time Rob and Russell are decked out in green, Stacy and Kassidy in red. Pre-game tailgating at McMahon Stadium features a mixture of both team colours, with fans good-naturedly kidding each other and having a great time. In 2006, when the Stamps banned Gainer the Gopher from the Western semifinal, two-and-a-half-year-old Russell showed up wearing a Gainer the Gopher suit. It worked. The Riders beat the home team 30–21.

To grow up in Regina is to be a football fan. Rider pride is as ingrained as a love of prairie sunsets. Once a Rider fan, always a Roughrider fan—through the glory years of Ron Lancaster and George Reed or the longest period of post-season futility in CFL history. I grew up eight blocks from Taylor Field. My friends and I spent hours on the high school grounds playing football, always pretending, of course, we were Roughriders.

The first real job I had was Roughrider water boy for the 1956–57 seasons. The general manager was Dean Griffing who had started the Calgary Stampeders 11 years earlier; the coach was Frank Filchock. The 1956 edition was one of the best clubs in CFL history, losing narrowly in the playoffs to the greatest team of all time, the Edmonton Eskimos of Jackie Parker, Johnny Bright, Rollie Miles and Normie Kwong.

Over the winter, several players retired and four all-stars were killed in a plane crash. The Riders went from a 10–6 contender to a 3–12–1 also-ran in 1957. When Griffing and Filchock were fired at the end of that disastrous season, so was I. I was 15 at the time, and in two short years I learned a great deal about pro football and life.

My dad, W.A. "Alex" Kelly, introduced me to the game. My first memory of a football game was in 1950, sneaking into Taylor Field with my brother Alex in the fourth quarter when the gate was open and the guard was gone, finding my dad and watching Tom "Citation" Casey of the Winnipeg Blue Bombers. I recall being sick in bed in 1951 when Mom and Dad came home and told me about the thrilling 19–18 Western final playoff win over Edmonton. My mother, Win, wore a white chrysanthemum with green ribbons.

While it is true the Green Machine wins a Grey Cup about once every generation, the Roughriders are never dull. What other team ever lost a crucial game when they were ahead with no time left on the clock?

Who else began a playoff game before a half-empty stadium only to finish with a full house? Or who had a coach who wore a tuque in July and in practice threw the ball blind-folded to his receivers during passing drills? Or lost a game because of a thunderstorm? Or won a playoff game because of the water boy? Or had three Hall of Fame coaches in seven years and still set new records for futility? What other team lost fan support because the general manager wouldn't take off his hat?

Through thick and thin (mostly thin), good times and bad (mostly bad), the love affair between Saskatchewan fans and their football team continues unabated and is unique in all of sport. In a way, the Riders are the personification of the Canadian Football League, an organization that's often at death's door but always able to defy the odds and live to play another day.

No one has worked harder for success than those who manage and support the Saskatchewan Roughriders. They hold pancake breakfasts, tailgate parties, "Meet the Players" nights, $300-a-plate dinners and an incredibly successful annual lottery conducted by legendary executive Tom Shepherd. During the offseason, coaches and players attend countless sportsman's dinners throughout the "Land of Living Skies."

When the club has been in danger of folding, fans rally around the team in the proud pioneering spirit that made the province great, except instead of holding a barn-building bee or helping an ailing neighbour get a crop off in time, the people in the district save their football team. They do it because nobody can imagine Saskatchewan without the Roughriders.

Thanks to the combination of the brilliant team president/CEO Regina boy Jim Hopson and success on the field that saw the team make the playoffs 10 straight years from 2001 to 2010 and appear in three Grey Cups in four years, 12 years into the 21st century, the Rider granaries are full with one bumper crop after another. But the good folks of Saskatchewan know full well that just when everything is coming up number one Durham, the lightning hits the outhouse and it's back to square one. That happened in 2011.

Fortunately, the Roughriders are as tough, determined and resilient as the people they represent.

It is not hyperbole to suggest that if Canada's team ceased to exist, the CFL would soon follow it into oblivion, and we as a nation would lose a precious part of our cultural heritage. The Saskatchewan Roughriders are more than just a football team. They are a treasured institution, loved by Canadians from coast to coast. Saskatchewan and Canada without the Roughriders? Like Paris without the Eiffel Tower. Unthinkable.

Green is the colour; the Roughriders are the team. Canada's team.

Chapter One

The Good Old Days

The Regina Rugby Club was born at a meeting on Tuesday, September 6, 1910, at City Hall.

The September 7 issue of *The Morning Leader* ran the headline:

RUGBY FOOTBALL IS NEXT ON LIST

Regina Club Organized

First Practice Called For Tomorrow

> *A list of invitees to the first workout at Railway Park was published. On Monday, September 12, officers were chosen. The premier of Saskatchewan, Walter Scott, was named Honorary Patron. Dr. Lorne Steele was the first president, W.G. Allen, vice-president and W.J. Bright, secretary-treasurer.*

Five days later, at the King's Hotel, Steele and Bright met with delegates from Moose Jaw and Saskatoon to form a provincial league. Regina and Moose Jaw were in, but Saskatoon was unable to make a commitment. The Regina Rugby Club looked forward to exhibition games against Moose Jaw.

The great tradition of Saskatchewan football began a few weeks later on October 1 in Moose Jaw. A special train left the Queen City at 1:30 PM for the Mill City to the west. Excursion tickets were $1.75.

The first game the Regina Rugby Club ever played was a loss, 16–6. *The Morning Leader* gave, in part, the following account in its October 3 edition:

> *Moose Jaw, October 2—The Regina Rugby Team came, saw but did not conquer the local rugby fourteen yesterday afternoon at the baseball grounds. The capital city boys were accompanied by 150 lusty-lunged supporters who made themselves heard throughout the game. The Moose Jaw folks turned out 600 strong to cheer their favourite sons on to victory…*

> *The score, 16–6, scarcely indicates the play as the Regina boys were in the game all the time and had the play in the Moose Jaw territory a good part of the game. The one great advantage the home team had was in weight. Every man on their line weighed 175 pounds, averaging about 20 pounds a man heavier than the Regina boys. The heavyweights certainly took advantage, repeatedly bucking for downs…*

> *The Moose Jaw 14 got away with a lot of offside interference on Referee Du Moulin. The latter, a few years ago was one of the best rugby officials in Canada but he seems to have neglected his football education since coming to the province. At one stage of the game, Scott of the Regina team so strongly objected to his decisions that he was ruled off for two minutes...*

Blaming the referee has been a time-honoured tradition of Saskatchewan football right from the beginning.

Members of the North-West Mounted Police (NWMP) Rugby football team (May 26, 1891). Regina's first organized rugby football team were members of the NWMP, who travelled to Winnipeg to play two games against the Winnipeg Football Club in 1888.

Moose Jaw scored two touchdowns and a convert to lead 11–0 at the half. They added an unconverted touchdown.

Regina replied with a single and a five-point TD.

The Moose Jaw 14?

Today's football fan would have found the game played in 1910 exceedingly strange, with 14-man sides and the practice of "heeling," whereby the ball was put into play by a linesman kicking it back to the quarterback with his heel. Twelve men a side and snapping the ball back through a player's legs did not become part of the game until 1921.

The quarterback was one of several players who handled the ball. Until the forward pass was introduced in 1929 by Jerry Seiberling and Ralph Losie of the Calgary Tigers in a game against Edmonton, quarterbacks scarcely resembled their modern counterparts. The positions were backs, halves, quarter, scrimmage, outside and insides. In 1912, the back was called the flying wing.

The scoring system was also different. Before 1921, "touchdown" meant the end of a play because the ball had been touched down on the ground. Carrying the ball over the goal line was a "try" and was worth five points. The convert was worth one point as it is today, but it was kicked from the 35-yard line. A field goal was four points, a free punt through the uprights was three points and a penalty kick was two. A "rouge" was a single point scored off a punt or a missed field goal when the receiving player was tackled in the end zone. A single was scored when the ball was kicked to or over the dead ball line in the end zone.

Earning a first down by gaining 10 yards on three successive plays hasn't changed, but back then you could make a first down, one time only, by losing 20 yards in three downs.

The Regina Rugby Club went winless in their first year of operation, the only time in their distinguished history they failed to win a game. The Saskatchewan champion Moose Jaw Tigers were supposed to play the Winnipeg Rowing Club for the Western Canadian championship but were told that because they weren't a member of the amateur association they were ineligible.

Only Regina could compete for Western football supremacy. And compete they did with great success.

The original colours worn by the Regina Rugby Club were purple and gold. In 1911 they changed to blue and white to match the Regina Amateur Athletic Association. The following year they adopted black and red, the colours they carried into gridiron battle until 1948.

The first victory in the history of the Regina Rugby Club came on September 23, 1911, over Moose Jaw, 15–11, at Regina's Dominion Park. The year 1911 also saw Saskatoon take part in the Saskatchewan league for the first time. They opened at home on September 30. The headline in *The Morning Leader* told a surprising tale:

RUGBY GAME AT SASKATOON ENDS IN AN UNSEEMLY RIOT LED BY POLICE.

REGINA PLAYER ARRESTED AND SOAKED

Score was 14 to 0 for Regina when mob broke out on the grounds.

SASKATOON POLICE LED ON THE MOB

Men Who Should Have Maintained Order Were Cause Of Riot.

With the game slipping away, Saskatoon Berry Pickers manager Harry Trusdale, a city police officer, saw an opportunity when a Regina player hit one of his players from behind. He charged onto the field to arrest the Regina player, Adamson, who protested loudly and profanely. The Chief of Police entered the fray threatening to take the entire visiting team into custody.

But then it was the cavalry to the rescue. Four Mounties arrived on the scene and whisked the Regina boys to safety. Adamson was arraigned by Saskatoon's "finest" in police court before a magistrate and fined $5.00 and cost.

When the shenanigans broke out, the referee called the game without declaring a winner. League officials later awarded the win to Regina who finished the season in first place with a mark of 3–1.

In 1912, the Regina Rugby Club under the tutelage of Fred Ritter won their first of four straight Western championships. They were 3–1 that year. They would not lose another regular-season game until 1929 when they were 3–1–1. They then went undefeated until 1936.

As was often the case over the first 50 years of Canadian football, controversy dogged Regina's first crack at the Western Canada championship and the Hugo Ross Trophy. (Winnipeg realtor Hugo Ross donated the trophy. It became a memorial trophy a year later when he went down with the *Titanic*.)

The post-season practice in those days was to guarantee the visiting team a share of the gate receipts to offset their travelling costs. Regina's opposition was the Winnipeg Rowing Club. Concerned about bad weather, a muddy field and Regina bringing more players and officials than necessary, Winnipeg, much to the chagrin of their own fans, said they would rather default than offer Regina a guarantee in writing to cover expenses. By the same token, they refused their opponent's guarantee to play in Regina.

"We won't take the cup by default," Fred Ritter told *The Morning Leader* on November 6. "We'll go and play them on their own grounds and we'll pay our expenses."

On November 9, 1912, Regina won their first Western championship, 5–0.

The Morning Leader printed several "Extras" that day that were sold out almost as soon as they reached the hands of the newsboys. Everywhere on Saturday evening, in the stores, the theatres, at private parties, everyone was talking about the great victory over Winnipeg. The following morning, one minister dispensed with his sermon to talk about the Regina Rugby Club.

The good citizens of the Queen City were as proud as punch.

The team went undefeated against Moose Jaw and Saskatoon in 1913, putting them into the Western semifinal against the Edmonton Eskimos at Dominion Park on November 8. Led by Freddy Wilson, Fred Ritter and Punk Thompson, the Queen City boys sent Deacon White's crew down to defeat 19–7. Ritter sustained a serious knee injury but stayed in the game until the end. In those days, the 14 starters were on the field the entire game. There were no substitutions for injuries.

Regina prevailed at home in the Western championship game, shutting out the Winnipeg Rowing Club 29–0 to retain the Western title and the Ross Memorial Trophy.

Freddy Wilson was the star. In the first few minutes, he punted, ran under the ball and fell over the Winnipeg goal line for a touchdown. It would be hard to imagine why the early game was exciting without passing. The answer was simple. Instead of the pass, players punted to teammates streaking down the field, catching the ball on a dead run.

After vanquishing the Winnipeggers, the streets of Regina were filled with revellers marching through town with burning brooms as torch lights. After the game, as was customary in those days, a banquet was held at the Commercial Club attended by the two teams as well as leading citizens and sportsmen of the community.

Winnipeg manager Eddie Chown congratulated the winners while bemoaning the lack of fan support for his team. He praised the winners for having everyone in town behind them. A downtown parade followed the dinner.

Football excitement grew when fans learned of the challenge of the Hamilton Tigers and their $1000 guarantee to go down east and play for the Grey Cup. Disappointment swept the city when the team said no.

Regina team manager Jack Mitchell explained that several players couldn't get time off work to go, and he didn't think they had much of a chance to win with Fred Ritter injured. The final deciding factor was the way the Grey Cup championship was arranged—the trophy was awarded to teams only from the intercollegiate or interprovincial leagues, both in the East. Even if Regina had won, they would not have been recognized as dominion champions.

During the first week of August 1914, hostilities broke out in Europe, and the Great War was underway. No province was more patriotic than Saskatchewan, and young men rushed to sign up to beat the Boche.

The 1914 football season began on September 26 with Regina defeating the Moose Jaw Robin Hoods 34–5. They followed that up with wins over Saskatoon, Moose Jaw and Saskatoon Varsity. Regina won the Western championship by beating Winnipeg 20–12. The stars were team captain Frank Townsend and Freddy Wilson.

In 1915, the war settled into the deadly stalemate that would characterize the conflict until the bitter end. More and more young men joined up and left Saskatchewan. Still, the Regina Rugby Club was able to field a team of veterans and won their season opener on September 25 against their only opponent Moose Jaw, 15–0. Two days later, Fred Ritter left the team for a coaching position in the U.S. Regina beat the Moose Jaw Robin Hoods four more times before facing the Calgary Canucks in the Western final at Dominion Park. A crowd of 1800, many in khaki, saw the home team prevail 17–1.

The 1916 season opened on Thanksgiving at Dominion Park with Tare Rennebohm scoring two touchdowns to lead Regina to a 23–2 win over Saskatoon. Rennebohm spent all his adult life with the team. After retiring as a player in 1927, he was the general manager, manager and finally equipment manager until his death in

1957. Tare suffered a heart attack in the last game of that season in Winnipeg. He died a few days later. His son had worked alongside him in the dressing room and took over when his father passed over to that great gridiron in the sky. Tare's wife sewed numbers on team jerseys and repaired them when necessary.

In Saskatoon on October 21, 1916, Regina won its 28th straight regular-season game 13–6, even though they were missing several stars. Other players who weren't in good shape came in shortly before the game. By this time, most of the players were in the army and on leave to play the game. Tare Rennebohm, Heinie Rogers, Jerry Crapper and Freddie Wilson led the way.

Moose Jaw didn't play that year and, on the basis of sweeping the series with Saskatoon, Regina was proclaimed the provincial champion.

And so ended the first phase of Saskatchewan football. From their inception through 1916 the Regina Rugby Club posted 20 wins against 5 losses. From 1911 to 1916, their mark was 20–2, and from 1913 to 1916, 14–0. They won four Western championships and five provincial titles. But after the 1916 season, play was suspended for the duration of the war.

The Glory Years

The Regina Rugby Club reassembled in September 1919. They were about to embark on one of the most incredible journeys in the history of sport. In the 16 seasons between 1919 and 1936, the team lost only six regular-season games. They finished 11 seasons undefeated, including four in a row, from 1919 to 1923.

Regina opened the 1919 season in Moose Jaw, trouncing the Millers 40–6 and then beating them again at Exhibition Park in Regina 36–1. They followed up with two lopsided wins over the University of Saskatchewan and a shutout against Saskatoon and finished the regular season at 5–5, having outscored their opponents 180–7. Coached by Jerry Crapper and Frank Townsend, the Regina Rugby Club was one of the greatest football teams in the 14-man era.

Next up was the Winnipeg Victorias on November 1 in Regina. Every Vic was a war hero and had been out of the game since 1914.

Regina's veteran club was fast, and they had an excellent quarterback in Neil "Piffles" Taylor, after whom the football stadium was named in 1947. Other stars were flying wings Nels Newbatt, Al Urquhart and Fred Wilson. Tare Rennebohm was a terror on the line. Regina won 12–0. In attendance were members of the 28th battalion, who were in Regina for a reunion.

Today, recruiting football players is a costly, sophisticated business. Not so in 1920. To assemble the team for that season, an announcement was placed in the September 1 edition of *The Leader* that the first practice would take place at the Exhibition Grounds at 5:15 PM. Canadian football accommodated the players' full-time jobs by scheduling practices after work. Young men were able to establish themselves in their life's work while enjoying a football career at the same time. CFL teams have gone back to that tradition.

The year 1920 marked the first time the Regina Rugby Club sold season tickets. When you bought a membership in the club, it came with admission to all senior and junior home games of the Saskatchewan Rugby Union. Season-ticket and membership drives have become a regular part of Roughrider football ever since, with new variations in the form of shares in the club and Saskatchewan Roughrider licence plates.

A new team joined the football wars that year, the Regina Boat Club. They practised at Regina College on Scarth Street and College Avenue and held their chalk talks at the boat club on Wascana Lake.

That year, the Regina Rugby Club had a surprisingly tough time with the cross-town upstarts but still prevailed 11–2 and 12–8. They beat Moose Jaw twice and wrapped up the provincial crown by shutting out Saskatoon 35–0.

They vanquished the Calgary Tigers 13–1 in the Western semifinal and prepared to face Winnipeg in Regina. Because several Vics couldn't make the trip, the team defaulted, and Regina was declared the 1920 Western champion.

Rule Changes

A new day was about to dawn in Canadian football. In 1921, the teams reduced the number of starters from 14 to 12. Rosters were set at 18 a side with substitutions allowed. The unearned try was eliminated, making all touchdowns worth five points. The ball was to be snapped back instead of heeled, and the quarterback was allowed to cross the line of scrimmage.

And for the first time, the Western champion challenged for the Grey Cup.

The first Grey Cup was played on December 4, 1909, when the Toronto Parkdales lost to the University of Toronto, 26–6. The Varsity squad did not receive the Cup until the following year. The Governor General of Canada, Earl Grey, wanted the trophy to go to the Canadian senior hockey champions, but Montréal businessman Sir Hugh Montagu Allan beat him to the punch and put up a mug himself. The Allan Cup is Canada's oldest hockey trophy.

Although Lord Grey agreed to award the trophy to the football champions, his staff forgot to have it made. The oversight was corrected—Birks jewellers got the job done for $48—and the Grey Cup was presented to the University of Toronto.

Grey likely never saw a Canadian football game. He returned to England in 1911 and died on August 29, 1917. He is best remembered for an off-hand gesture of the donation of a trophy that bears his name.

For the people of Saskatchewan, the Grey Cup is as important as the Holy Grail itself.

The big event of the 1921 season was an exhibition game in September between the Regina Rugby Club and the Hamilton Tigers. Grandstands holding 3000 were placed along the gridiron and as many tickets were printed.

The eastern team arrived in the Queen City on September 19. The Rotary Club threw a luncheon for them and they were entertained at the Capital Theatre, which had opened only weeks earlier at 12th Avenue and Scarth Street. The Tigers dined on duck, courtesy of the Regina Rugby Club at 8:00 PM, following the game. All citizens were invited to the dinner to be held at the Regina Trading Company's banquet hall.

The game was played at the Mounted Police barracks. The weather put a damper on ticket sales, so to meet Hamilton's guarantee, teams of volunteers canvassed the entire community and sold 600 additional tickets.

The contest was a dandy with Hamilton winning 15–6. Tigers coach Liz Marriott praised the home team as the toughest they had faced.

In 1921, Regina beat Saskatoon for the provincial title, but the losers protested the game. The Saskatchewan Rugby Union ordered a new final, and Saskatoon won the contest 9–6. Later, Saskatoon lost to the Edmonton Eskimos, who in turn lost the first Western challenge for the Grey Cup 23–0 to the Toronto Argonauts.

Regina sailed through the 1922 season undefeated but once again faltered in post-season play, losing to Edmonton 13–8.

In 1923, the Regina Rugby Club lost a regular-season game for the first time in 11 years, dropping a 4–3 squeaker at Cairns Field in Saskatoon. A week earlier, they had handled the Quakers easily, winning 15–5 at Park Hughes (Regina) and then again in September by a score of 7–0. They also shut out Moose Jaw and then defeated the Winnipeg Vics 11–1 in Regina before a record crowd.

Grey Cup, Here We Come

The Saskatchewan Roughriders, nee Regina Roughriders, nee Regina Rugby Club, would represent the West in the Grey Cup 18 times through to 2010, with the first in 1923. Because the Canadian Rugby Union (CRU) was controlled by the Ontario and Québec Rugby Football Unions, the Grey Cup was played in the east, usually in Toronto, until 1955 when Vancouver became the first Western team to play host. Until then, the Western champions were at a disadvantage, not only from a home-field perspective but also because the trek east was expensive. Regina was the smallest city to compete for the national crown.

A committee of leading citizens was struck to raise funds for the trip. If the Grey Cup gate was big enough, all team expenses would be covered, but attendance depended on the weather, which could be rather nasty in December.

Regina's opponent would be Queen's University.

On the eve of their departure for Toronto, Regina coach Jack Eadie was moved to tell *The Leader:*

> If Queen's can show any marked superiority over the Regina club, they will be hailed as a team of supermen. The Regina club is without flaws or blemish, as far as I can see. They have taken their training more seriously than any team I have ever been interested in, and win or lose, they are sure to win the admiration of eastern fans next Saturday.

The team arrived in Toronto on November 28 and went straight to the King Edward Hotel. They held practices Thursday and Friday at Varsity Stadium and pronounced themselves ready for their moment of glory.

Opinion in Toronto was divided. Some thought Queen's would have trouble adjusting to Canadian Rugby Union rules, which were different in blocking and interference from university statutes. Others felt that Queen's stars Pep Leadlay and Harry Batstone would overwhelm the Westerners. They were right.

Queen's won 54–0. Regina was lucky to get nothing. The team was introduced to end runs and blocking, unheard of in Western Canadian football. Queen's devastating use of those tactics changed the game.

An important ritual following gridiron contests today is awarding the game ball to the most deserving individual on the winning team. In 1923, in a manner similar to a bride throwing her bouquet, the winning captain tossed the game ball in the air, and the players fought for possession. Bill Creighton fought off all challengers to come up with the ball, which he proudly took back to Regina.

On "Roughriders"

"Regina Rugby Club" was an awkward title. Every other team had a nickname. Early in 1924, the directors of the Regina Rugby Club decided they wanted a nick-name, too.

There is no definitive answer as to how the team got its new name. Since the 1890s, Ottawa footballers had been called the Rough Riders. In 1924, they dropped the name in favour of "Senators," and the Regina

Rugby Club picked up the name "Roughriders." Three years later, Ottawa re-adopted their former moniker.

According to some sources, the Roughriders name came about when a contingent of Canadian volunteers fought with Teddy Roosevelt in the Spanish-American war. His troops were called the Roughriders. The unit's colours were red and black. Some of those soldiers later played with the Regina and Ottawa football teams and wanted the Roughrider name. Roosevelt's Roughriders was one word, not two, so it seems that the Regina Roughriders were named after the heroes of the Spanish-American war, leaving the Ottawa Rough Riders to be named after the lumberjacks who rode logs down the Ottawa River.

For the first two years, it appeared the name change had been a bad idea. In 1924, the Roughriders had four victories against two losses, winning the provincial title in a hard-fought 6–2 win over Saskatoon at Cairns Field. After that win, the Riders went to Winnipeg a week later to meet the Vics. Even before the train left the station, Regina was in trouble: their star Howie Milne couldn't go because of business obligations.

Early in the first quarter, Jack Rowland cracked a bone in his left shoulder. But in a gritty display of courage, Rowland stayed in the game until halftime. He was soon joined in the infirmary by back Dan Dojack, centre half Scotty MacEachern and quarterback Pete Dolan. The final score was 22–5 for Winnipeg.

In 1925, the Riders played only one game, a win over Moose Jaw before losing the Western final to Winnipeg. Moose Jaw dropped out that season because they couldn't get players, and Saskatoon didn't field a team.

The following year, Regina beat Winnipeg and the University of Alberta to win the Western Canada championship. Because the East didn't declare a champion until December 4, scheduling the Grey Cup a week later, Regina refused to travel to Toronto. Ottawa won its second straight title, defeating the University of Toronto 10–7.

In 1927, the Roughriders beat Moose Jaw three times, knocked off Winnipeg and then eliminated the University of British Columbia. They declined to go down East because it was too expensive, and they didn't think they could win.

In 1928, the Roughriders, Moose Jaw Maroons, Winnipeg St. John's Saints and the Winnipeg Tammany Tigers formed the Tri-City Rugby Football Union. Howie Milne coached Regina with Tare Rennebohm as general manager.

The Roughriders went undefeated, outscoring the opposition 125–11, surrendering but a single touchdown.

On October 27 the Roughriders hosted the Saints in the final. A crowd of 1500 turned out in the bitter cold to watch Fred Wilson, Greg Grassick and quarterback Fritz Sandstrom lead the Riders to a 12–1 victory.

The trip down East was special because two Queen City teams could vie for a national championship. The Roughriders and the Regina Pats were eligible to represent the West in the battle for the Canadian

Junior Rugby Championship. Roughrider coach Alvin Ritchie also held that position with the Pats.

The Roughriders would face the Hamilton Tigers. Hailed in the *Toronto Star* as "the most formidable machine ever turned out by the Bengal breed in the jungle under the mountain." (There is a big hill in Hamilton they call a mountain.) The Cats were listed at five-to-one to win the Dominion championship.

Hamilton officials insisted the Grey Cup be played on their home field, even though 17,000 fans could be accommodated at Toronto's Varsity Stadium. The Hamilton grounds were enlarged to hold 12,000. Tiger officials were willing to sacrifice the difference in gate receipts to give their fans a chance to watch the game at home.

The Roughriders boarded the CPR Imperial Limited and headed for the Golden Horseshoe. Twenty players averaging 165 pounds and 25 years made the trip along with coach Ritchie, secretary-treasurer Tom Hanway, manager Tare Rennebohm and trainer Jiggs Durand.

The only major concern was Freddy Wilson's "slightly" fractured left ankle. Although the great veteran could walk without any trouble, running was another matter and kicking was probably out of the question.

The team arrived in Hamilton on Friday, November 30, and after checking into the Royal Connaught Hotel, proceeded to the Hamilton Amateur Athletic Association (HAAA) Grounds for a full-dress workout. They then retired to their quarters to await the big day.

The Hamilton Tigers were undefeated in 1928, outscoring opponents 146–20. Their stars were future Hall of Famers Huck Welch, Pep Leadlay, Cap Fears, Jimmy Simpson, Ernie Cox and coach Mike Bodden. This is not to say that some Regina players weren't worthy of Hall of Fame status. The selection committee members were mostly from the East when the Canadian Football Hall of Fame opened in Hamilton on June 19, 1963. Geographic bias prevailed until the late 20th century.

The only men from the era of 1910–48 who made it into the Hall as Roughriders were Al Ritchie, Piffles Taylor and Claire Warner, all as builders. The fact that the Roughriders didn't fare well in Grey Cup games confirmed the Eastern bias.

Although a hard-fought game, Hamilton won the 1928 Grey Cup 30–0. Ritchie didn't come home empty-handed, though. His Pats won the junior title.

The teams met again for the national championship in 1929. The Riders went 3–1–1 that year, including a scoreless tie in Saskatoon where Harry Pullen's Quakers became the first team in Regina football history to shut them out, even holding fullback "Dynamite" Eddie James, already being called great at the tender age of 21, to a handful of yards.

Against a background of headlines describing the stock market crash of 1929, the Roughriders downed Winnipeg St. John's 19–3. Heavy snow followed by a thaw had turned the field into a quagmire. The Riders felt a sense of vindication over St. John's. That season, for the first time in five years, they had lost a regular-season game, to St. John's, and some critics said they were on the decline. By handling a gutsy St. John's team in terrible playing conditions, they proved the kings of the gridiron weren't dead yet.

According to a decision made earlier by the Western Canadian Rugby Union (WCRU), the final would be played at the home of the winner of the semifinal between the Manitoba and Saskatchewan champions. Calgary objected, saying the final was supposed to be rotated among the three provinces, and it was Alberta's turn. The WCRU gave it to Regina because Alberta had declined to play in the Western final the last five years.

The Calgary Tigers were considered to have the best chance in years at dethroning the perennial champions. They were coached by former Rider great Fritz Sandstrom and led by Buck Billings, late of Toronto Balmy Beach. Their quarterback was master passer Gerry Seiberling from Drake University.

Yes, passer! In 1929, the forward pass came to Canadian football, although it wouldn't truly revolutionize the game for another 20 years. Perhaps that was because of the rules.

The passer had to be five yards back of the line of scrimmage when he threw the ball. The pass could not be completed within the opponent's 25-yard line. If the pass went incomplete, punting rules would be in effect, and the opponent could pick up the ball and run. Seiberling completed the first-ever forward pass to Ralph Losie in a game against Edmonton on September 21.

The Roughrider executive met at the King's Hotel on Monday, November 7, to plan for the Thanksgiving clash against Calgary. (In those days, Thanksgiving moved around the fall calendar.) To avoid the terrible playing conditions in Winnipeg, it was agreed they would keep the field swept clean of snow each day before the game. If it snowed on Thanksgiving, they would cover the gridiron with sawdust.

Because Calgary was given a hefty financial guarantee, ticket sales were pushed hard. Admission was one dollar for adults, 50 cents for students. For the first time, they charged for parking, a dollar per vehicle.

At dawn on Thanksgiving and Remembrance Day, November 11, there was a nip in the air and ice on the ground. Playing on a frozen, slippery field, Regina defeated Calgary 15–8 before 2000 fans. Dynamite Eddie James scored two touchdowns for the locals while Tiger Fritz Sandstrom was serving a 10-minute penalty. The most spectacular play of the day occurred when Fred Brown intercepted a Gerry Seiberling pass and returned it 55 yards for a touchdown. The Riders took advantage of their breaks and won the right to face the Tigers in Hamilton again.

Although the Riders hadn't employed the new weapon during the season and playoffs, they furiously practised the forward pass for two weeks in preparation for their rematch with Hamilton. Catching the Easterners by surprise, they gave them all they could handle before bowing 14–3, the smallest margin of defeat in East-West Cups to date.

Regina completed 8 of 11 passes. Southpaw and snapback Jersey Jack Campbell threw nine of them and Angus Mitchell two. There was no attempt to fool the opposition. When they wanted to pass, Campbell had a teammate assume his duties as centre and he took the snap and threw it. The Tigers didn't know how to defend it.

Hamilton threw only one pass. Huck Welch tossed the ball to Jimmy Simpson who lateralled to Cap Fears who ran to the end zone. The referee wouldn't allow it because Simpson caught the ball within the Regina 25-yard line. The first touchdown pass in Grey Cup history would have to wait.

As the citizenry celebrated New Year's Eve at the Saskatchewan or Kings hotels or at the brand-new, just opened Trianon Dance Palace, they had no idea of the terrible times that lay around the corner.

Chapter Two

The Depression and War

It was 1930. The Great Depression had arrived. The only activity that prospered during the Dirty Thirties was Roughrider football, with four Grey Cup appearances in five years.

Back at his familiar position as head coach was Al Ritchie, dubbed the "Silver Fox." An Ontario native who moved to Regina in 1911, Ritchie was everywhere on the sporting scene. His day job was with the Government of Canada Customs and Excise Department, but his true passion was coaching baseball, hockey and football. He won two Memorial Cups and that national junior football championship.

The Roughriders outscored their opponents 102–12 in 1930 and shut them out five times. Undefeated in the regular season, they defeated Winnipeg, Calgary and Vancouver in the playoffs to advance to the Grey Cup where they would face Toronto Balmy Beach.

Or would they?

As usual, the Eastern excursion was up in the air. The Rider executive debated whether or not to send the team to the Grey Cup for the third straight year. Weighing the cost against the fact that the West was making a better showing each year, they finally opted in favour of the trip, and the team resumed workouts.

Regina was even money to win their first Canadian championship because the Balmy Beachers were badly battered by the Bengals in the Eastern final. Most of the stars of the old gold-and-blue were on the limp.

The Riders pulled out of Union Station full of confidence, unlike their previous pilgrimages when they didn't know what to expect and were in awe of the entire experience. This time they thought they had a good chance to win the championship. Balmy Beach was considered an inferior team to the Tabbies who had outscored the opposition, 295–35. Hamilton blamed their playoff demise on injuries and fatigue brought about by their extensive exhibition tour of Western Canada. They played 12 games when most teams only played six.

During the Westerners' trip to Toronto, the Canadian Rugby Union issued a statement that the forward pass would not be permitted in the Grey Cup game because both teams had not used it during the season. While the Western Interprovincial Football Union (WIFU) and Big Four teams (Toronto Argos, Montréal, Hamilton Tigers, Ottawa Rough Riders) used it, Balmy Beach, champion of the Ontario Rugby Football Union (ORFU), did not. Apparently, the rule had been on the books all year, but for some reason, the executives in

Toronto "forgot" to let the WIFU know about it. This was an example of the underhanded tactics the East pulled on the West, so determined were they to prevent their country cousins from winning the Grey Cup.

The Roughriders almost won anyway. Balmy Beach prevailed 11–6. The game was played in a sea of mud made even worse by driving rain. But despite the horrific conditions, Fred Brown made history when he scored the West's first touchdown in Grey Cup competition.

For the first time, Regina football fans were able to follow the game on their radios. Through a special hook-up between CKCK in Regina and CHWC in Toronto, the game was broadcast from Varsity Stadium and relayed to Regina over a telephone hook-up, and Foster Hewitt of the *Toronto Star* did the play-by-play.

In addition to the broadcast that had been arranged by the *Leader-Post,* a complete progressive scoring summary was maintained on the paper's bulletin boards on the front of the building on Hamilton Street. At the same time, the switchboard operator handled a deluge of calls from fans anxious to know what was going on. The operators gave out the scores a few minutes after they had been heard on the radio in the CKCK studio located in the same building. A loudspeaker installed in a window on the first floor enabled the fans in the street to follow the game.

Regina fans were proud of their team. The 1930 edition of the Roughriders had put up the fiercest fight of any Western opponent. In four tries for the Cup, they had improved each time out, the margin of defeat shrinking. When the train bringing their heroes arrived at Union Station at 9:50 AM on December 10, a huge crowd was on hand to welcome them home.

In 1931, the Canadian Rugby Union approved the forward pass for all rugby unions, whether they wanted to use it or not, with the rule that if a team threw two consecutive incomplete passes, they would receive a 10-yard penalty. Also, if a pass went incomplete within the opponent's 25-yard line, the offensive team lost possession.

Another rule change affected converts. The scrimmage line for converts was changed from the 35-yard line to the five-yard line. In addition, a drop kick, place kick, run or pass could be used. Converts went from one extreme to the other. Before 1931, a converted touchdown was a rarity. From then until now, a miss is highly unusual.

The 1931 Roughriders went 5–0, clinching their seventh straight provincial crown by beating the Saskatoon Quakers in front of 1200 fans at Exhibition Park. Quarterback Angus Mitchell, nicknamed "Little Napoleon" because of his brilliant play calling, recorded the first touchdown pass ever scored in the Queen City. Scrimmaging on the Quaker 30, Fred Goodman took the snap and found Mitchell wide open. He ran unimpeded into the end zone.

Spectators were eager to see the Roughriders' new acquisition, American import Curt Schave, make his debut on a Regina gridiron, after starring for the teams in Moose Jaw and Saskatoon. The former North Dakota athlete lived up to his advance billing by dazzling the crowd with his running, kicking and passing ability.

The year 1930 marked the beginning of Western Canadian teams actively recruiting Americans to play for them.

Regina faced Manitoba champion Winnipeg St. John's in one semifinal; the Vancouver Athletic Club and the Calgary Altomah-Tigers clashed in the other.

Expecting a close tussle in Winnipeg, the Roughriders recorded their greatest triumph ever, outscoring their foe 47–5. In a glimpse of things to come, the Riders wore green-and-white uniforms, borrowed from the Winnipeg team because they had inadvertently left their own behind in Regina.

Calgary won the other semifinal but lost at Regina 26–2. In their fourth straight Grey Cup appearance, the Roughriders faced the Montréal Amateur Athletic Association Winged Wheelers in the Québec metropolis on December 5.

Montréal had adopted the forward pass in a big way, bringing in quarterback Warren Stevens from Syracuse. He threw to Frank Robinson for the first touchdown pass ever recorded in the Big Four.

As usual, the Grey Cup could not be played without conflict. This time it was about referees. Regina wanted one of the officials working the game to be from the west. Howie Milne was travelling east with the team, expecting to work the contest. Montréal, however, objected, citing lack of precedent for including a western official and pointing out that the Roughriders were challengers who had no say in such matters. Clearly the Big Four and the Ontario Rugby Football Union executives believed the Cup belonged to them and the Western Interprovincial Football Union was allowed to play for it.

The Winged Wheelers were wrong about the referees. According to custom, in the Grey Cup the two competing teams chose the officials. Because the teams could not agree, the Canadian Rugby Union made the decision. The referee would be Joe O'Brian from Montréal, with Regina's Milne as the umpire. Tom Barton, also from Montréal, was the linesman.

The field was frozen, and snow was falling gently, adding to the drifts already on the gridiron. The temperature at game time was −11°C. Some players resorted to wearing coonskin coats over their uniforms.

Montréal led 7–0 at the half on a Huck Welch single and a Pete Jotkus touchdown set up by an Eddie James fumble.

In the third quarter, Montréal made history when Warren Stevens completed the first Grey Cup touchdown pass, 24 yards to Kenny Grant. As the quarter ended with the Wheelers leading 13–0, the Montréalers went into a huddle. Were they planning a sneak play on the ensuing kickoff? (In those days, the team that scored received the kickoff.) Actually, no. Stevens had split his pants, and a new pair had been rushed in from the bench.

In the final 15 minutes, the Wheelers scored nine more points. Montréal won its first Grey Cup, 22–0. It was the Riders' fourth consecutive defeat.

The 1932 Roughriders once again rolled over provincial opposition before dispensing with Winnipeg and Calgary to win the West and head down east for the fifth straight year. Once again, they would meet the Hamilton Tigers.

Because of injuries, the Tigers were no better than even money to prevent the West from winning its first Grey Cup. The game was played on December 3 under almost perfect conditions—warm, no wind, a fast track. The temperature was a balmy 8°C.

Although out-played, the Tigers won 25–6. The difference was six Roughrider turnovers.

Winnipeg Wins

The next season saw more imports from North Dakota, Wisconsin and Minnesota. The Winnipeg Rugby Club and St. John's joined forces, calling themselves the Winnipegs. With no other provincial opposition, the merged Manitobans played exhibition games in the northern U.S., giving them a good idea of what talent was available. Future Hall of Famers Carl Cronin, Greg Kabat and Russ Rebholz crossed the border. Regina imports Curt Schave, Austin De Frate and Bill Mjogdalen came from neighbouring North Dakota.

Regina went 5–1 in the regular season and prepared to meet the Winnipegs on November 4 in the Manitoba capital at Carruthers Field on, as usual, a snow-covered gridiron. Despite blizzard-like conditions the day before the game, advance ticket sales exceeded $1000. Unfortunately, the Winnipegs ended Regina's seven-year run of Western championships with a decisive 11–1 victory.

Winnipeg went on to defeat Calgary 15–1, beginning a 34-year run as a dominant team in the Western Conference. The ORFU champions had a berth in the Grey Cup. To qualify to meet them, Winnipeg was ordered to play Toronto, winners of the Big Four. The Argos won 13–0 and also won the Cup by edging out Sarnia 4–3.

A special incentive to Regina football was offered in 1934. The Canadian Rugby Union had decided that year's Grey Cup game would be played at the home of the Western champion for the first time. Determined to be the hosts, with Greg Grassick at the helm, the Riders were 6–0 during the regular season, outscoring the opposition 156–25. But even though they were possibly the best Roughrider team of that era, they almost didn't make it past the semifinal.

At Exhibition Park, Winnipeg and Regina battled through 50 minutes without scoring a point. Then Rider quarterback Ralph Pearce completed the first pass of the game, a 20-yard strike to Steve Adkins, followed by Ted Olson's 40-yarder to Paul Kirk, bringing the ball to the enemy 25-yard line. With time a precious commodity, Olson punted into the end zone. Russ Rebholz tried to kick the ball back, but it was blocked. Ted Lydiard fell on it for a touchdown and an 8–0 victory. Then it was onto BC to play a two-game set against the Vancouver Meralomas. They won the opener 22–2, the second game, 7–2.

In a decision that surprised no one in Western Canada, the Canadian Rugby Union reneged on its promise to hold the game in the west. Twenty-one years went by before the Grey Cup was contested outside Ontario.

The Riders headed to Toronto to face the Sarnia Imperials. Although the Roughriders were better than their opposition, once again turnovers did them in. Ralph Pearce fumbled the first punt of the game, leading to the first of five Bummer Stirling singles. The ball went out of the end zone, and the game was delayed while the police recovered it.

A mishandled snap led to a turnover on downs early in the second quarter that Sarnia immediately converted into a touchdown. Turn about being fair play, Regina blocked a punt on the Imperial five that Ted Olson ran in. The Roughriders trailed 11–5 at the half.

In the third quarter, Andy Young fumbled a punt on his goal line. Sarnia scored easily. The Rider goose seemed cooked; they were down 17–5. The never-say-die Riders fought back with a single and a touchdown. Stirling added three singles. Sarnia won their first Grey Cup, 20–12.

Rules, Rules, Rules

The game of football changed dramatically in 1935. Because of the presence of so many Americans on western teams, the WIFU adopted some American features. Under the new rules, teams could use the forward pass anywhere on the field, eliminating the restriction against throwing within the opponent's 25-yard line. But officials didn't completely clear the way in what is now called the "red zone." If a pass on third down went incomplete in that area of the field, the opposing team took possession at its own 25-yard line.

In another change, the kicking game was modified by disallowing points for punting the ball out of the end zone. This rule had practical purposes: games were delayed while someone retrieved the football, and too many miscreants were making off with costly pigskins. Fences later removed the need for the rule.

In a rule that remains in effect to this day throughout the CFL, the WIFU allowed the team that had a touchdown or field goal scored against it to have the option of kicking off or receiving.

The blocking (called "interference" back then) rules were changed, allowing backs to block five yards past the line of scrimmage. Penalties to prevent a defensive player from interfering with a receiver in the end zone were established. When the defending team interfered with the receiver of a pass thrown over the goal line, the attacking team was awarded the ball half the distance to the goal line and a first down.

The Roughriders, with Al Ritchie back as head coach, were undefeated during the 1935 season, outscoring the opposition 135–13. But they lost the semifinal to Winnipeg who, after eking out a 7–0 win over the Calgary Bronks, won the first Grey Cup for the West by defeating Hamilton 18–12. Fritz Hanson, Greg Kabat and Bud Marquardt made touchdowns for the Manitobans, and Hanson was a one-man wrecking crew, ably assisted by Dynamite Eddie James. All but Marquardt are in the Hall of Fame.

Griff

In 1936 Dean Griffing arrived on the Canadian football scene as the coach of the Roughriders. In 1945 he
founded the Calgary Stampeders before returning to
Saskatchewan as general manager in 1954. He was
inducted into the CFL Hall of Fame in 1965.

A big barrel-chested man, once accused of biting
an opponent, Griffing pointed to his bridgework and
denied the charge, allowing, "I might have gummed
him up a little bit," which was a minor matter in the
days when players pooled their money for the first to
draw blood.

Griffing's Riders had a mediocre mark of 3–2–1,
barely outscoring their opponents 52–42. For the first
time since their inception in 1910, Regina did not finish
first. That honour went to defending Grey Cup champions Winnipeg who won the opening game of the
total point series 7–4. The Roughriders won the second
game 20–5, the round 24–12. They regained their
status as Western champions after knocking off the
Calgary Bronks 3–1.

The East was not amused when Winnipeg won the
Grey Cup in 1935. Believing the balance of power was
shifting because of the widespread use of American
imports in Western Canada, the Eastern-dominated
CRU restricted their use. They ruled that no player could
compete unless he had lived in Canada for a year. He
could play only if he had taken up residence in the
league city before October 1 of that season. The WIFU
ignored the rule.

Regina's five imports, including player/coach Dean Griffing, were declared ineligible for Grey Cup play. Regina refused to make the trip east without them. Western officials announced Winnipeg would take Regina's place. "No way!" said Regina. "We'll play the Grey Cup without our Americans." They sent a telegram to CRU president Bobby Hewitson to that effect, only to be notified the WIFU had withdrawn their challenge, and no western team would play for the dominion title. Sarnia then won their second and last Grey Cup, defeating the Ottawa Rough Riders 26–20. It would be 15 years before the Western Roughriders would return to the big game.

Throughout the early Dirty Thirties, the good people of Regina could take pride and solace in the winning ways of their football team. But not in 1937. Just as that was the worst year in Saskatchewan history economically, the Roughriders for the first time lost more games than they won (2–6) and failed to make the playoffs. The next year wasn't much better, with the team going 4–4. Griffing's third-place team lost the semifinal to the Winnipeg Blue Bombers who went on to beat Calgary before losing 30–7 to Toronto and Red Storey's incredible fourth-quarter, three-touchdown performance in the Grey Cup before a record crowd of 18,778.

When war broke out in 1939, the Roughriders were embarking on a 12-game schedule with Winnipeg, the Calgary Bronks and the Edmonton Eskimos. The Blue Bombers finished first at 10–2, the Riders second with a 6–6 mark. Regina was upset by the Bronks, 24–17.

Winnipeg won the final and their second Grey Cup 8–7 over Ottawa.

With young men joining up to fight the Nazis, Roughrider ranks thinned and, in 1940, at 2–6, the team had their worst record since 1910. The following year, they lost the first of three finals to Winnipeg.

Regular play resumed in 1946. Regina missed the playoffs that year and the year after, bringing to a close the story of the Regina Roughriders, nee Rugby Club. Between 1910 and 1947, they won 16 Western championships and appeared in seven Grey Cups. They outscored their opposition 2310 to 980. Their record was 115–53–1.

It was their golden age.

The modern age was about to begin.

Chapter Three

Green Is the Colour

In 1948, when the teams in Moose Jaw and Saskatoon ceased operations, the Regina Roughriders became the Saskatchewan Roughriders, although it took a few years before the term "Regina" was discontinued entirely. The name "Saskatchewan" wasn't officially adopted until April 1, 1950. In an account of a game in 1948 against Calgary, both "Regina" and "Saskatchewan" are used throughout the *Leader-Post* story. By the mid-1950s, the team was mostly known as the Saskatchewan Roughriders.

Also, in 1948, in order to take advantage of a bargain, the team discarded their red-and-black uniforms in favour of green and white. Rider executive Jack Fyffe found two sets of green-and-white jerseys on sale in a Chicago store. Because the price was low, Fyffe snapped them up, and the "Kelly Green" and White tradition so completely identified with the Wheat Province began. True to the Saskatchewan creed, a penny saved is a penny earned.

Two important football developments happened after World War II, both somewhat related. In 1948, Calgary's Les Lear revolutionized the Canadian game by unleashing an all-out passing attack. When Lear, the first Canadian to star in the National Football League, brought Keith Spaith, Woody Strode and Ezzert "Sugarfoot" Anderson to Calgary, the modern era of football began. The Stampeders went undefeated in 1948, still the only CFL team to do so, and won the Grey Cup.

The other post-war development was the collapse of the American Football Conference after the 1949 season. This freed up a number of imports who would become stars in Canadian football. Before 1949, the imports came right out of college. Certainly that continued with All-Americans like Johnny Bright and Jackie Parker who came north after graduation, but for a while, import ranks were dominated by gnarly, old pros. At that time in football history, the CFL paid better than the NFL, and the Canadian dollar was worth more. Of course, the Americans played both on offence and defence, seldom leaving the field.

Most of the 1946 Roughriders came from the Regina junior teams or right out of high school. Some were veterans from other WIFU teams. Regina finished last in the West in '46, winning only two of eight games. But the foundation was laid for future success with Canadians Johnny Bell, Sully Glasser, Pete Martin, Len Ortman, Wayne Pyne, Roy Wright and Toar Springstein.

Improvement was not immediate. When the team lost its fourth of five games in 1947, Ken Preston stepped aside as coach in favour of Fred Grant, a 22-year-old Virginian who played at Wake Forest and Alabama and was a star in the 1946 Rose Bowl game. He was 2–1 the rest of the way. Joining the team that year were guards Art McEwan and Chuck Radley and end Bob Pelling, stalwarts for several years to come. Three more came aboard in 1948, including lineman Mike Cassidy, halfback/kickers Del Wardien and Ken Charlton.

Racism in Regina

Gabe Patterson was the first black person to play for the Roughriders. From all indications, it was not a happy experience. A black man in Regina was an object of curiosity in a place where blacks were seen only in travelling minstrel shows or on baseball teams.

Jackie Robinson broke the colour barrier in major league baseball in 1947, followed later that season by Larry Doby in Cleveland. Gabe Patterson arrived in Regina that same year.

He wasn't the first black American to play north of the border. Tom Casey played for the Hamilton Wildcats in 1940. Herb Trawick and Virgil Wagner were among the original Alouettes in 1946, and Les Lear brought Woody Strode and Sugarfoot Anderson to Calgary. Strode, the man in the movie who handed the rifle to John Wayne when he shot Liberty Valence, played a key role in breaking the colour barrier in the NFL. Imports began arriving in Western Canada in the early 1930s, most from border states. After World

War II, increasingly, the imports came from the Deep South, the bastion of racism and segregation.

Gabe Patterson lived a lonely life in Regina. His only solace was playing football. The story persists that at the 1948 team wind-up party at the Regina Golf and Country Club, when Patterson walked in, his coach Fred Grant walked out. But the Alabama native had his defenders, among them veteran Ken Charlton. "[Grant] was great," the Hall of Fame halfback enthused. "He was one of the better guys that came from the States to coach up here that understood our game well. He was a good coach and a real good guy."

As for the incident with Gabe Patterson, Charlton stated, "I don't want to get involved in that. It was a personal thing between the two of them."

Some claimed the incident never happened. No one bothered to ask Patterson for his opinion.

Roughrider-Stampeder Rivalry Begins

The 1948 campaign opened with an exhibition win over Toronto Balmy Beach Indians. Tickets to the brand-new grandstand at Taylor Field went for $1.50.

The final standings almost tell the whole story about that amazing season.

TEAM	W	L	T	F	A	PTS
Calgary	12	0	0	218	61	24
Saskatchewan	3	9	0	133	137	6
Winnipeg	3	9	0	81	234	6

The Riders took the playoff spot over Winnipeg on the basis of points for and against.

Calgary surrendered five points a game, the best record in modern Canadian football history. But Saskatchewan's 11 points per game against wasn't exactly chopped liver, either. They were becoming a very good football team. In fact, 1948 really told a tale of two seasons.

The Riders lost the home opener to Calgary 12–1 on August 25 and lost again to the Stamps on Labour Day, 14–8. Calgary won both ends of a back-to-back series on September 25 (13–12) and October 2 (12–11). Calgary won again two weeks later in Regina, 8–7. Three wins by three points. Between that game and a post-season tie, the Horsemen beat the Riders 19–0. Five out of eight games between the Roughriders and the only team in Canadian football history to go undefeated were close.

View of the stands and refreshment stand at Taylor Field, 1953

The most disgraceful moment in Saskatchewan football occurred during the Labour Day game. With Calgary and Saskatchewan tied in the fourth quarter, and scrimmaging from their own 25, Rider quarterback Johnny Cook went back to pass.

"I was playing left corner linebacker," recalled Stampeder Jim Mitchener, "and Keith Spaith was behind me. They threw a pass and Keith tackled the fellow who caught it, Gabe Patterson. He dropped the ball and I picked it up and ran for a touchdown. They were so angry. They thought it should have been complete. The fans started throwing rocks at us and we had to put our helmets on and march arm and arm to our bus. Talk about bush league football."

The rest of the regular season went by without incident. On to the playoffs.

The first game of the Western final took place at Taylor Field on Saturday, November 6, before 7000-plus fans in Regina. The result was a 4–4 tie, and although they were undefeated, the Stampeders were upset with themselves because most of the game was played in the Saskatchewan end. Back at Mewata Stadium in Calgary, the Stampeders romped home 17–6 and went on to their first Grey Cup appearance, defeating Ottawa 12–7 and inventing the Grey Cup festival in the process.

The Edmonton Eskimos returned to the Western Conference in 1949, this time for good. They were 4–10 their first year under Annis Stukus. They would not experience another losing season for 12 years.

Five years after returning to play, they won the first of three straight Grey Cups.

That 1949 season saw the Stampeders go 13–1, their only defeat a 9–6 loss to the Roughriders in Calgary. The loss ended the longest winning streak in CFL history, 22 games, a mark that still stands. Their record over two seasons, including playoff games and Grey Cups was an incredible 28–3–1.

With coach Fred "General" Grant telling the faithful, "We are out to win and will win," and the Calgary papers calling him "Corporal Grant," enthusiasm for the first game in Regina was at a fever pitch. For the playoff, the Riders introduced a new wrinkle, a mascot called Ruffie. A goat bedecked in a white-and-green blanket, Ruffie was tethered at the Rider bench during the game.

Despite all the enthusiasm, it looked like business as usual when Calgary won the first game of the two-game total-point series 18–12. But Saskatchewan took the return match, 9–4.

More than 400 raucous supporters made the trip to Calgary for the Remembrance Day clash. Wearing straw hats with green-and-white ribbons, they arrived in the Foothills city by train, plane, bus and automobile. Several young men hitchhiked. The train package was popular. For $29.50, you got a return ticket, a berth, a reserved seat at Mewata Stadium and a football favour.

At halftime, the "Stubble Jumpers" as they called themselves, were given a tremendous ovation from the 14,000-plus Calgarians in attendance. They joined in a community sing-song with the home-town fans belting out, "Bronco Busters from the Valley of the Bow!" and "Calgareeee!"

The Stampeders dominated the game through the first three quarters, although they didn't have much to show for it—a lead of 4–1. The never-say-die Roughriders mounted a furious comeback. Doug Beldon threw a 39-yard strike to Johnny Bell. Keith Spaith ran up to make the interception but it caromed off his hand into Bell's waiting arms at the 10. He scored unmolested.

On the Riders' next possession, Beldon found Matt Anthony wide open at the enemy 50. He lugged it to the 37. Beldon hit Bell at the 16. On the next play, Bob Early, finding his way around right end blocked, reversed his field and headed to the other side away from the goal posts for a loss of a yard. On the second down, Beldon got the ball back in front of the posts but lost eight yards in the process. (There were no 15-yard hash marks at that time.)

With seconds left on the clock, the Riders lined up for a 33-yard field goal that would win them the right to go to the Grey Cup. Buck Rogers missed it, but Les Lear of the Stamps was called offside, giving the Riders another shot, this time five yards closer. In came "Dead Eye" Del Wardien whom the Stampeders had cut in 1947. He missed, too. Johnny Bell tackled Pete Thodas in the end zone for a meaningless single point. Calgary won the round 22–21 and headed to Toronto where they lost the Grey Cup to Frank Filchock's Montréal Alouettes, 28–15.

The curse that has bedevilled Saskatchewan football for generations was born.

In 1950, Les Lear's Calgary Stampeders fell into the cellar with a mark of 4–10. They made the playoffs only twice during the decade. The Bombers returned to form under the dynamic quarterback "Indian" Jack Jacobs who led them to first place, winning 10 and losing four. Saskatchewan and Edmonton had identical 7–7 records. In the playoffs, the Eskimos won in Regina, 24–1. Winnipeg won the West, losing the infamous "Mud Bowl" Grey Cup 13–0 to Toronto.

With the semifinal loss to the upstart Eskimos, it had been 16 years since the scourge of Western football, the Roughriders, had been to the Grey Cup. The drought would soon be over, ended by the most popular man to ever don the green and white.

Chapter Four

Dobberville

Montréal had the Rocket, New York had the Babe and Edmonton had number 99. No matter how great these players were, it is hard to imagine a more passionate love affair between a city, a province and an athlete than that between Regina, Saskatchewan and Glenn Dobbs, the long, tall Tulsan who led the Riders out of the football wilderness to the Promised Land.

Licence plates with "Dobberville" adorned vehicles from one end of the province to the other. At recess, children followed Dobb's son all over the Herchmer School grounds, anxious to bask in his reflected glory. Everywhere he went, Dobbs was mobbed by hordes of adoring fans. The coming of Glenn Dobbs in 1951 to a province with a population of under one million and a city of only 71,319 souls, was the greatest thing to ever hit the old Pile of Bones, even greater than the Royal Visit on October 10, 1951, of Princess Elizabeth and her new husband Prince Philip.

Dobbs' presence in Saskatchewan was the result of the greatest president in Roughrider history, R.A. (Bob)

Kramer. Elected to the Canadian Football Hall of Fame on May 1, 1987, Kramer was a businessman who owned the Caterpillar Tractor dealership in Regina. He headed up the team executive from 1951 to 1953 and came out of retirement to lead it again from 1961 to 1965 when the team was in danger of folding. He not only saved the franchise, he ushered in its golden age.

Glenn Dobbs explained how he succumbed to Kramer's siren song.

> I had retired from football after four years in the All-America Conference and I came home to settle down in Tulsa. We had a small stock farm south of town with 20 head of cattle. I thought, "Well, this is it."

> Somehow or other, Mr. Bob Kramer, who was one of the most wonderful men I've ever met in sports, found out I was available. They were hunting for somebody to come up to Saskatchewan and play football. He and his wife came down to Tulsa. He called and invited me to come and visit with him. He wanted me to come and play quarterback that year. That was in 1950.

> I told him I would be interested except I had signed a contract do to the broadcasts for Oklahoma State University and so I wouldn't be available for the 1950 season.

> He said, "We need a quarterback and we need to get you up there to play football." He was so nice and so kind that I just tried to talk as nice as I could and yet I had to be firm because I had signed a contract with the radio station for a year. Back in our day, when

you gave your word or signed a contract it meant something.

He said, "Well, I've got to get your name on a contract. If you play, will you play with us?" I said, "All things being equal, yes." And I signed a contract to that effect.

I liked Mr. Kramer and I liked his ideas and how hard they worked. It was kind of a Green Bay operation. The whole province owned the team.

My family and I decided the next year I would play for him. I belonged to the Chicago Bears by this time. I had been the number one choice of the Chicago Cardinals and the next year George Halas made a deal for me. I called him, told him I was going to play again. He made me an offer. I said, "Sir, that is nowhere near what I made in the American league." Saskatchewan made me an offer. I told Mr. Halas what the offer was. All he had to do was match it. He passed. That's how I became a Roughrider.

The first Tulsa University player to make the U.S. College Football Hall of Fame did not regret the "Papa Bear's" legendary parsimony.

I enjoyed Saskatchewan. As far as people and players were concerned, it was just like the closeness and friendliness of high school days. We really enjoyed it. We went to church with them. We went to parties with them.

I was raised in a small town of about 4500, called Frederick. Everybody knew everybody and were friends. We were just normal, everyday, southwest-type people.

We all enjoyed our friends in Frederick and those people in Saskatchewan were the same to us, they felt the same. So we just felt right at home.

We loved it and it was a mutual thing. We felt bad when we'd lost a game but the next day on the street the people said, "Don't worry about that, you've done all that you can do."

They just filled the ball park up. They came from all over the province. I still [1997] get letters and calls from up there.

It would only be natural for his talented teammates to resent the implication of all Dobbs' adoring fans that the Roughriders were a one-man show. "No, not at all," said Ken Charlton. "He was a super guy. Glenn was a real, real good guy. I don't think anybody on the team resented him for the publicity he got."

There were five new imports, including Dobbs. The other four also came from the defunct American Conference—Jack Russell and Jack Nix on the ends, centre Red Ettinger and tackle Martin Ruby. The only hold-over was Al Bodine. Russell, Ettinger, Ruby, Dobbs and Bert Iannone made the All-Star team. Dobbs led the league in punting with an average of 44.2 yards.

Gone was coach Fred Grant, replaced by Harry "Black Jack" Smith.

The 1951 Roughriders lost six games. They won eight to finish in a three-way tie for first with Edmonton and Winnipeg. Dobbs described his team:

We worked hard that year. I always worked hard as a player. I had to because I was not a heavyweight.

I weighed 200 pounds. I was 6-foot-4 and I played both ways.

We were not an overwhelming team. We were only allowed six Americans. And darn, Jack Russell, the big end, got hurt and we had trouble at centre when Red Ettinger got hurt.

Some of our Canadians were older. Toar Springstein was in his second last year. Ken Charlton, the perennial halfback was close to the end of the line, just like a lot of us were. Kenny was a hard-working dude. We were all the same type of guys. We knew we didn't have all the ability and we worked hard.

Saskatchewan opened the season at home on August 25 against Calgary. Dobbs boomed five singles in a driving rainstorm to win 8–1. The next night at the Quarterback Club, the "Loquacious Lithuanian," Annis Stukus, coach of the Eskimos, said, "This is my year." He also announced he was going to sign a rookie import named Roland Miles.

The rivalry with Edmonton was hot all year but was based on mutual admiration and respect. The Riders won three of the four regular-season meetings between the teams.

Edmonton won the sudden-death semifinal over Winnipeg 4–1 on the strength of a Stukus field goal. What followed was a typically thrilling Western final.

In the first of the best of three, Edmonton came from behind to draw first blood when Jimbo Chambers ran 95 yards for a touchdown to give the hometown Eskimos a 5–11 victory. Back in Regina, the Riders evened the series, winning 12–5 and setting up the rubber match two days later, the third game in six days.

It was a showdown between two old pros, Glenn Dobbs and Frank Filchock. The "Dobber" won out, barely. Eskimo hopes died when Chambers was brought down near the 10-yard line after a 65-yard run. Whew! By virtue of their 19–18 triumph, the Roughriders were heading to the Grey Cup for the first time since 1934.

In the dressing room after the game, the players went looking for Black Jack Smith to give him the traditional dunking in the shower. "You were wonderful!" he shouted at them as the players grabbed him from the top of a bench. "There may have been better football games than the one today, but nobody ever played as hard as you did. I'm proud of you all. You're my boys!"

Glenn Dobbs was the happiest man of all. He said he never wanted to win a game as much as that one.

"It's the fans. The people up here have been wonderful. I played college football and had a turn at the pro game. I was in Los Angeles a long time and nobody cared much about footballers off the field. I came up here and every door was open to me. The other boys who came in will say the same thing. We had to win. The fans deserved it."

Guard Pete Martin had joined the club out of junior in 1946. He went around the dressing room on crutches, congratulating his teammates. Big tears rolled down his cheeks.

"We waited such a long time for this but it was worthwhile," he said. "I always wanted to play on a Grey Cup team and here I am with a broken leg." Martin never played again.

Always thankful for any blessings, the prevailing mood of fans in the province was win or lose the Grey Cup, they were happy just to be there. But, of course, deep down they really wanted to win.

The Riders' opponent was Ottawa.

Hogtown, Here We Come!

Calgarians created the Grey Cup festival in 1948 by turning staid old Hogtown on its ear, riding horses down Bay Street, flipping flapjacks at city hall and generally having a rip-snorting good time. From 1948 on, westerners have made the pilgrimage to the site of the Grey Cup to cheer on their representatives in their effort to win the Holy Grail of Canadian football. In 1951, over 1000 fans filled two special trains for the trip to Toronto. The journey took two days and nights.

Ken and Val Charlton described the event. "It was super," said Ken. "The train was loaded with people. It was like a big party all the way down. It was great."

Mrs. Charlton chimed in: "It was absolutely beautiful but the players didn't party. A porter came through the train and said, 'Ssshhh, these are all the players' wives, they're a bunch of nuns.' The players were in another car. We were all at the back and it was just a ball. I rode on the bread truck in the parade."

Eighteen-month-old Bobby Kramer in Winnipeg greeting the Roughriders enroute to the 1951 Grey Cup in Toronto

The Grey Cup Parade was held on the morning of the big game. The Saskatchewan float naturally promoted agriculture and wheat. Val Charlton and others threw little loaves of bread to the thousands lining the parade route. The night before, Myrtle Bainbridge, a student at Balfour Tech, was crowned Miss Grey Cup.

The Roughriders were handicapped in their eighth quest for Lord Grey's trophy by injuries. The day before the game, they held a secret workout. Jack Russell ran up and down for a while but had to give up when his knee wouldn't respond. Del Wardien missed the workout with a sprained ankle. Even their good luck charm was on the limp. Old Jack Wedley, a defensive end who had been on six Grey Cup–winning teams, five with the Argos and HMCS Donnacona in 1944, sprained an ankle in practice.

It was windy at kickoff time, the temperature around the freezing mark, and the field was in good condition. Ottawa won the toss, electing to receive. Saskatchewan had the wind. On his first possession, Dobbs threw a long bomb to Charlton at the Ottawa 25-yard line, but just as he was about to catch it, Bobby Simpson tripped him from behind right in front of the referee who ignored the obvious interference. Dobbs then quick-kicked (a punt on second or first down) an 80-yard single. On the next series, Ottawa's Howie Turner fumbled a lateral from quarterback Tom O'Malley, recovered at the Saskatchewan 54-yard line by Chuck Radley.

Charlton made four yards before Dobbs quick-kicked again, but Ottawa was charged with roughing the kicker. Sully Glasser ran for six and two yards. On the third down, Dobbs punted the ball into the end-zone stands. Leading 2–0, Saskatchewan wouldn't score again until the fourth quarter. Ottawa scored a converted major to lead 6–2 after 15 minutes.

Early in the second stanza, Mickey Maguire fumbled a punt giving Ottawa possession at the Saskatchewan 35. O'Malley promptly threw to a wide-open Alton Baldwin who took one step into pay dirt. Minutes later, Bobby Simpson intercepted a Dobbs pass at the Ottawa 10, stopping Saskatchewan's deepest drive of the game. Ottawa was ahead 12–2 at the half.

The easterners added another touchdown in the third quarter. Trailing 19–2, the Roughriders fought back.

Ottawa added a single to start the final quarter. A few plays later, Maguire recovered a Benny MacDonnell fumble at the Ottawa 30. On a third-and-10 gamble, Dobbs found Jack Nix on the five-yard line. He went over for the touchdown. Red Ettinger converted, making the score Ottawa 20, Saskatchewan 8.

MacDonnell fumbled again on Ottawa's next possession, recovered by Mike Cassidy at the Ottawa 39. It was Charlton for 9, Bodine for 20, Glasser for the TD. Ottawa 20, Saskatchewan 14.

Saskatchewan was closing the gap. Mr. Momentum was dressed in green and white. Then Maguire fumbled a punt at his own seven-yard line. With 30 seconds left, Ottawa kicked a single. The final score was Ottawa 21, Saskatchewan 14.

Maguire was disconsolate. His first fumble had led to an Ottawa touchdown. The second resulted in a single, but more importantly, deprived the team of the ball when they desperately needed to mount a final drive and had Ottawa on the run. Maguire's slender body was racked with sobs. The tall Tulsan Dobbs, loomed over him.

"Look, kid," said Dobbs as reported in the *Leader-Post* on November 26, 1951, "You didn't lose that ball game for us. We all lost it. The guys in the backfield and the guys on the line. We all did something wrong. I did a lot of things that were wrong. I threw a lot of passes that were pretty poor. No one man ever lost a game, just as no one man ever won it. Cut it out. Do you hear?

Cut it out. Forget those fumbles. You're all right." He tousled Maguire's hair and walked away.

Most agreed the physical beating the Riders sustained during the Western final was the key factor in their defeat. "We had a lot of injuries," recalled Charlton, "but they all played, except Jack Russell, but not as well as we could have. It made a helluva difference."

"The main problem," explained Dobbs, "was Jack Russell being hurt and then for some reason, the coach Harry Smith decided all of a sudden on game day that Russell wasn't going to play. So they took the left end, Jack Nix, and moved him over to the right end and took Johnny Bell off the bench and put him at left end. Instead of having a new man in one spot, we had two new ends in new spots, just a couple of days before the game. That, to me, was the biggest problem we had."

By all accounts, Dobbs put on one of the greatest displays of punting ever witnessed in a Grey Cup or any other game. Ottawa great, Hall of Famer Bobby Simpson said, "I was catching punts at the time. There was quite a wind that day. On his first punt, he was standing on his 15-yard line. I'm back on my 15-yard line. He kicked it very, very high. I'm standing on my 15-yard line and I never moved. The ball was still going up when it went over my head. It went over the end zone and landed 12 rows up in the bleachers. I had never seen a kick like that before in my life."

"Yeah, I kicked them pretty good," Dobbs allowed. "But I was paid to do that."

Miss Grey Cup 1951, Myrtle Bainbridge (bottom centre with hat), with unidentified individuals at the Grey Cup celebration in Toronto. Saskatchewan lost to the Ottawa Rough Riders 21–14.

On Grey Cup day, the All-Canadian team was announced. Martin Ruby made it, as did Dobbs, only one of three Rider quarterbacks to do so; the others were Ron Lancaster and Kent Austin.

When the Roughriders arrived back at Regina's Union Station on the evening of Tuesday, November 27, they were welcomed home like conquering heroes by thousands of rabid fans. What a wonderful year it had been. What gridiron glory lay ahead? They could hardly wait. But it was not to be.

From Dobberville to Loserville

The year 1952 was a disastrous one for Saskatchewan on and off the field. Excessive rain turned wheat fields into rice paddies. A terrible plague of hoof-and-mouth disease struck the province's cattle, with entire herds destroyed and buried in mass graves. Sheep and swine were also slaughtered, as were goats, including the Roughrider's mascot, Ruffie.

The defending Western champions struggled from day one. Sully Glasser was the team's leading rusher with only 267 yards.

The good news was the arrival of a raw rookie from the Saskatoon Hilltops named Ron Atchison and an eager young offensive lineman from the Montréal junior ranks, Reggie Whitehouse, as well as receiver Harry Lampman from Queen's. Seeing more playing time in 1952 was high school graduate Bill Clarke, the 1950 Canadian School Boys Curling Champion out of Regina's Scott Collegiate.

Gone was Harry Blackjack Smith. Asked why Smith was fired, Ken Charlton was succinct. "Why? He did a lousy job, that's why. He didn't do a good job with the club we had."

Smith's successor was Glenn Dobbs. Although he had never been a head coach before, Dobbs had no reservations about taking the job.

"No, because they had been turned down by quite a few people. Evidently a lot of people knew about our shortage of manpower. They just couldn't get anybody interested. At the last minute they talked to me about it and I said, 'Well, sure, I won't mind doing it because I had been with Harry and we had all his plays.'"

The Riders had suffered through the worst season in their history up to that point, winning only three of 16 games and finishing last. Dobbs was replaced by Frank Filchock who had been fired in Edmonton, even though he took the Eskimos to the Grey Cup. After defeating Winnipeg in the Western final, Filchock gave the Eskimo executive an ultimatum: pay him more money or he wouldn't take the team to Toronto. They agreed to his terms. After losing the Cup to Toronto 21–11, they fired him.

Although Dobbs had no objection to surrendering the coaching duties to Filchock for 1953, in the end, he felt an enormous sense of betrayal.

"I took the job that one year just to tide them over," Dobbs recalled ruefully. "They asked me to start looking around. Joe Aguirre who had played with us in Los Angeles was a good friend of Filchock's. They wanted the coaching job. Filchock and Aguirre got after me to help Frank get the head job. I was happy to do it. I didn't know Frank very well, other than just as a competitor and a player.

"I thought he would do well there and I would come back and be the old man at quarterback while they were breaking in somebody new. It didn't work out that way. Every time I played it seemed that I was on the second unit. I got my knee hurt. Then it started getting well and I put on a brace. Then I hurt it again over at Calgary. It was an up and down year."

Mostly down.

And so the Glenn Dobbs era came to an end.

"It was a labour of love for us up there," he reminisced 43 years later. "We just had all the good things in the whole wide world. I'm sorry I got my leg hurt real bad and I couldn't finish up like I wanted to. It took me a couple of years to get completely over my knee injury. It was a great time in our lives. Mr. Kramer offered me a job to stay up there and work with his corporations. But I came home and went to work on my farm, raising cattle."

Later, Dobbs became the athletic director at Tulsa. He died on November 12, 2002, at the age of 82, in Tulsa.

Chapter Five

Triumph and Tragedy

The year 1953 was an important one in Canadian football. The Schenley Awards were begun with a single category, Most Outstanding Player. Edmonton's running back Billy Vessels was the first recipient. In 1954, Blue Bomber Gerry James became the inaugural winner of the Most Outstanding Canadian Award. Tex Coulter of Montréal got the first award for lineman in 1955. Those were the categories until 1972 when a rookie award was created. Two years later, a defensive player award was created, with the lineman award going to offensive linemen only. Special teams were recognized in 1999.

G. Sydney Halter, a distinguished gentleman from Winnipeg, became Canadian professional football's first commissioner in 1953.

Harry Peter "Bud" Grant joined Winnipeg from the NFL Philadelphia Eagles. An NBA star with the Minneapolis Lakers, as well as a brilliant receiver, Grant was named Minnesota's Athlete of the Half Century. In addition to coaching the Bombers to four Grey Cup titles in six tries, he led his home state Minnesota to four appearances in the Super Bowl. A member of the CFL and NFL Halls of Fame, Grant is equally proud of both honours.

Also arriving on the scene in 1953 was Bernie Faloney who quarterbacked the Eskimos and Tiger-Cats to the Grey Cup on four occasions. Jackie Parker came north the following year. Vessels, Parker, Faloney and Johnny Bright, to name a few, were legitimate All-Americans.

In 1953, two Franks arrived in the Queen City. Frank Filchock became the head coach and Frank Tripuka tried out at quarterback. At training camp, Filchock had to choose between the great veteran Glenn Dobbs and NFL cast-off Tripuka who was in the prime of his athletic life. Although Dobbs felt he was relegated to second-string status, Filchock chose him over the much younger Tripuka, even though Dobbs was nursing a knee injury during the pre-season. Despite being the great hero of 1951, Dobbs had an off year in '52, and many fans felt the newcomer's time had come. After the personable Notre Dame graduate took over from Dobbs, the only quarterback in Rider history to suffer as much abuse as Tripuka was Ron Lancaster, the greatest of them all, proving once again that the prophet is indeed without honour in his own land.

At any rate, Tripuka was cut from the team. The next night, August 29 against Calgary, Dobbs went down with a career-ending knee injury. The back-up Richard King was inadequate, so Filchock had to fill the breach. He took to the field in an old-fashioned, battered helmet covered with adhesive tape, winning several games before Tripuka could be re-signed. Filchock had two noteworthy accomplishments, setting a record for consecutive completions and bringing about a change in the rule book.

The change in the rulebook came about as a result of the Riders protecting a 10-point lead against Winnipeg in the fourth quarter of a very windy game at Taylor Field. Rather than punt into the breeze, Filchock conceded four safety touches to preserve the win. The rule was changed so that if a team conceded a safety with less than five minutes remaining, that team had to kickoff. Now, the team giving up the safety has to kick-off regardless of when the two points are surrendered.

In 1953, Frank Filchock had a pretty good team. At one end was the NFL's 1952 leading receiver Mac Speedie; at the other end was Baylor star Stan Williams. Rookie Bobby Marlow out of Alabama led the team in rushing, 'Bama mate Jon Wozniak anchored the defence at middle linebacker. Finally, the foundation of what would be one of the greatest offensive lines of all time was signed, including centre Mel Becket from Indiana and guard Mario DeMarco from Miami, Florida.

Speedie, Marlow, Wozniak, Mike Cassidy and Martin Ruby made the All-Star team.

Because homebrews outnumbered imports by four to one, teams won with Canadians. A great crew came on board in 1953, among them defensive ends Paul Anderson from the Hilltops, Gord Sturtridge from St. Boniface and Doug Killoh from the Regina juniors, as well as Lee Munn from McMasters and halfback Moe Martin from Montréal.

The class of the Western Conference in 1953 was Edmonton, coached by now legendary Darrell Royal and quarterbacked by Claude Arnold. The Eskimos finished on top with a mark of 12–4, the first of five consecutive pennants. The Riders were second at 8–7–1, followed by the 8–8 Blue Bombers. Winnipeg edged Saskatchewan 60–23 in the two-game total-point semifinal and then knocked off Edmonton before losing the Grey Cup to Hamilton 12–6.

In 1954, Ken Carpenter signed on with the Riders. A brilliant halfback from Oregon via the Cleveland Browns, Carpenter made the All-Star team three times, led the West in scoring in 1955 with 90 points on 18 touchdowns and was the team's leading rusher in 1956 with 727 yards.

The other new import was Larry Isbell, a back-up quarterback, defensive back and left-footed punter. The Baylor graduate still holds the records for most punts and yardage in a playoff season, 46 hoofs for 2089 yards. He has the second-longest punt, 83 yards, in CFL playoff history. Isbell led the league in 1954 with an average of 46.3 yards and was best in the West two years later. Next to Ken Clark, he is the greatest punter in Roughrider history.

Quarterback and defensive back Ron Adam and guard Ray Syrnyk were signed from the Hilltops, as well as George "Lefty" Tait from Fort William.

The BC Lions, led by the flamboyant Annis Stukus, joined the Western Conference in 1954. Their slogan was, "The Lions Will Roar in '54."

"We roared alright," said Stukus. "Mostly in pain." They won only a single game that year, a 9–4 win over Calgary, a loss that cost the Stampeders a playoff spot.

Edmonton signed the Maryland's All-American quarterback Bernie Faloney as well as Mississippi All-American and U.S. College Hall of Fame halfback, Jackie Parker. All-American lineman Roger Nelson came up from Texas.

In 1951, the Stampeders traded Norm Kwong to Edmonton for Reg Clarkson, who didn't last a season in red and white. Calgary had also come to the conclusion that Johnny Bright was injury prone and shipped him north in 1954. Kwong, the "China Clipper," played 10 seasons in Eskimo livery, Bright 11. Together they gained 18,735 yards, scored 146 touchdowns and won three Grey Cups for the green and gold, the most dynamic duo in Canadian football history.

The Eskimos of '54, '55 and '56 can be counted among the greatest football teams of all time. Many would rate the 1956 and 1981 Eskimos as the greatest teams in CFL history. Filchock's Roughriders were just about as good.

In 1954, at 11–5, the Eskimos tied Saskatchewan for first place. The Riders were 10–4–2. Although the Riders beat Edmonton three out of four games, the Esks got first place because they had one more win. Once again, the Roughriders faced their old nemesis Winnipeg in the semifinal.

On a bitterly, cold night in Regina on a frozen field, the first of the two games ended in a 14–14 tie. Frank Tripuka played in Winnipeg but was ineffective. "I tore up that groin muscle of mine," he said. "I worked out prior to the game. They tried to shoot it with novocaine to kill the pain but 15 or 20 minutes went by and I couldn't stand it anymore."

His replacement Larry Isbell played valiantly, but the Roughriders lost 13–11. The Eskimos scraped by Winnipeg in three very close games before winning one of the most exciting games in Grey Cup history over Montréal 26–25.

At the end of the season, Hall of Famer Ken Charlton retired, along with Nellie Green and Chuck Radley. With 10 wins against six losses, the 1955 Roughriders won the most games in their history, 10, but still finished second to the 14–2 Eskimos. Although a much better team than the Blue Bombers, once again the Riders came up short in the two-game total-point semifinal, losing the first game at home 16–7. They won in Winnipeg 9–8 but lost the round 24–16.

In 1956, the Big Four and the WIFU joined together as the Canadian Football Council, the prelude to the formation of the Canadian Football League two years later. The value of a touchdown became six points, the belief being two field goals should not equal an unconverted touchdown.

The 1956 Saskatchewan Roughriders were one of the greatest teams of all time, acknowledged as such by friend and foe alike. It was their misfortune to be up against the Eskimos of Bright, Parker and Kwong, but the Riders fought some tremendous battles with Edmonton that year. The Eskimos won the first encounter at Clarke Stadium 15–3. But the Riders replied 31–4 in Regina and then whipped the champions 33–7 in the Igloo. The Eskies then got revenge at Taylor Field, 37–17.

The 10–6 Riders finished second to the 11–5 Eskimos, and hearts in their throats, prepared to face the Blue Bombers for the fourth straight year in the semifinal series. If only they could remove the Winnipeg whammy, they had a good chance to get by Edmonton and make it to the Grey Cup.

Thanks, in part to the water boy, they battered the Bombers badly.

Coaching Winnipeg was Allie Sherman, who later went on to fame and fortune in the NFL with the New York Giants. Sherman was renowned for introducing entire new offensive sets before a game, hoping to fool the opposition with plays they had never seen.

The night before the game, the Riders practised first at Taylor Field. Sometime after returning to the dressing room at the Exhibition Grounds, the water boy noticed he had left a ball behind, a Spalding J5V worth about $30. By the time he got back to the field—about seven blocks away—the Bombers had finished their workout and returned to the Hotel Saskatchewan. The missing ball was near the visitors' bench. Beside the ball was a binder. When he opened it, the water boy immediately recognized Allie Sherman's playbook.

Back at the dressing room, the water boy put the ball away and was heading toward the door with the binder when Frank Filchock spoke up. "Hey, kid," he said, "whatcha got there?" He always called him "kid."

"Oh, hi, coach," the water boy replied. (He always called him "coach.") "Mr. Sherman left his playbook on the bench, so I thought I'd drop it off at his hotel on my way home."

Filchock rushed over. "No need," he said. "I'm going that way in a few minutes. I'll make sure he gets it."

The next afternoon, Saskatchewan clobbered the Bombers 42–7. No matter what Winnipeg ran, the Riders were ready for it. No matter what defence they threw up, Frank Tripuka was able to solve it. The outstanding play of the game came late in the second quarter. The Riders were third down and one yard to go at the Winnipeg 46-yard line. Both teams lined up for a quarterback sneak or a handoff to Marlow. Tripuka promptly threw a pass over the middle to Ken Carpenter, who was so wide open he could have crawled into the end zone. Winnipeg had all 12 men up. The Riders lost game two in Manitoba 19–8 but took the series 50–26. Being totally prepared for Winnipeg was completely out of character for Filchock.

The Flinging Frankies

Born in 1917 in Crucible, Pennsylvania, a small town south of Pittsburgh on the Monogahalia River, Frank Filchock went to university at Indiana and served in the navy during World War II. He played for the Washington Redskins and New York Giants before coming to Canada. He was the first player in Giant history to sign a multi-year contract.

Filchock was unquestionably one of the greatest passers who ever lived. He didn't look much like an athlete, with a funny-shaped head, big ears and twinkling eyes on top of a short, rotund body. Adding to the absurdity was his penchant for wearing a little red tuque during practices, even in July, with a cigar clenched between his teeth. If during scrimmages there was a dearth of completions, Filchock would step behind the centre and tell the receivers what patterns to run. He would then don a blindfold and start passing. He seldom missed. After one of those demonstrations, the Rider attack improved considerably.

The biggest rap on Filchock was that he didn't take the game seriously enough. He favoured touch football over scrimmages with full gear. Some thought his training camps were country clubs. However, 25 years later, Hugh Campbell and Don Matthews introduced the same ideas into their operation, eschewing hitting in practice. The result was fewer injuries, which Campbell believed was an important factor in the team's great success.

Hall of Famer, the late Frankie Morris who played and worked with some of the best coaches in the game, said, "We ran what everyone thought were really short practices and our actual practice was short. But we were always out ahead of time and did a lot of things, including a touch football game which meant we did a whole lot of running."

Morris' teammate Normie Kwong agreed. "Filchock was one of the boys. He was a lot of fun to play for. I had a streak of fumbling the first time I carried the ball in three games in a row. The practice after the third game that happened, he came out and presented me with the ball and taped it to my arm and made me carry it the rest of the day that way. I don't think I fumbled the rest of the year."

Said Frank Tripuka of Filchock:

> *He couldn't tolerate team meetings or looking at scouting reports. Yet other teams were doing it. Possibly if we had done so, we would have been better than we were.*

> *But he was one of those guys who just thought meetings and film were extra-curricular stuff. He thought having someone up in the press box was a waste of time. He figured you were professionals and when it came time, you went out and played the game and that was it.*

> *Frank would always keep you free and easy and you had your fun but you didn't really go into a game completely prepared. Many a time, I'd come to the sidelines after running three or four plays and he and I would start talking about what they were doing. This should all have been done before the game. We'd do it during the game. Frank would ask where this guy was playing, what that guy was doing. Then we'd check the end to find how their opponents were playing them.*

> *After running some plays, I'd be checking with everyone on the offensive line to see what was happening. Then I would plan my offence from that. This should all have been done before the game from the film.*

[The only time the team watched film was when it was raining and they couldn't practice. And even then the emphasis was on hilarious miscues rather than strategy.]

> *But that is how it was with Filchock. You weren't prepared. Once you got going and he could see what they were doing, he could set up an offence to meet it. He was great at that. You'd go in at half-time and he would make up a play and say there was no way they could ever cover. You'd try it and he would be right. But this should have been done before the game. When I played for him in Denver, he was the same way. He hadn't changed a bit.*

"We had some good teams," said trainer Sandy Archer, "but poor coaching. We had guys like Frank Filchock who coached off the top of his head. If we had had a coach like Eagle Keys in the '50s, it would have been a different story."

Ron Atchison had a different view. "He was a great guy. I thought Filchock was probably the greatest genius in football that I had ever seen. He used to go scouting and never took any paper or anything. He just smoked cigars. He'd come back and it was all in his head. I loved that, actually. We never had any books at all until after he left. He'd run practically everything on the field. He would show you what was to be done."

Most practices ended with a rousing game of keep-away touch football. Filchock also liked to have players line up in teams of five or six facing each other five yards apart and kick the football back and forth between them. Regarded as just an enjoyable activity to break the monotony of practice, it was a great way to develop hand-eye coordination and foot agility.

A comic in the dressing room, Filchock's faithful companion was Suds, a Weimaraner he took hunting at every opportunity. The owner-operation of the concessions at Taylor Field was a man named Spud Legget who the coach didn't particularly like. On occasion when Spud came to the dressing room and was rapt in conversation with a player, Filchock would whisper, "Piss on him, Suds, piss on him." The dog would sneak up on Leggett, lift his leg and obey his master's command.

Ahead of his time or behind, prepared or not, all agreed Filchock had a brilliant football mind and was fun to play for. He was also successful, with a career record of 57–50–6. The Riders made the playoffs five of his six seasons as a head coach. Filchock's team made it to the Western final twice, the Grey Cup once. The Roughriders fired him after his only losing campaign in 1957.

Frank Tripuka isn't in the Hall of Fame, but he was a superb passer and field general. Born in 1928, he was raised in Bloomfield, New Jersey. Tripuka shared quarterbacking duties with Johnny Lujack and the Fighting Irish at Notre Dame. He turned pro with the Detroit Lions in 1949 and came to Saskatchewan in 1953 after stints with the Chicago Cardinals, New York Giants and Dallas Texans. Money was the major reason for the move.

"Coming up here," Tripuka explained, "you were getting twice the salary they were paying in the National Football League. I was playing in the NFL for around $12,000. Rider president Sam Taylor asked me to come here and said, 'Name your salary.' I just quickly doubled what I was making, added a thousand and said, 'Twenty-five.' He said, 'Come on ahead,' and that was that. I know it doesn't sound even close to what they are paying now, but everything being equal, I was very content."

Regina has been a tough place to play for quarterbacks. Despite his passing prowess, or perhaps because of it, Tripuka was considered one-dimensional because he didn't run very often. "They pay Bobby and Kenny good money to run. They're experts at it. I'm getting paid to throw," he said.

Paul Dojack, the greatest referee who ever lived, said, "One time it was second and three or four yards to go and Tripuka took off up the middle. Everyone stood around watching him because they didn't believe their eyes. When he was finally tackled, it took a few seconds for me to blow the whistle I was so stunned at what I had just witnessed." The rap against his running and passing successor Ron Lancaster was that he didn't win the big one.

Tripuka figured it didn't matter what you did. "The few cry babies you had, you just didn't pay attention to. You're going to get those no matter where you play."

Glenn Dobb's successor was balding, slouch-shouldered with a big nose and a large toothy grin. He spoke with a "New Joisey" accent. He wore kid's shoulder pads so as not to hinder his throwing arm. He looked awkward and ungainly. The odd time he did run the ball, he looked like a blind man feeling his way along. Despite the more than occasional chorus of boos directed his way, Tripuka was always cheerful and positive, especially about the people who often tormented him.

When asked what he liked best about playing in Regina, Tripuka quickly replied, "Oh, the friendliness of the people, the enthusiasm. You were part of the community which wasn't the case when you played in the NFL. There you got lost in the shuffle. You had a few enthusiastic fans but nothing like they were in Regina. Everyone took an interest, it was their team, you were their player. That made a big difference."

Those beyond the dressing room walls could not truly appreciate his total contribution to the team. Respected for his great intelligence and throwing arm, Tripuka's teammates looked to him for leadership, knowing he would find a way to win. He was an excellent athlete, successful at all levels. It ran in the family, too. His son Kelly starred in the National Basketball Association for many years.

Frank Tripuka completed 1090 passes in 1930 attempts for 15,506 yards. He had 87 touchdown passes and a percentage completion rate of 56.5. He is the fourth-ranked passer in Roughrider history behind Lancaster, Kent Austin and Darian Durant. He led the Western Conference in passing four times and was the all-star quarterback twice. He was as fine a human being as you would ever want to meet.

Tripuka remembered what fun they had as a team. Reggie Whitehouse played 15 years for the team. Although highly regarded by his peers, he was never an all-star. One day, Whitehouse hid Tripuka's trousers in the back room. When Frank came out of the shower, he looked everywhere for his pants, but Reggie kept a straight face. Finally Tripuka put on his boxer shorts, shirt, tie, socks, shoes and sports jacket and walked out of the dressing room and drove home.

Tripuka laughed and said:

Bobby Marlow would lie stomach down on the sidelines. One day Freddie Hamilton snuck up behind him, piled some paper under his foot and lit it. You should have seen him jump!

Mario DeMarco was always pulling some stunt on somebody. I remember one day I got Tare Rennebohm to give me a couple of long nails and I nailed Mario's shoes right to the floor while he was in the shower room. They were brand new work shoes because he was working at the gas station then.

He came over and just about had a fit. He laughed that off. There was always something like that going on around the locker room. All the guys on the team were very close, you know, like Sully Glasser. He went into the shower with his lit cigar in his mouth.

Jon Wozniak and I lived together when our wives didn't come up with us the odd year. The same with Kenny Carpenter. Kenny was always my roommate on the road. It was like one big happy family.

The 1956 best-of-three Western final opened in Regina on Saturday, November 10.

It was a well-played contest that saw the Eskimos in the lead 22–16 with less than three minutes to go. Tripuka led the team down the field to the Edmonton four-yard line. The minute flag was up. On the first play, he gave the ball to Sully Glasser who got to the two-yard line. Bobby Marlow took it to the one and, on the last play of the game, he crashed into the end zone to tie the game at 22. Whitehouse kicked the convert, making the final 23–22 for Saskatchewan. On the bus back to the Exhibition Grounds, the gruff, ever so rough and tough Martin Ruby was crying like a baby, tears streaming down his face.

The next two games were played in the Igloo, the first on the Wednesday, November 15. In game two, the Riders were leading 12–8 in the second quarter and had a chance to put the Eskimos away.

Tripuka recalled that night at Clarke Stadium. "I threw Harry Lampman a touchdown pass and it was called back. Then we tried a field goal and missed that. From that point on, the game turned right around, just before the half. In the second half, it was all Edmonton and they ended up beating us 20–12. But I always felt had that touchdown been allowed that Harry Lampman caught, we had them. But we didn't and that was that."

Former Eskimo quarterback and Alberta premier Don Getty remembered it well:

> *We had a halfback named Earl Lindley who broke his shoulder in the first game which we lost in Regina. In order to get the same offensive punch coach Pop*

Ivy switched Jack [Parker] to halfback. Ivy made the decision to play me at quarterback which I was extremely nervous about because it was really sudden death. But I also looked forward to it because nobody wants to sit on the bench. We won that game, 20–12. It was probably the hardest hitting football game I can remember. In the next game, we really got the jump on them. I threw three or four touchdown passes.

Four days later, on a cold, miserable night, the home-towners recovered Doug Killoh's fumble in game three on the opening kickoff and put it in the end zone. Getty led the Esks to a 51–7 win and then pummelled the Montréal Alouettes 50–27 to win their third straight Grey Cup. The two games combined represented the greatest offensive performance in CFL post-season history.

The outcome was no surprise to Ron Atchison. "They ran around us as if we were on ice. I discovered after that they had honed out their cleats. Those were the days you were allowed to use aluminium cleats. They used maybe a $5/8$-inch drill and just honed out the top of them so it left a real sharp edge around them. The rule was you couldn't do that. They ran around us just like nothing. That's how they beat us that time." It wouldn't be the last time the Roughriders would be done in by footwear.

Frank Tripuka believed this fine group of players could have done better if Filchock had been a better coach. They also could have done better if racism hadn't prevailed. While the Eskimo had stars like Johnny Bright and Rollie Miles, the Bombers had Tom Casey, Leo Lewis, Ernie Pitts and Calvin Jones, the

Stampeders had Sugarfoot Anderson, Woody Strode, Chuck Anderson and John Henry Johnson, the Riders were either lily-white or had the token "black" on the team. Eighteen years after Gabe Patterson, George Reed would compare Regina to Alabama.

In 1956 the only black player on the team was Jon McWilliams from Nebraska, a fleet-footed receiver, so fast down field on punt coverage he usually ran by the returner. A shy but friendly individual, he almost always left the dressing room alone. In 1957, halfback Sam Wesley from Oregon was the sole non-white on the team. He didn't play much. He stood over by the side of the bench, talking to the water boy saying, "They must be saving me for the Grey Cup."

Milton Robichaux, an end from Trinity, Texas, on the team, was typical of the white Americans. He cursed Abraham Lincoln for making him and Sammy Wesley brothers.

Common comments in Regina were, "You have to have two of them" or "They're not like other people," as if they were animals in a zoo.

"I remember trying to find out why there were no blacks on our team," said Ron Atchison. "They had one black ballplayer here when I arrived. The women chased him so much the executive said they'd never have another one."

Times have changed. In the 1950s, there were one or two blacks on the team, the rest of the imports being white. Today, it's the other way around.

The Plane Crash

Despite losing to the Eskimos in the 1956 final, the Rider faithful were full of optimism. With no retirements contemplated, the future looked bright, even though Winnipeg was getting stronger, and the Eskimos were showing no signs of age.

Without a Grey Cup to celebrate, and because a dozen Riders were in the line-up, Saskatchewan fans turned their attention to the Second Annual All-Star game, staged at Empire Stadium in Vancouver by the Shriners and the CFL before 13,546 fans.

The two starting quarterbacks were Tripuka and Sam "the Rifle" Etcheverry of the Montréal Alouettes. They were such great passers that the game was an aerial circus, despite driving rain and ankle-deep mud. The West won 35–0.

Selected to play, among others, were Mel Becket, one of a long line of great Saskatchewan centres and defensive end Gordie Sturtridge. The day after their triumph, they boarded a Trans-Canada Airlines plane destined for Calgary, Regina and Winnipeg. Also on board was a Blue Bomber all-star Calvin Jones and Roughriders Ray Syrnyk and Mario DeMarco, who had gone to the coast to watch.

They never arrived. The plane smashed into BC's Mount Slesse on December 9, 1956. All 62 people on board went to a wintery grave, the worst aviation disaster in Canadian history up to that time. The bodies were never recovered. All the players who died were unique individuals in their own right.

Gordon Sturtridge came to the Roughriders from Winnipeg, where he was with the Bombers in 1949 but never got into a game. He sat out a couple of years, attempting a comeback in 1953.

Coaching the Blue Bombers was George Trafton, a member of the NFL Hall of Fame, reputedly a driver for Al Capone in his younger days. It seems Trafton made a serious error in judgement about the young Mr. Sturtridge and cut him from the club, muttering something to the effect that he would never make a football player.

Sturtridge joined the Riders in 1953 and promptly won the Rookie of the Year Award for the Western Conference. Two years later he won the first Stack Tibbets Award for the Roughriders' outstanding Canadian. Sturtridge made the All-Star team in '55 and '56.

Gordie's father was so incensed at the treatment he had received in Winnipeg that he offered his offspring 100 dollars every time he managed to knock the Bomber's prize quarterback Indian Jack Jacobs onto the seat of his pants. Until Jacobs left the league in 1954, he had no more persistent adversary than Gordie Sturtridge who accepted $100 bills from his delighted father. In the process, he became one of the finest defensive ends in the league. Sturtridge was at the height of his powers when fate dealt him a cruel blow.

Sturtridge was always sparring with Tare Rennebohm over his equipment. If his T-shirt, socks and jock weren't the newest or whitest, he wanted to exchange them. He wanted to be able to see his face in his shoes. He loved a practical joke and was good at playing them.

Two weeks before the All-Star game, Gordie gave me (the water boy and author) a ride home from practice. He had a beautiful 1956 Ford that impressed me to no end. I said to Gordie, "Boy, I sure like this car!" He replied with a laugh, "When I die, I'll leave it to you."

Mario DeMarco was one of the best blocking guards in the country in 1956. When Frank Filchock left Edmonton to coach Saskatchewan, Mario went with him. Three times an all-star, the Miami, Florida, product was an inspiration to his teammates on and off the field.

Those privy to the dressing room are the only ones who can really know who the leaders of a team are. In the case of the 1956 Roughriders, DeMarco, Jon Wozniak and Tripuka played that role. DeMarco had a kind word for everyone, especially when things weren't going well.

Tripuka looked back at 1956. "It just wasn't the same after the plane crash. Many times I've thought about DeMarco. He was such a good-natured soul. Some of the things he would do, years later you still laugh about them.

"He opened up a gas station with Mel Becket. They didn't know the first thing about automobiles or servicing cars. He ended up unknowingly pouring motor oil into the transmission.

"Gosh, I miss him. Mario was one of a kind. He never had a bad word to say about anybody."

DeMarco's partner on the line, as well as in business, was Mel Becket from Indiana. A shy man who kept to himself, Becket earned the respect of his teammates and opponents with his work on the field. The two remain united in death. In their memory, the Western Conference named the offensive lineman award the DeMarco-Becket Memorial Trophy.

Redwater, Alberta's Ray Syrnyk was their linemate. A hardworking guard from the Winnipeg Junior program, Syrnyk was a steady, dependable starter. Another quiet man, he enjoyed a reputation off the field as an individual always ready for a good time. He went out to Vancouver to have fun.

The Trans-Canada Airlines North Star, Flight 810, left Vancouver shortly after 7:00 PM. It was last heard from at 7:35 PM near Hope, BC, when the pilot radioed that an engine had failed and he was turning back. Subsequent rescue operations were hampered by extreme turbulence and bad weather.

Fateful decisions were taken that All-Star weekend. Calvin Jones missed the original flight because he slept in. A Blue Bomber official said he was squeezed aboard the plane that went missing. Eskimo all-stars Frankie Anderson and Rollie Miles, as well as club president Moe Lieberman were booked on the flight but changed their reservations to an earlier one.

The head referee for the all-star game, Regina's Paul Dojack, was scheduled on Flight 810 but changed his plans to visit a niece who was to meet him in Vancouver. She didn't show up. He left Monday. His TCA Viscount had trouble landing in Regina because of a snow storm. On a second try, the plane was guided in by radar.

Waiting anxiously in Regina for news of the flight was Mrs. C. Jarques who was babysitting the Sturtridge children—Vickie, five; Valerie, six; and Gordon, 15 months. Mrs. Jarques had been told the children's parents would be home about 6:00 PM. Gordie wired from Vancouver airport that the flight had been delayed because of bad weather and that they would not be home until 10:30 PM.

It fell to Ron Atchison to let the children know something was wrong:

> I was a pretty good friend of Gord's. My most vivid memory was when the babysitter phoned us here about seven o'clock in the morning and she was hysterical. The wife and I went over and we pretty well knew that something was pretty serious.

> So I told the children that the plane was down but nobody knew what had happened to them. I gave them that much. I never said they were dead or anything. Those are my most vivid memories—the stress the babysitter was under and, of course, the long wait before it [the plane] was discovered.

The day after the crash, Mildred Sturtridge's parents, Mr and Mrs. Edward Alford of Winnipeg, arrived in Regina to look after the children. Interviewed on the Tuesday by the *Leader-Post*, Mr. Alford said as the merry cries of the children echoed throughout the house, "We still haven't told them the full story yet. We are still not certain what the situation is ourselves. If the worst comes, we shall be taking the children. We would break the news to them gradually."

Valerie Sturtridge, a resident of Winnipeg, confirmed that her maternal grandparents raised them. She has no memory of being told about the plane crash.

"Actually, I don't," she said. "It's strange, but I sort of don't have too many memories of my childhood at all. I think that's a defence mechanism more than anything else, but I don't actually remember the day…that someone sat me down and said, 'They're not coming back.' It's really strange. My sister I think is pretty much the same. I don't have any memories of my mom and dad at all."

Sandy Archer said, "The one [memory] I remember was Harry Lampman went out there. I can't recall whether he played on the team or whether he just went out. When he came back, he told me the story that he was ready to fly back, and the guy from Winnipeg, Calvin Jones, wanted to get back and Harry said, 'Being single, it didn't matter to me,' and so Harry traded tickets with them.

"Ray Syrnyk wanted to go out there [to Vancouver]— he wasn't playing in it—he didn't have any money but he was in a card game the night before and he won enough money to get a ticket to go out there, so he went."

Bill Clarke remembered it a bit differently. Because the game was to be played in Vancouver, Clarke and Bobby Marlow were taken off the All-Star team and replaced by hometown Lion heroes By Bailey and Norm Fieldgate. Clarke and Marlow were going to go to the coast anyway but lost too much in the poker game to Sandy Archer and Syrnyk, who then took Clarke's ticket.

At a Regina party a few days before the All-Star game, Gordie Sturtridge presented his wife Millie with a new mink coat. Bill Clarke had painful memories of that evening so many years ago.

"Millie told us that flying out to Vancouver was her first-ever flight. She said she was really afraid of crashing. I told her not to worry, that you just fly into a mountain and splat! That's it. You won't feel a thing. I've never said that to anyone since."

The Roughriders took a long time to recover from the plane crash. It wasn't only the matter of losing four talented ballplayers. All teams have experienced that through injuries, retirement and now free agency. Mario DeMarco, Ray Syrnyk, Gordie Sturtridge and Mel Becket were deeply missed. Young male athletes think they are immortal. These players were young men who had died and were left behind. Death hits young people harder because it is contrary to the established order of things. A pall of gloom settled over the dressing room.

"Losing guys like DeMarco, Mel Becket, Gordie Sturtridge and Ray—they were such a big part of the team," recalled Tripuka. "They were definitely, unquestionably friends. It just wasn't the same after the plane crash.

"And, of course, Jon Wozniak retired, called it quits. Martin Ruby was finished. When you lose guys like that out of your starting line-up, it just can't be the same. It is impossible to be the same. You can't replace men like that overnight."

In 1957, halfback Alex Bravo, Oklahoma tackle Leland Kendall, receivers Harry Lampman and Jon McWilliams, as well as Canadian backs Bernie Bucholtz, Rod Pantages and Pete Thodas, did not return.

From Bad to Worse

New players on the scene included halfback Jack Hill, a Robert Duvall lookalike who at Utah State the year earlier was the second highest scorer in college football. He came to collegiate and pro football later in life because he first fulfilled his obligation as a Mormon missionary.

Continuing the religious theme was Baylor All-American Bill Glass, both a defensive tackle and a preacher. He came to the CFL because his Baptist beliefs prevented him from playing on Sunday, the favoured day of the NFL. He performed poorly in Rider livery and asked to be released from his contract to devote his time to God. As soon as GM Dean Griffing agreed, the Reverend Bill overcame his devotion to the Fourth Commandment and signed with the Cleveland Browns.

Also arriving in 1957 was defensive tackle Buddy Cockrell from Hardin-Simmons in Texas. When the weather turned cold, he asked for a pair of long handles. After some explaining, Tare Rennebohm finally realized he was asking for a suit of long underwear. Canadian Len Legault joined the team in 1957 and played nine years, the only bright recruiting light that season.

Losing 13 veterans out of any team's line-up would spell disaster. Add in the dreadful psychological impact of the plane crash, and you have a pretty grim year. There wasn't much Frank Filchock or any other coach could do.

It was a two-team league that year. Edmonton finished on top at 14–2, taking all four games against the

Riders and outscoring them 121 to 36. Saskatchewan finished last at 3–12–1.

The Riders averaged 22 points a game in 1956 and 17 points the following year. The decline was most noticeable on defence, going from surrendering 17 points a game to 27. No team had given up 438 points before. Two years later, Saskatchewan broke their own record for futility by yielding 567 points. They established the still-standing record of 710 points-against in 1991. When the Roughriders have a crop failure, it's spectacular.

It seemed that in just about every game, the opposition scored on their first possession. The sight of Len Legault, Ron Atchison and Bill Clarke trudging dejectedly to the sidelines time after time is etched in memory as is the quiet of the locker room, players sitting slump-shouldered against the wall, peeling off a sock or sweater and throwing it at the laundry hamper. More and more meetings were held where the grim-faced club president Don McPherson would come into the dressing room with GM Dean Griffing and sit down with Frank Filchock. Four years in a row, the team had experienced success, had held their own against the best in the west. For most of the players, as well as Griffing and Filchock, losing was a new and unpleasant experience.

Frank Tripuka, Stan Williams and Larry Isbell (punting) had the worst year of their distinguished careers. With a great passing quarterback, the leading receiver was Ron Dundas with only 38 catches for 625 yards.

At the end of the season, the Rider executive decided to clean house. Filchock and Griffing were fired.

Filchock learned of his dismissal on the radio when returning from a hunting trip with Suds.

The year 1958 marked the beginning of the 19-year stewardship of Ken Preston as general manager. Although he came to be regarded as one of the best in the business, success didn't come easily or early, even though he made the playoffs his first year in the front office.

His new head coach was George Terlip. Thirty-five years of age when he came to the Roughriders, the Elkhart, Indiana, native had played at Notre Dame, winning three national titles in 1946, '47 and '49. He played for the Buffalo Bills and Cleveland Browns after which he coached college football at several U.S. schools. He had been Frank Clair's backfield coach at Ottawa in 1957.

Terlip faced a massive rebuilding job. Sam Wesley, Charlie Hatch, Galen Laack, Buddy Cockrell, Milt Robichaux, John Witte and Bill West all left after one year. Veterans Stan Williams, Sully Glasser, Moe Martin, George Tait and Tom Donnelly retired.

But a good nucleus remained, including Tripuka, Carpenter, Marlow, Isbell, Legault, Whitehouse, Harry Lunn, Atchison, Clarke, Wahlmeier and Ron Adam.

The most exciting acquisition was Chester "Cookie" Gilchrist, a teenager from New York State who had played with the ORFU Kitchener-Waterloo Dutchmen. Incorrigible off the field and on, Jake Gaudaur brought him to Hamilton in 1956. Although Gilchrist made the Eastern All-Star team both years he toiled for the Tabbies, a frustrated Ti-Cat brain trust shipped him to

Saskatchewan. After one year in green and white, he went to the Argos for two years.

In 1961, Gilchrist joined the Buffalo Bills in the American Football League (AFL). He was the leading rusher in the AFL and scored five touchdowns against the New York Jets on December 8, 1963. He led the Bills to two league titles. He was an all-star every year he played on both sides of the border.

Gilchrist came to pro football straight out of high school. A huge man, in addition to being a punishing runner, he was a devastating tackler on defence who loved to unleash a blood-curdling yell at his opponents, scaring them half to death. Cookie cooled down at half-time by showering in his uniform. He became the first Roughrider to rush for over 1000 yards—1254.

The biggest story of 1958 was Jack Hill who set a new CFL scoring record of 145 points. Hill had 16 touchdowns, 36 converts, four field goals and a single. The 16 TDs were also a record that stood up until Hugh Campbell caught one more in 1966. Hill led the West with 60 catches for 1065 yards, the only receiver in the country to break the 1000-yard barrier. He made the All-Star team along with Gilchrist, Ken Carpenter and Larry Isbell. The year 1958 was the apex of his career. He never came close to those numbers anywhere again.

The '58 Roughriders reduced their points against by 114 and scored 44 more than in 1957. At 320 points for, they were second best in the league. The Bombers were the class of the league, going 13–3, the still mighty Eskimos second at 9–6–1. Saskatchewan was three points behind, 7–7–2. Given their offensive weapons, they should have done better. Perhaps the coaching was to blame. Replacing Filchock with Terlip was going from one extreme to the other.

Said Frank Tripuka:

> *Typical of some of these new coaches who take over, they get a little radical. George was one of those kind of guys. I think there is a certain discipline you have to have on a team and rules you have to abide by but George went kind of crazy. Some of those meetings of his, two hours at a time. Up to a certain point you have to have that but George went over the deep end. The funny thing is, if we could have just found a happy medium between an organized guy like Terlip and a free-wheeling guy like Frank Filchock, I think you would have found a successful formula. It had to be someplace between the two.*

Halfway through the season, Terlip signed NFL quarterback Al Dorow who only stayed a fortnight and no wonder. In one game Terlip alternated quarterbacks on every down, bringing in the play from the bench. This was completely foreign to Tripuka.

"That's when I got a little angry because I was always brought up with the fact that I was the guy who was going to call the plays. But Terlip wanted to send stuff in. And he sent some crazy stuff in. He was the man and you had to obey him. He was the coach."

Edmonton won the semifinal round, 58–12.

At season's end, the American nucleus of Tripuka, Marlow, Bobby Mulgado, Carpenter, Hill and centre Neil

Habig remained. Larry Isbell retired, as did Canadians Harry Lunn and Fred Hamilton.

Rock Bottom

The next year was an unmitigated disaster, the worst season in the club's history, except for their first in 1910. Going 1–15, they averaged 13 points a game while surrendering a record 35 points per game. Two of the three worst defeats in Roughrider history occurred in 1959, losing 55–0 to the Eskimos on August 24 in Edmonton and 61–8 to Winnipeg five days later in Regina. Imagine! Being outscored 116 to 8 in one week!

Only Neil Habig made the All-Star team. One of the few bright lights was the arrival of Gene Wlasiuk from the Winnipeg Juniors who became the Riders' career leader in punt returns and punt return yardage. He is ranked eighth all-time in the CFL, remarkable considering no blocking was allowed then.

Frank Tripuka wanted out:

> *The funny thing about my football career is that I never thought I'd be playing that long. Every year I played, I said this is the last one. I'm going to be staying home.*
>
> *I reached the point in '59—of course, things weren't going well—and I thought it's about time I called it quits. I said to George Terlip, "I'd just as soon stay closer to home, if it could be worked out. I'd like to be traded."*

Terlip had come from Ottawa. He was the backfield coach under Frank Clair. He talked to Clair and they worked out a trade.

> *So I went to Ottawa, but Clair and I never got along. It was just like mixing salt and pepper. He and I— nothing. That was probably one of the most miserable years I ever spent in football. Finally, when Terlip got fired with five or six games left, Sam Taylor called me in Ottawa to see if I wanted to come back here and take over as head coach. I said, "Yeah, I'd be happy to." Anything to get out of Ottawa.*

> *That's how I came back and finished the season coaching. Then they offered me the job for the 1960 season and I said no. I just had no ambition whatsoever to coach anymore and that was that.*

The player that Ottawa sent to Saskatchewan for Tripuka was defensive lineman Jim Marshall. The following year, the Riders needed a quarterback, so they traded him to Cleveland for Bob Ptacek. When the NFL expanded, the Minnesota Vikings plucked Marshall from Cleveland's unprotected list. He went on to become a great star for Bud Grant's four National Football Conference champion teams, a feared member of the Purple Gang. He held the NFL iron man record, appearing in 282 consecutive games, a mark only broken in 2009 by Minnesota quarterback Brett Favre.

Tripuka was reunited with Dean Griffing and Frank Filchock in 1961 as the quarterback of the fledgling AFL Denver Broncos. After Tripuka's release in 1963, he appeared in green and white for the last time, helping coach Bob Shaw groom a promising youngster named Ron Lancaster. He then retired to New Jersey.

Tripuka's successor as head coach in Saskatchewan was the great Rider veteran Ken Carpenter.

In the last home game of the 1960 season, the Roughriders, at 2–11–2, couldn't see a playoff spot with a telescope. The opposition was Edmonton. It was a cold, grey day. The Eskimos had defeated the Riders 19–1 and 29–6 in their first two encounters. In the third meeting at Clarke Stadium, the score was 9–2 for the green and gold. In their final game in Regina in November, the Roughriders played the game of their lives and scored nine points in the final quarter to lead 11–10. With seconds remaining, Edmonton lined up for a desperation field-goal attempt. It would be 51 yards into the wind. Tommy Joe Coffey drove the ball toward the uprights, a line drive that just trickled over the crossbar. Final score: Edmonton 13, Saskatchewan 11. It was that kind of year.

The 1960 Riders were stronger defensively with Illinois All-American Bill Burrell joining Atchison and Clarke on the defensive line. Regina native Larry Dumelie began a distinguished eight-year career in the defensive backfield after graduating from Arizona. Ken Don and Bob Ptacek were linebackers. That line-up reduced points against by 145. Unfortunately, they scored seven fewer points than the previous year. The offence was hopeless with Ptacek at quarterback.

Retiring after the 1960 campaign were Canadians Ron Adam, Ron Dundas, Doug Killoh and Vic Marks. Receiver Vernon Vaughn had to retire as well after being diagnosed with cancer. He died soon after and was buried in his Roughrider uniform. Also leaving was Bobby Marlow, the fourth leading rusher in team history behind George Reed, Mike Saunders and Wes Cates with 4291 yards. Coach Ken Carpenter came out of retirement as a player and joined the Rider alumni in Denver.

Three wins in two years. They say it is always darkest before the dawn. The good people of Saskatchewan were about to enjoy a spectacular prairie sunrise.

Chapter Six

From the Outhouse...

Few decades in human history have been as momentous as the 1960s, a time full of upheaval and change. The Civil Rights Movement, the Anti-War Movement, the Student Movement, the Separatist Movement, the Women's Movement. Hemlines went up, drugs went down. Make love, not war. Drop in, drop out.

These were exciting times in Saskatchewan, too. The province became the world's biggest producer of potash, just discovered at Bell Plaine, Esterhazy and all around Saskatoon.

The CFF-NDP government of Premier Woodrow Lloyd introduced the Medicare Plan that became Canada's most sacred social program.

Dief the Chief was the province's favourite son; Tommy Douglas and Ross Thatcher did battle in Mossbank, Saskatchewan, enthralling a radio audience of hundreds of thousands. Regina's Golden Mile Plaza opened in 1960. The beautiful Wascana Centre project was begun and the University of Saskatchewan, Regina

Campus, opened its first new buildings on the wide-open prairie.

Yes, as Bob Dylan sang, "Times They Are A-Changing."

On the football field, too.

While the Riders struggled through the first season of the '60s with a mark of 2–12–2, the big story in the CFL unfolded in Calgary, where the Stampeders opened the brand new and beautiful McMahon Stadium on August 15. Ungracious guests, the Grey Cup champion Blue Bombers rained on Calgary's parade by winning 38–23. To fill the new stadium, George McMahon had hired NFL legend "Stout" Steve Owen, late of the New York Giants. At that time, his record of 151–100–17 made him the third winningest coach of all time in the NFL behind Curly Lambeau of Green Bay and the Chicago Bears' George Halas.

Owen had coached the Giants from 1931 through 1953. He won the NFL championship twice. He accomplished the nigh impossible by coaxing the rag-tag Stampeders into the 1960 playoffs, only to be trampled by the Eskimos 70–28 in the semifinals.

The Giant legend had come to the CFL in his early 60s, although he looked much older. But Calgary wanted a younger man for their football team so they fired Owen after one season, replacing him with Glenn Dobb's brother Bobby.

R.A. "Bob" Kramer, back in charge of the Roughriders, believed the team needed a real coach, rather than an inexperienced one learning on the job like Ken Carpenter. Kramer brought Steve Owen to Regina.

Stout Steve's down-home philosophy was perfect for the prairie province. "Football is a game played down in the dirt and always will be."

Owen's approach to defence was simple. "Football was invented by a mean son-of-a-bitch and that's the way the game's supposed to be played."

Kramer had the coach he wanted. He turned his attention to the first of the "Save Our Roughrider" campaigns. The club was teetering on the edge of bankruptcy. Only 4908 season tickets had been sold in 1960. In February 1961, the Riders staged a huge pep rally at the Regina Armouries. Guest speakers included one of the famous Four Horsemen of Notre Dame, as well as the new head coach. The appeal went out to the faithful. Just over 1000 new season tickets were sold, enough to carry the team through another couple of years. It had to, because after missing the playoffs in 1961, ticket sales dropped back to 4603—305 less than the beginning of the decade.

In Owen's first year, the team went 5–10–1, finishing fourth. Their leading receiver was former Stampeder Jack Gotta, traded by Calgary to the Green and White in 1960 for a running back named Lovell Coleman. Coleman became the fourth leading rusher in Stampeder history. A great player and coach, Gotta was one of the most beloved characters in Canadian football. He led Saskatchewan in receiving for three straight years. He won four Grey Cup rings as an assistant and head coach and revitalized the Stampeders in the late 1970s. Coming to Saskatchewan seemed perfectly natural to him.

*When I was growing up in northern Michigan on
the Wisconsin border, there was only one place that
really played football and that was Green Bay. Regina
was much more booming than Green Bay ever was.
Like Green Bay, football has always been so dominant
in Regina. It was a great, great feeling. I grew up in
a football environment. Everyone played basketball
and baseball to stay in shape for football. When it
came to Regina, as great a hockey centre as it is and
the number of great hockey players who have come
from there—other than the guy from Floral* [Gordie
Howe]—*football was so dominant, football was king
like it was in Green Bay so I felt really good about it.*

According to Gotta, Steve Owen laid the ground-
work for future greatness. He brought a new attitude,
a sense of true professionalism to the franchise.

*Steve Owen was great. He was so observant. He'd
pick up things and say things to me like, "Jack, on
that last cut, you should perhaps be pushing that
defence a little bit deeper and then make your cut
because of the zone they're in." I had such great
respect for him because of his background that when
he'd say things, I was listening.*

*He made you fully aware of being fundamentally
sound in everything. Do this better, do that better. He
never glorified anybody. He brought the game away
from the individual to the team concept. Everyone
has to contribute. I really appreciated that.*

Wayne Shaw signed for $2000 in 1961. The Davidson,
Saskatchewan, native who would be a star linebacker

with the team for 12 years, also thought highly of Stout Steve.

"I liked him. He was a funny guy. They used to say he drank a bottle of scotch a day. But Steve took our team that only won two games and made the playoffs in 1962. Remember, we didn't have Ronnie and George in '61 and '62."

And Shaw admired Jack Gotta: "I loved Jack. He was a character. I was upset with the way the press in Regina did him in when he was the head coach there [1985–86]. He was one of my favourite guys. I always looked upon him as a really nice guy. He was one of the few Americans who treated everyone the same."

Five Riders made the 1961 All-Star team: Ron Atchison, Bill Clarke, Jack Gotta, Neil Habig and Bob Ptacek. The team quarterback in 1960 and 1962, Ptacek made the '61 dream team as a linebacker.

Ptacek had the distinction of blowing both his Achilles tendons in late 1962. He injured the first on the football field. After a rehab of over six months, the doctor pronounced him fit, and he resumed his daily workouts that included a rousing game of racquet ball, in the course of which he blew the other Achilles. The Michigan alumnus retired in 1965.

Owen's quarterback in 1961 was Dave Grosz. The Oregon Duck completed only 42.7 percent of his passes for eight touchdowns. He was much better throwing the ball to the opposing team, racking up 20 interceptions. In '62, Ptacek was back at the controls, completing 60.7 percent of his passes for 2317 yards, 15 majors and only 10 interceptions.

The new star on the scene in 1962 was a fleet-footed halfback named Ray Purdin from Northwestern. After being humiliated in Hamilton 67–21 (the most points ever scored on a Roughrider team) on October 15, 1962, Purdin was heard to comment outside Civic Stadium, "Let's get on the bus before they score another one."

That was the lowest point in an otherwise successful year. Owen's Roughriders made the playoffs for the first time in four years, the first of what would be 15 straight post-season appearances, a record eclipsed only by the Edmonton Eskimos.

In the playoffs, the Stamps won the semifinal round 43–7. All-Stars that year included Neil Habig for the fourth year, Ray Purdin, Bill Burrell, Garner Ekstran and, for the third time in a row, Ron Atchison. Habig and Purdin were All-Canadians. Things were looking up.

Steve Owen, winner of the 1962 Coach of the Year Award, retired to New York and was replaced by the volatile, dictatorial Bob Shaw for the 1963 season. A huge bear of a man, Shaw played with the Cleveland Rams and Chicago Cardinals before completing his career with Calgary and Toronto. He had been a fine receiver, an excellent place-kicker and a Stampeder all-star in 1952. He stayed in Saskatchewan for two years, and then amid much fanfare and great expectations, left to right the listing good ship Argonaut. After two frustrating years in Toronto, he served as an assistant at New Orleans, Chicago and Buffalo. Shaw returned to the CFL in 1976 as general manager of the Tiger-Cats. He soon re-established his reputation as a tough guy by firing his personally selected head coach,

George Dickson, because the team was winless after four exhibition and two regular-season games.

For most of Shaw's players in Regina, his two years in Saskatchewan were the longest two years of their careers. Canadian Bob Good from Thunder Bay via Oregon State said, "We played well under Shaw because we detested him and wanted to show him." Shaw made no bones or apologies about the tactics he employed.

"It's difficult to say how to motivate football players," Shaw said.

> Really, it's different strokes for different folks. I think that sometimes you have to throw fear into a player. You get to know your players. Some need a pat on the back or a chewing out. It just depends on the player. No one works to their full potential. I think they can be pushed to their full potential by different kinds of motivation.
>
> You have to be honest. They know that if they don't work up to their potential there is no place for them on our football team. The sad situation is when a player can't be honest when he has an opportunity to perform and can't do it but also can't look himself in the mirror and admit he can't do it.

All-Star Ron Atchison, who would rather have a root canal than criticize a fellow coach or player said, "Bob Shaw had diarrhea of the mouth. He talked so much it got so we didn't pay any attention to him. Shaw was a hard guy to take. He was the only coach I ever had that literally cried after a game. He took everything personally."

Jack Gotta: "I found him a hard guy. Certainly he was highly opinionated. It was his way, and if you were faltering a bit, it could be pretty dramatic."

George Reed: "My first pro coach was Bob Shaw. I would have quit football if he had stayed. He didn't treat us like men."

Not everybody was negative. When discussing coaches, Dale West said, "Steve Owen was a great defensive coach. Bob Shaw did a really, really thorough job. The main thing with pros is they figure that you know it when you get there so not a whole lot of time is spent on fundamentals. It is more of a package and trying to work around what your strengths are.

"In the basics, Shaw was a pretty good guy. A lot of us had difficulty with his temperament but that's neither here nor there. I think he was a reasonably good football coach."

West was being exceedingly generous considering Shaw's determination to end West's career. Shaw's wife played a major role in decision-making with the ball club. She told her husband that West had been partying the night before a game, although that wasn't true. Shaw, in the manner of "bring me John the Baptist's head on a platter," decided to cut West. But the next night, West had three interceptions against Hamilton. He played another five years.

The player closest to the coach is the quarterback. Ron Lancaster played two seasons for Bob Shaw. "He was different. He was a tough coach to play for in a lot of ways. He put together a pretty good football team over those years. But basically it was the guys who were there in 1963 when I got there and the guys that were acquired during that time who all decided to stay and made it a pretty good place to play football.

"He was sound, all his stuff was good. He was a tough guy to play for. That's all I'll say about it." (Other players say Ronnie despised him.)

The 1963 season saw a change in the balance of power in the Western Conference. Plagued by injuries, Winnipeg finished out of the playoffs for the first time since 1949 and only the third time in the team's distinguished history. Beset by retirements, bickering and bad management, the mighty Eskimos fell into the basement with a mark of 2–14, their all-time worst year. On the rise were the Calgary Stampeders under the direction of Bobby Dobbs, finishing second with 22 points, two behind Dave Skrein's first place BC Lions. The Roughriders actually regressed by one point, finishing third at 7–7–2. Both saw-offs came against Calgary, 4–4 and 33–33. Calgary won the other encounter 17–16 in Regina.

The Wizard of Wittenberg

There were some new dogs on the block. Ron Lancaster arrived in a trade with Ottawa. Also in the line-up were George Reed, Ed Buchanan and Hugh Campbell. The nucleus of a dynasty would soon be in place.

Roughrider general manager Ken Preston should have been charged with grand larceny for his "steal" of Ron Lancaster.

"I was traded to Saskatchewan for not very much— I think the waiver price [$500]—but I'm not sure.

There were no players involved. The only deal was if they didn't want me, I went back to Ottawa. I always say I went for a broken helmet with no face mask."

Lancaster was born on October 14, 1938, in Fairchance, Pennsylvania. He grew up in Clairton, a few miles south of Pittsburgh. John Hufnagel and Tom Clements lived just down the road.

Lancaster attended Wittenberg University in Springfield, Ohio, graduating with a Bachelor of Education degree in Physical Education. On June 6, 2000, Lancaster received an honorary doctorate of laws degree from Brock University. Doctor Lancaster explained how he came to Canada.

"George Terlip was the general manager in Ottawa at that time. He had been my offensive coach with my college coach who was Bill Edwards. They were at Vanderbilt together. When they left there, Coach Edwards came back to Wittenberg as the athletic director and head coach. George ended up in Ottawa as the GM. Coach Edwards thought I should try pro football. He talked to George, and George signed me."

Ottawa already had a quarterback, a Canadian kid named Russ Jackson. Although the myth persists that they detested each other, "It became apparent in Ottawa," explained Lancaster, "that they weren't believers in the two quarterback system, nor were Russ and myself. Both of us were young, early in our careers and both of us wanted to play. They had to make a decision. Russ was in his third year when I got there and he had kind of proven that he was the starter. That made one of us expendable, and I was the guy."

Lancaster didn't jump for joy:

> *I wasn't real enthused about going out there to Regina at the start because I didn't really know anything about it—I'd only been there once. I kind of always wanted to play in Hamilton or Toronto, being closer to home and stuff. But I wanted to play. In those days, there was no such thing as free agency and all that junk, not that it would have mattered anyway, because my philosophy was that's part of the game—you get traded or sold, you just pack up and go. And that's what I did.*
>
> *Once I got out there, I kind of enjoyed it. It wasn't bad. I didn't live there at first. I went up in '63 and '64 and we liked it so we moved there in 1965.*

The other member of the dynamic duo came just as cheap as Lancaster.

"Originally, Vancouver had my rights," recalled George Reed, "when I came out of Washington State. They traded my rights to Saskatchewan. So I went to Saskatchewan. In those days, the money was as good as the National Football League and they offered me more money to come up here and that's how I got up here."

Halfback Ed Buchanan was picked up from the Stampeders for $500.

Arguably the three greatest games in Roughrider history are the 1966 Grey Cup, the 1989 Grey Cup and the second game of the semifinal against Calgary in 1963.

The Stampeders had clobbered the Green and White 35–9 at McMahon Stadium on Saturday, November 9, 1963. The Roughriders returned to Regina for the rematch. Somehow it seemed appropriate that the game would be played on Remembrance Day. Remembrance Night, actually.

Trailing in the series by 26 points, Saskatchewan had to win the second game by 27. The Roughriders opened the game with a sleeper play. "Ray Purdin went 95 yards," exulted Lancaster. "When we hit the sleeper play, a perfect play, and then we got another quick seven and the feeling on the bench was 'We've got a chance.' I think the momentum started and picked up from there."

Did it ever! Before the smoke cleared, the Roughriders won the game 39–12 and the round by a single point. They were returning to the Western final for the first time in seven years.

"The most incredible thing about it," said Lancaster, "was that we started the game with nobody in the stands and finished to a full house. It was unbelievable. We play on Saturday in Calgary and get beat up pretty good, and we go home and play Monday night, which everyone assumes is going to be the end of the year. It's November, a night game, it was cold. When we went out on the field there was nobody there, and when we started playing the game there was nobody there, but as soon as things got interesting, when we came back out for the second half, it was starting to fill up and at the end of the game, it was packed."

Those in the press box and the top rows of the stadium could see the cars streaming toward Taylor Field from all over the city. In fine 1960s fashion, a happening was taking place.

No one expected it.

Recalled the King of the Quarterbacks; "I think probably deep down inside, even a lot of the players didn't expect us to come back and win. Realistically, before the game no one thought we had a chance. But things happen in a football game that cause momentum to swing, and it swung our way. Once we got a couple of touchdowns, the game and series became reachable. Then everybody got fired up and excited; we played hard and ended up winning.

"But I really don't believe that at the start of the game we believed we could do it. We always felt we could beat Calgary but not by 27 after you've lost to them by 26. That doesn't seem right. I'd say the mood was let's win the ball game, go out and play hard. We always played hard. Things worked out pretty well."

Said Jack Gotta:

We believed we could do it if everyone played their best. One guy wasn't going to do it. You get a feeling that it could happen and that built throughout the game. The guys who were there were those kind of players who believed they could do it. As the game progressed, I felt we were getting stronger mentally.

Spirit, heart, courage elevate a man above another at testing time. All of that came together. Nobody had to say anything. Everybody just rose to the occasion. Games like that sustain you through the tough times. In the dressing room at half-time, guys were saying "We can do it, we can do it!" You don't want to be in the dressing room that long, you just want to get back at it. Let's not come down.

"Regina had a good football team," allowed Stampeder quarterback Jerry Keeling. "It was just one of those days when everything went wrong for us. We didn't play well. That was a real tough one because we had such a big lead. We probably went in thinking 'Just protect the lead and not do anything too bad.'"

What about the sleeper play? "Purdin just came off the bench and stepped onto the field. No one saw him. They changed the rules after that so the player had to come to the hash marks."

"Winning a game, coming back from that far down, you've got to be a little bit lucky, which we were, and they were a little unlucky, like Larry Robinson missing [four] makeable field goals. But nevertheless, it was a heckuva football game and we ended up doing something I don't think anyone expected us to do," said Lancaster.

"We got a little bit lucky at the right time, made some plays when we had to. They made some miscues. That's generally how football goes."

Bring on BC!

In their 10th season as a franchise, the Lions had made the playoffs for only the second time. But they did it up big, finishing first. They had players such as "Peanut Butter" King Joe Kapp, "Will-o-the-Wisp" Willie Fleming, Norm Fieldgate and Tom Brown.

The first game of the best-of-three finals was played on a crisp, grey day at Taylor Field, the Lions winning 19–7. Both teams looked forward to escaping the bitter prairie cold for the friendlier climate on the West Coast. But always gracious hosts, the Lions made sure the farm boys would feel at home by providing a snow storm for the second game, won by the visitors 13–8. Game three was a blowout, 36–1 for BC.

Lancaster described the bursting bubble.

> *The difference then was that you played the first game at home and then you'd go on the road for the next two. You didn't alternate it. We played the first one at home and lost. We played out there on Wednesday night. The surprising thing was everybody looked forward to playing in BC in November because of the weather, and then we played in a snowstorm. Yet we got a touchdown late in the game and won 13–8. Now we have to play on Saturday. We were pretty beaten up by Saturday, but they were a better football team, too. The game was over early. They got us down early and didn't let up.*

Seven Roughriders made the 1963 All-Star team, including Garner Ekstran (also All-Canadian), Ron Atchison, Bill Clarke, Al Benecick, Neil Habig, Dale West and Wayne Shaw. Rookie George Reed led the team in rushing with 751 yards. Gotta was the leading receiver. Martin Fabi was the CFL's number one punter with a 44-yard average.

Saskatoon native Dale West had arrived in Regina the year earlier, after a collegiate career at Arizona and the University of Saskatchewan. He signed for $3500.

"God, that was great!" he exclaimed. "The minimum was $2000. But you were only working four or five months. I did fine. I have no regrets about it."

On August 15, 1963, on a Thursday night, the Riders defeated Hamilton 5–3 in a driving rain storm. West had three interceptions that night, sharing the record with three others for most picks in a game by a first-year player. West also set a record for interception return yardage in a single season. West beat out established stars Harvie Wylie (Calgary), Norm Fieldgate (BC), Oscar Kruger (Edmonton) and Henry Janzen (Winnipeg) for the 1963 Western nominee for Outstanding Canadian, losing the Schenley Award to Ottawa's Russ Jackson.

In 1964, the Riders compiled their best record, 9–7, since 1956. New to the team was defensive back and Weyburn, Saskatchewan, native Hank Dorsch from Tulsa; Bob Kosid from Kentucky; Georgia guard Nat Dye; Jim Worden, a big tight end nicknamed "The Hog" from Wittenberg; receiver Gord Barwell from the Saskatoon Hilltops; and massive offensive tackle Clyde Brock out of Utah State.

Ray Purdin retired, his career as brilliant and short as a falling star. Two reasons were given for his departure.

"He didn't get along with Bob [Shaw] very well," explained Lancaster. "He just decided to say the heck with it. He was offered a job as a recreation director of a city in Michigan. He just decided it was time to move on."

Under new coach Neil Armstrong, the Edmonton Eskimos were twice as productive in 1964, winning four games instead of two. Winnipeg experienced the worst year in their history, at 1–14–1. CFL and NFL Hall of Fame coach Bud Grant winced at the memory:

The longer you are in coaching, the more humble
you become. You find out there are no geniuses in

*the coaching profession and certainly not yourself.
The team that will win is generally the team with the
best players and not the best coaches.*

*In 1964 we lost, at various times, nine players who
were out for the season. We started with a record of
1–1–1 and then we proceeded to lose 13 in a row. The
next season, seven of those nine players came back
from their injuries and they played the whole year
and went to the Grey Cup.*

*So any ideas I ever had about being a genius coach
were dispelled right there. You get the best players,
that's the big hurdle.*

*There are some coaches who can mess up with the
best players, but there are no coaches who can win
championships with the poorest players.*

While Edmonton was setting a record for most
points surrendered, 458, the Lions set the still-standing
record for fewest surrendered in the modern era, 10.8 per
game. They went on to win their first Grey Cup,
defeating Hamilton in Toronto 34–24.

The Stampeders, bent on revenge, were delighted to
face third-place Saskatchewan in the playoffs. In game
one at Regina, touchdowns by Eagle Day, Ted Woods
and Jim Dillard plus a Larry Robinson field goal gave
the visitors a 24–8 lead after three quarters of play.
But then Lancaster, the "Little General," went to work.
With Reed and Buchanan on the ground and Hugh
Campbell in the air, Lancaster completed 28 of 35 passes
and engineered four fourth-quarter touchdowns to pull
out a 34–25 win, and in the process, setting a record
for fourth-quarter points in a playoff game. The legend of

the "Wizard of Wittenberg," who pulled rabbits out of a hat with dramatic last-minute comebacks, was born.

The Roughriders continued to dominate back in Calgary, opening the scoring with an unconverted touchdown. Then the roof fell in. Calgary won the game 51–6, the round 76–40.

"We won by nine the first game," said Lancaster.

> We went there with a nine-point lead. You think things are going to work out. We marched down the field and scored first. They scored 51 points after that. I remember early in the third quarter Shaw telling me I'd better get hot or we'd be going home. I was thinking, 'Man, we might as well go home.' We couldn't get anything going after that first drive.

> I remember in that game Ted Woods returning a kickoff. He came around over near our bench and got hit, flipped up and over in the air, landed on his feet and ran for a touchdown.

> I'll tell you right now—things aren't going your way when they get hit, flip in the air, land on their feet and go for a touchdown. I don't remember much else about that game. I just remember we got killed.

All-Stars that year were Ed Buchanan, Hugh Campbell, Al Benecick, Dale West, Bob Ptacek, Wayne Shaw and Ron Atchison. Buchanan with 1390 yards was All-Canadian. Teammate George Reed had his first 1000-plus season, running for 1012 yards. Neil Habig made the dream team for the sixth straight year and retired along with Jim Copeland and Don Walsh. Jack Gotta went to Montréal. To the relief of most and the regret of none,

Bob Shaw departed for Toronto. His replacement was the stoic, quiet, controlled former head coach of the Eskimos and assistant to Shaw, Eagle Keys. The "Big Bird" from Turkey Neck Bend would usher in the greatest era in Saskatchewan Roughrider history.

The son of a carpenter, Keys is actually from Tompkinsville, Kentucky, a few miles west of the Cumberland River and north of the Tennessee border.

So what about Turkey Neck Bend?

Eagle Keys laughed. "Turkey Neck Bend was a little place in the river about seven miles from Tompkinsville. People used to ask me where I was from and I'd say Tompkinsville. And they'd say where in the world is that? I finally got to saying Tompkinsville is near Turkey Neck Bend so they wouldn't ask my any more questions. I used it up here one time and the media picked it up."

After graduating from Western Kentucky University at Bowling Green, Keys played semipro ball in Paterson, New Jersey. A teammate was Tom "Citation" Casey, and his coach was Allie Sherman. Keys joined the Montréal Alouettes in 1949. Three years later, he headed west to join his buddy Frank Filchock in Edmonton. Keys made the All-Star team at centre three years in a row. He became forever enshrined in football legend for his courageous play in the 1954 Grey Cup.

Early in the second quarter against Montréal, Keys broke his leg. Despite his injury, he limped out on to the field to snap the ball for a Bob Dean field goal and two converts. Contrary to persistent mythology, he did not snap the ball for the convert that won the game after

Jackie Parker tied the score with a scintillating fumble recovery and run. Bill Briggs performed that honour.

As Keys explained, because of the injury, his playing days were over, setting the stage for one of the most successful coaching careers in CFL history.

"I'd always figured on coaching. I broke my leg in 1954 in the Grey Cup and I had retired from playing because my leg wasn't completely healed. Pop Ivy was the coach at Edmonton. We only had one assistant and he made me his assistant. But I mean I always felt I was going to coach. That was the first job I had with Ivy in 1955. I replaced Sam Lyle as head coach of the Eskimos in 1959."

The following year, Keys' Eskimos upset the best team in Blue Bomber history to face the Ottawa Rough Riders in the Grey Cup. An injury-riddled bunch of brave Eskimos went down to defeat 16–6.

The great Eskimo dynasty was crumbling. Normie Kwong retired after the 1960 season. Rollie Miles followed in '61 and Johnny Bright two years later. A forerunner of the shocking Wayne Gretzky trade, Edmonton traded the legendary Jackie Parker to Toronto in 1963.

After the 1963 season, another cornerstone of the dynasty departed when Eagle Keys was fired, a victim of the club's 2–14 record as well as a number of players' wives who leaked information to the media about discontent in the dressing room. An honest man without guile, Keys was deeply hurt, leaving Edmonton a sadder but wiser man, especially when it came to trust.

In 1964, Bob Shaw hired Keys as his assistant coach. The Big Bird took over in 1965.

More pieces to the Grey Cup puzzle were put in place when New Mexico's Jack Abendshan, a guard and place kicker, signed, along with linebacker Wally Dempsey from Washington State, defensive back Ted Dushinski of the Hilltops as well as Regina boy, receiver and punter, Alan Ford, who played his university ball at College of the Pacific. All are on the Plaza of Honour.

Calgary was the class of the league in 1965, finishing first at 12–4. Bud Grant's Blue Bombers bounced back to an 11–5 mark, good for second place. Saskatchewan was third at 8–7–1, four points better than the defending champion BC Lions that they had eliminated from playoff contention with a magnificent pass-and-run play in Vancouver on October 24. Scrimmaging from his eight-yard line, Lancaster faked to Reed and threw deep to a streaking Gordie Barwell for the touchdown. At 102 yards, it was the longest touchdown pass of their careers.

For the first time, the Western semifinal would be a single-game, sudden-death affair. On a cold, Winnipeg day, late in the fourth quarter, trailing the Bombers 15–9, Lancaster had tight end Jim Worden wide open in the end zone. The ball hit the upright. "If I'd been trying, I'd have never hit that goal post in 100 years," number 23 remarked ruefully. (And modestly.)

Four Riders were All-Canadian that year: George Reed, Hugh Campbell, Ted Urness and Al Benecick. Dale West and Clyde Brock made the Western All-Star team.

Campbell led the league in receiving with 73 catches for 1329 yards and 10 touchdowns.

The Great George Reed

But the big story of 1965 was George Reed. The Renton, Washington, native set a new rushing record by running for 1768 yards. He won the Schenley Award for Most Outstanding Player. Beginning in 1965, 12 of the next 13 years saw either Lancaster or Reed carrying the Roughrider colours for Most Outstanding Player Award, the exception being Tom Campana in 1975. No wonder they referred to it as the George and Ronnie Show.

Reed's performance down the stretch that propelled the Riders into the playoffs was particularly impressive. After he retired, Reed looked back on that remarkable year.

"It was my best year stats-wise. It was my best year from the stand-point of the team because we had to win a couple of games at the end of the season to get into the playoffs which meant a lot to the team. The game against BC, I had 268 yards and then I followed it up with about 150 against Edmonton."

His game against the Lions represents the second-highest single-game rushing total in CFL history, just behind Ottawa's Ron Stewart's 287-yard performance in 1960.

Reed continued, "1965 and '66 were great years because I was a marked man and no one could stop us. To me, that's what I was. The one year, 1966, Paul Dudley got hurt, all we had in there were guys blocking, and I knew Eagle was just going to feed me the ball. The difference between gaining 1400 yards or 700 yards is very minimal. You can get an extra 20 yards here or there. Certain games were tougher than others or meant more. I think my last year, 1975, before I retired was probably as good a year as I had. I wound up with almost 1500 yards and I thought I played very well."

Reed rushed for 751 yards his rookie year. But you could see what was to come.

Jack Gotta agreed:

> He was never a showboat type of guy, just an intense guy. When he hit the hole, you went holy mackerel! Can a guy really have that much power and quickness and strength?

> When I coached, I always wanted to find a back like George. If it was a third and one and you could have any back to give the ball to, George Reed would be the one. If you had to make that one yard or the season's over and the coach is fired, George Reed gets the ball in my books.

Reed ran behind an exceptional offensive line: centre Ted Urness, guards Al Benecick and Jack Abendshan, tackles Clyde Brock and Reggie Whitehouse. One of the greatest defensive players in Canadian football history, Wayne Harris of the Calgary Stampeders said, "They had a great offensive line, and, of course, George Reed, Lancaster and Hugh Campbell. They were a very balanced football team, very strong. You could have probably named an all-star offensive line and you wouldn't have a better line than what they had in those days."

George Reed (left; number 34) playing against the Edmonton Eskimos, 1960

Of course, a good back makes the linemen better. George Reed agreed: "An offensive line always likes to block well. In Saskatchewan our theory was you get off and engage the defensive line but don't worry about where I'm at because a lot of times I start off over to the right and I wind up way back to the left. Of course, with the yardage you gained, it made the offensive linemen look good. It made their blocks easier because they knew all they had to do was stay with them and I would find a hole."

Maybe yes, maybe no. Ralph Galloway blocked for Reed from 1969 through 1975. Three times an all-star, the 6-foot-one 250-pound offensive lineman from Southern Illinois said, "Anybody knows George Reed is going to carry the ball nine times out of 10 on short yardage situations. If there is any motion whatsoever in the backfield prior to a play, a linebacker knows which way Reed is going. It is therefore very difficult to make a cut-off block on a linebacker who knows where the play is going."

According to Bud Grant, Reed was not the best full-back who ever played professional football. That honour he reserved for Cleveland's Jimmy Brown. Grant thought Reed could keep pretty good company in the pros: "George Reed is probably the second best fullback to ever play the game," he said after taking his Minnesota Vikings to their fourth appearance in the Super Bowl.

Arguably the greatest Roughrider of them all, it is ironic that such an incredible talent almost didn't play professionally at all. "Playing pro football was never part of my thinking when I was in college," Reed said in 1974. "Nobody drafted me in the National Football League, but then someone from the BC Lions talked to me about playing ball in Canada. They mustn't have thought much of me, though, because they traded me right away to Saskatchewan for a draft choice or something."

While at Washington State, Reed played 55 minutes per game during his junior and senior years. He was a Pac-Eight All-Star but the pros thought he was too small for a full back at 6 feet and 195 pounds and too slow to be a halfback. Reed wasn't all that disappointed about not playing in the NFL.

"Naturally, you aim for the NFL when you're a kid in high school and college, and it would have been nice to have played in my own country and in front of my own people. However, my best living can be made here, and we're happy here, although we do miss being around more black people."

In 1997 he said, "I was up to 11 different NFL teams that tried to get me to come down and play but I never went down. I came close to going to Denver in 1969, but I changed my mind and decided I would stay in Canada."

George Reed was, and is, proud of his race and his heritage. He got into trouble in Regina in the mid-1960s by describing the Queen City as "worse than Alabama" as far as blacks were concerned. Given the attitudes in the CFL at that time about blacks who spoke their mind on race and other issues, it goes without saying that Reed would have been run out of the league if he hadn't been such a superb player. "No question about that," reacted Reed. "That's just the way it is up here."

Reed rejected the cherished Canadian notion that racial prejudice didn't exist north of the 49th parallel. "I have no illusions about that," he said during an interview in 1964 at his workplace, Molson's on Dewdney Avenue where he was employed as a sales representative. "If I wasn't George Reed football player, most of the people who glad-hand and welcome me wouldn't give me the time of day. When we moved to Regina, a long time went by before anyone on the block would talk to my wife. My kids were subject to constant abuse as well—name calling, that kind of thing. But if you're black, you come to expect that kind of treatment whether in Regina or Seattle or, yes, Alabama."

Later, Reed would be president of the CFL Players' Association, fighting for higher salaries. That was typical of the man. Although a superstar, he believed in fighting injustice wherever he found it, including underpaid Canadians. "You can't treat players like dogs anymore," Reed said at the time. "If you holler and drive people, they'll resent it and rightfully so. If you kick players around, they'll rebel. And you can't go around paying people peanuts anymore either. We get a minimum guaranteed salary of $10,000 a year. Last year [1973] there were quite a few guys playing football for less than $4000 a year." The minimum salary in 2012 for all players is $30,000.

Reed was often let down by those who should have been more supportive.

Bud Grant recalled:

> I was at a banquet one time in North Battleford and George Reed was there along with Jesse Owens and Ernie Banks. Reed got up and said he didn't know if he was going to stay in Regina, he wasn't getting a good deal. He might leave and go to the NFL. We got into the car after the banquet to go back to Saskatoon, and Jesse Owens just read the riot act to Reed.

> He said, "You dumb nigger, you're the dumbest guy I've ever seen. You've got the world right in your hand in Regina. All those people worship you and you're out there cutting them down." He went on for half an hour, just cussed him out something terrible for the lack of appreciation for where he was and what he was doing and what it meant to those people. "You just threw cold water in their faces. They're proud of you, they're proud of their team and you're standing there telling them you're not sure if you want to

stay there. You're the dumbest guy I've ever met in my life."

George Reed didn't have to apologize to anyone for his courage in the face of racial adversity. As trainer Sandy Archer can attest, he gave everything to Saskatchewan Roughrider football.

"He played with a lot of injuries. He had the turf toe that you hear about. They had to shoot that twice a game. Imagine getting a needle stuck in your toe twice a game. Really painful. He played and never missed a game. Today a guy would be out anywhere from three to six weeks."

Like all good trainers, Archer was a father confessor, counsellor, sympathetic ear. "On game days, George Reed would come about an hour earlier than anyone else and we'd sit and talk and he'd tell me things. I'd give him my opinion.

"We'd take a drag on the same cigarette which early on between negroes and whites—you know what that means. He did it all the time with me. He'd tell me his woes, and I'd try to give him whatever advice I had."

At the end of the 1965 campaign, the great Bill Clarke retired to go on to bigger and better things in the game of life. Lineman Len Legault did the same, becoming a full-time teacher. Punter Martin Fabi packed it in after four seasons. Arriving on the scene were tackle Tom Benyon from Queen's; safety Bruce Bennett, an All-American from Florida; Hilltop linebacker Cliff Shaw, brother of Wayne; Concordia defensive end Don Gerhardt; Ed McQuarters from Oklahoma via the NFL;

defensive tackle Moe Leveque from Les Alouettes; and Toronto flanker Gil Petmanis.

Also returning was Jack Gotta, this time as an assistant coach. Jocko described what happened. "Right after I got done with my mediocre playing career, I went back down to the States. Eagle had taken over from Bob Shaw. I called Eagle and said, 'It has always been my desire to be a coach. And if there is such good fortune that there is an opening on your staff and you haven't got somebody in mind, I'd certainly be interested in coming up.' He called me and said, 'Yeah, c'mon.' And I got the job as an assistant.

"That was such good fortune because it is such a difficult thing breaking in at any level of coaching. For Eagle to have the faith in me that he did to hire me was one of the greatest things of my life. I told Eagle I was indebted to him forever because that's what I wanted to do, coach football."

Asked why he hired Gotta, a man with no coaching experience, Eagle succinctly replied, "Well, he wanted a job." He went on. "Jack had been a good offensive and defensive player. When you can only have two coaches, you want somebody that can work both ways. Jocko did a good job."

Keys' other assistant was Jim Duncan, an intensely private man who went on to lead Calgary to a devastating win over the Riders in 1970 and their second Grey Cup victory in 1971.

It is assumed that the general manager provides the coach with the players. That wasn't the case back then. Asked how recruiting was done, Keys replied,

"The head coach did most of it. Most of the time we only had two assistants and we'd send them on certain scouting missions. But the head coach actually did most of the scouting. We didn't have a personnel director."

What about general manager Ken Preston? "As far as recruiting of players, Ken never did that. He'd just sign the players that had been around for a while, you know, for the next year. I didn't sign those players, I signed new players to contracts."

But did Preston and Keys had regular meetings to discuss team needs? "Not really," replied Keys. "I mean we talked and we were in the same team office building, but as far as discussing player personnel and so forth, no, we didn't do that."

Keys' offseason recruiting priorities had been the defensive line and secondary, which he succeeded in shoring up with Gerhardt, McQuarters and Bennett. The usually reserved Keys was moved, at the beginning of the regular season, to say, "We are further advanced this year than last season at this time. We have pretty good balance and I think we have a good chance of going all the way."

The Big Bird was right on.

Chapter Seven

To the Penthouse

The Roughriders opened the 1966 season in Edmonton with a 40–13 win, followed by a 38–14 whipping of Winnipeg, moving Bomber quarterback Ken Ploen to remark, "That club played like mad dogs. I don't think I've ever been hit so hard, so often. If that team stays healthy, there is no doubt they will be the team to beat."

The next victim was BC, falling 16–14. On August 17, they received a dose of humility by losing 26–1 in Calgary. The Roughriders returned home to lose 18–17 to the Eskimos. Then came a Labour Day encounter with Montréal at Taylor Field.

The Als were coached by Darrell Mudra who had a PhD in Psychology from the University of North Dakota. The night before the game, he sat down with the United Press International (UPI) stringer and team owner Ted Workman. Mudra argued that by using psychology he could get his players to put out 10 percent more effort than the other team, and that is why they would win. The next day against Saskatchewan, the

Alouettes lost a squeaker, 44–0. Mudra's team finished 7–7, so his theory worked half the time.

The Riders then hit a rough patch, losing 29–7 in Hamilton and two days later, 18–8 at Ottawa, playing without the injured George Reed, Al Benecick, Ed Buchanan and Moe Levesque. Then came an 11–11 result in Winnipeg, followed by a loss at home to Calgary, 35–18. The Riders had one point to show for their last four games. Were they sliding back to oblivion? No. They rallied, and for the first time in 15 years, Saskatchewan finished first with a record of 9–6–1. Also for the first time in 15 years, Ottawa topped the east. The last time that happened, in 1951, Ottawa beat Saskatchewan in the Grey Cup.

Winnipeg beat Edmonton 16–8 in the semifinal and prepared to open the final against the Roughriders in Regina. Sandy Archer could hardly wait.

"My first year I went to the Grey Cup. That's when Glenn Dobbs was the quarterback in 1951. It looked like we were never, ever going to go again. I remember Eagle Keys saying before our playoff games, 'We're going to win this thing.' I just couldn't believe getting there because we were always second best."

The Roughriders had finished third in 1965. With only one more win, they finished first in '66. What made the difference?

"When Eagle took over in 1965," Lancaster explained, "he put a team together without trying to rebuild it. He added to what we already had to make it a better football team. He fixed some spots and instilled confidence that the people who were there could get the job done.

I think the players respected him for that. He added whatever missing pieces were needed and as a result put together a pretty good football team for about eight years.

"That first year in '65, we just didn't get it done in the playoffs. In 1966, 9–6–1 was good enough to finish first. The first place bye was really important. It then was just a matter of doing it."

Ed McQuarters

Said Eagle Keys, "We had the addition of three or four players that I think made a lot of difference. We went steadily up from the first year I was there, as long as I stayed there. In my last year we were 14–2. I think the addition of Ed McQuarters, Bruce Bennett, Don Gerhardt, especially McQuarters and Bennett, made a lot of difference. No doubt about it. McQuarters was really outstanding."

Ron Atchison agreed. "You know in football a lot of people talk about what the offence does. I'm still convinced it's the defence that wins ball games. If you don't have a good defence, you're not going to win anything.

"Our defence was the best I remember it, and that was mainly because of one man, Ed McQuarters. He was a one-man wrecking crew. He was one the one guy who led us further than we'd ever been before. He had that power. He could disrupt a whole team because he had such great strength and speed. He was a very hardworking ballplayer."

Lancaster was equally enthusiastic. "That was quite a big acquisition for us because he was as good as any defensive lineman I'd ever seen play the game. And that goes right up to today [1999]. To put him on that defensive line, that becomes a threat because he was the kind of guy you had to be aware of all the time. If you weren't, he was going to get to the quarterback and he could outrun most of them. When he came onto that football field, it helped everyone on the team. When they doubled teamed him, someone else was open."

According to an article in *Sports Illustrated* by Jack Olsen that depicted the St. Louis Cardinals as a seething cauldron of racism, the talented McQuarters was cut because he refused to play the role of an "Uncle Tom." Described by Olsen as one of the best defensive linemen in the NFL, McQuarters was shipped out for refusing to accept racism. After retiring from the Roughriders, McQuarters denied that was so.

He explained how he ended up in a Rider uniform:

> *I was drafted by the Dallas Cowboys out of Oklahoma University. I was contacted during the off-season and told that my rights had been traded to the St. Louis Cardinals. Okay, no problem.*
>
> *I got to St. Louis, went through the first year on the taxi squad, played the last three games of the regular season. I thought that was nice of management because in order to be eligible for a pension, you had to play at least three games. They activated me just so I could have that first year's pension. I came back the next year and I was the last cut in training camp the second year.*
>
> *At that time, Jim Champion was the assistant defensive line coach at St. Louis and he had coached*

before in the CFL and he was also a good friend of Eagle Keys. He called me in and said, "Ed, there is a team in Canada you can play with if you're interested in going to Canada for football." I said, "Yeah, yeah, why not?"

I guess he contacted Eagle and then Ken Preston called later and said they were making arrangements to bring me to Saskatchewan. That was all fine, the time went by, and finally my plane tickets came in September and that's how I got here.

But I was told by Eagle himself that they had brought me in with the idea of trading me to Edmonton for a defensive back John Wydareny. But once I got here and looked pretty good and could help them out, they kept me and the trade never happened.

Keys laughed. "No, I don't think that's true. You're always looking, but I don't ever remember us acquiring him for that. Jim Champion told me about him and I got him up here."

Big Ed on the Big Bird: "Eagle was quiet. He had a way of not saying much, not only during practice throughout the week but even during games. He didn't say much but he had a way of looking at you that you knew what you should be doing and you'd be in trouble if you didn't. That's the one thing that stuck in my mind about Eagle, the way he looked at you to get the performance out of you he thought he should be getting out of you."

McQuarter's contribution in the 1966 Western final would be enormous.

Bombers Blitzed

The first game of the final was played on a bitterly cold night in Regina on November 13. The Roughriders got down to business early. On the opening drive, Garner Ekstran, playing tight end, made an acrobatic catch at the Winnipeg 38-yard line. That was as far as they got, and at 4:09, Jack Abendshan's field-goal try went wide for a single.

The Bombers went three and out. With Alan Ford joining Reed in the backfield, the two alternated carries down to the enemy 11-yard line. On second and five, Lancaster faked to Reed and threw to the back of the end zone to a wide-open Gordie Barwell. Near the end of the opening quarter, Abendshan kicked the Riders into an 11–0 lead.

Defence was the order of the day with the Bombers unable to pick up a yard in the first 15 minutes. Half-way through the second stanza, Ken Ploen finally got Winnipeg untracked, moving on three successive first downs to the Rider 43. Then the most patient man in football tried to get back in the game with one dramatic stroke by throwing a strike to Billy Cooper in the end zone. Bob Kosid leapt in front of the receiver and grabbed the ball. Cooper tried to pull the ball from his grasp, but Kosid held on for dear life. In the last minute of the half, Kosid intercepted again, leading to a 33-yard Abendshan field goal to close out the first 30 minutes with Saskatchewan leading 14–0.

In an effort to spur the troops on to victory, a large contingent of the 1951 Roughriders were introduced at half-time. It must have worked because the Cereal

Kings shut the Bombers down in the third quarter, during which there was no scoring. Ed McQuarters looked like a Bomber regular, so often was he in the Winnipeg backfield.

In the last quarter, Ploen and Cooper teamed up for a touchdown. The final score was Saskatchewan 14, Winnipeg 7.

Roughrider hearts stopped when centre Ted Urness collapsed leaving the field after the game. He had been helped from the field late in the game but pronounced himself fit and returned to action. He was rushed to the hospital where he underwent tests. He was kept over night with a slight concussion but was expected to suit up for game two.

After the game, Keys said, "The win is satisfying, but right now I'm so worried about Ted that it doesn't feel like we won. It was a good one to win, of course, but especially because we could pass in the cold weather and our defence came up so darn big. They were just great, weren't they?"

Bud Grant agreed, to a point. "I wasn't surprised with the way their defence played. The game went just about according to the book. It might have been different if Ken Neilson had hung on to that long pass at the five-yard line or the interception in the end zone had been ruled a simultaneous catch. The officials had a good day, those clowns! It must have been because they were on national TV."

The rematch was three days later in Winnipeg.

Ed Buchanan running with the football, against the Calgary Stampeders, 1960

Rider fans' hopes were buoyed when they heard that halfback Ed Buchanan would be back in the line-up after a lengthy absence because of torn knee ligaments. He could have played the first game, but Keys opted for an extra import on defence. However, Paul Dudley sustained a bruised kidney, resulting in Eddie B's return.

Despite losing the opener in Regina, Bud Grant's Blue Bombers were confident and favoured to win. His post-season record was impressive, winning nine out of 10 playoff games. The Riders were not afraid. They had not lost to Winnipeg all year.

The two teams staged a thriller in game two on a cold, windy night at Winnipeg Stadium. When all was said and done, it was two Eds who made the difference, as the Riders won 21–19 and returned to the Grey Cup for the first time in 15 years.

Trailing late in the third quarter 12–4, Ed number one made his contribution. George Reed picked up two first downs to get the ball to his own 37. On the next play, Ed Buchanan carried the ball off right tackle and didn't stop until he made it to the end zone 73 yards away. With 15 minutes to go, the score was Winnipeg 12, Saskatchewan 11.

The Bombers had opted to take the wind in the third quarter. By the time the final frame rolled around, the wind had picked up considerably.

The first victim of the wind was Ed Ulmer. After the defence threw Dave Raimey for successive losses, Ulmer's punt travelled only 21 yards. Three plays later, Abendshan kicked a 43-yard field goal, pulling the Riders into the lead. But Ploen struck back, driving the Bombers to the Saskatchewan 47.

Then Ed number two made his contribution.

Bud Grant had defensive end Billy Whisler going both ways in order to keep McQuarters out of the Blue Bomber backfield. That proved to be a fatal mistake.

"We had a blitz on," McQuarters recalled. "The blitz called for me to go outside, and Don Gerhardt was supposed to loop in behind. Instead of the offensive lineman dropping back in pass protection, he fired out. I think he blew his assignment. When I started to loop around, he was right there. He sort of knocked me off stride so I ended up being out of position, but Don was where he was supposed to be and hit the quarterback, Kenny Ploen. Wally Dempsey also hit Ploen, and the ball hit the ground and, because I was out of position, I saw it. It took one bounce, I was there and sort of scooped it up and took off."

Sixty-five yards later, he was in the end zone, and the Riders were ahead to stay.

"It happened because I was out of position," asserted McQuarters. "The strange thing about it, the Grey Cup was over, we're back in Regina at a party and Eagle said to me, 'You know, Ed, if that had been the regular season, you would have got a zero on your grade because you were out of position.' The zero turned into a Western final win for us and a trip to the Grey Cup."

After the game, Keys shook hands with all his players and then met the press. "The big difference was Ed Buchanan's return," he said. "He took a lot of pressure off George Reed. I thought Buchanan's touchdown in the third quarter was the turning point in the game." Buchanan had 125 yards on 16 carries.

Called "The Hog" because of his size and manners, Jim Worden's demeanour hid a lively football mind. Said Buchanan, "Jim told me at half-time that he had discovered a weak spot on the left side of the Winnipeg line."

After getting by the initial rush of tacklers, "I looked up and saw Worden ahead of me. I stopped for a second and he threw a beautiful block. Then I just kept running."

Two days later, the Western All-Star team was announced, including 11 Roughriders. On offence were receivers Hugh Campbell, Jim Worden and four of five members of the line, Jack Abendshan, Al Benecick, Clyde Brock and Ted Urness. Lancaster and Reed were in the backfield. Defensively, Garner Ekstran, Wayne Shaw and Bob Kosid were picked.

Reed, Campbell, Brock, Benecick and Worden were All-Canadian. Ron Lancaster was runner up for the Schenley Most Outstanding Player Award to Russ Jackson of Ottawa, even though he had better numbers.

The Green and White were pleased their Grey Cup opponent in Vancouver would be Ottawa, established as seven-point favourites. They had something to prove. Feverish preparations began the day after the win in Winnipeg. Pacific Western Airlines provided charters to the coast, good news in light of a pending strike by Air Canada. Six flights were available and filled. Regina's city council approved a $2000 expenditure to send a float for the Grey Cup parade. Premier Ross Thatcher announced a $2500 grant to assist the Regina Lions and Police Boys' Bands.

The Riders left for Vancouver on November 22. Eagle Keys allowed that they were pretty confident, which, coming from the taciturn Turkey Neck Bender, was practically a guarantee of victory.

Ottawa arrived that evening after an 11-hour odyssey made necessary by the airline strike, that took them through Chicago to Seattle and a bus ride north to downtown Vancouver.

To accommodate the media, the league ruled out closed practices. No problem. Keys just moved his team around to different practice sites, three days, three different fields, inadvertently forgetting to let the press know where they were going. The coach's reason for doing so had nothing to do with preventing Ottawa from discovering new wrinkles in the Saskatchewan offence. As Keys explained, it was part of a week-long isolation strategy. "We felt we were better off keeping the players away from everything we could. Pop Ivy more or less taught me that in 1954 when we went to Toronto and we moved around a little bit. That's the reason I did it here."

Keys wanted the players focused on only one thing: victory.

> *To go to a Grey Cup is great, but the thing to do is win it. That's the thing we stressed more than anything in order to achieve anything we had to win. Unless you're prepared to dedicate yourself to the Grey Cup game, you don't deserve to win. If you don't prepare and discipline yourself, you'll lose it because of mistakes. And you don't want to make mistakes and lose because you went there to have a good time.*

Ron Lancaster:

> *You remember your* [Grey Cup] *losses more than your wins. They stick with you longer. The Grey Cup is something you shoot for each year from training camp on. When you lose a Grey Cup, it puts a damper on your entire season. Even though you did win your Conference and you got to your objective, you didn't win it. The thing that bothers you is that there are so*

many football players who in their whole careers never get to a Grey Cup.

While Ottawa whooped it up in downtown Vancouver, Keys had the Riders in neighbouring Burnaby. A good thing, too, because just as in 1963 when the Cup was held in Vancouver, a riot took place at the conclusion of the Grey Cup parade, the Friday night before the game. It took 150 police officers and the K-9 corps to quell the vandalizing mob. Police arrested 689 people.

"Eagle had us out of town," said McQuarters. "We were totally focused because everybody was expecting big things from us. We were isolated. I do remember the wives being upset because they were told, 'Stay away from your husband. This is Grey Cup time. You can see him anytime.' That was Eagle's way." The Riders referred to their digs as The Monastery.

Recalled Ron Atchison, "We did the smartest thing I think that Eagle could have done. He took us way out of town when we were in BC. We were in a quiet place. It was the best preparation we could have had for that game. I think it made quite a difference.

"We were there for maybe four or five days before. He made the first night one o'clock curfew and every night after an hour earlier. He gave you time to go out with your wife and take in some of the festivities around town. Every night the time got shorter until we had a nine PM curfew. Eagle's preparation was excellent."

"We prepared," Lancaster said. "There was no question Eagle Keys would never change the way we did things all year. He was a believer in doing certain things, and we prepared for that game the same as any other. We had curfews at night, we had meetings in the daytime, we had our practices. You try to keep things as normal as you can. Try not to make any great big radical changes."

Roughrider strategy against Ottawa was simple. Their greatest strength was the offensive line of Whitehouse, Brock, Abendshan, Benecick, Urness and Worden. It opened the holes for George Reed and Ed Buchanan. It protected the quarterback. In addition to The Hog, Lancaster could throw to Alan Ford and Hugh Campbell.

The Riders would run, run, run and run some more, not only to advance the ball and score but also to eat up the clock. Ottawa liked to go with a spread line by splitting defenders outside, giving Reed and Buchanan the opportunity to find gaps and capitalize on blocking angles.

Despite the presence of Russ Jackson, Whit Tucker, Ron Stewart, Bo Scott, Ted Watkins, Jay Roberts and Jim Dillard, Keys felt the opposition's greatest strength was their defence. His ace in the hole would be the Wizard of Wittenberg.

Keys was the first coach in the CFL to have his quarterback use audibles. Ron Lancaster wouldn't call the play until he was behind the centre and had a chance to see Ottawa's defensive formation. "I think it's our only chance against a defence that has no weaknesses," Keys explained. "When we beat them in 1965, 80 or 90 percent of Lancaster's play were audibles. He'll do the same tomorrow."

Lancaster was ready several days before the big event. "I'm ready right now," Ronnie said that Thursday, "and I was ready yesterday. I don't like to get all psyched up for a game. I was jazzed up for the last one with Winnipeg, and I was so tight, I thought I played lousy. I just hope I can go into this game relaxed."

On game day, when it came time to introduce the players, they were incredibly tense. A timely pratfall may well have been the turning point in the greatest day in the history of Saskatchewan sports.

When the announcer called out number 53, Jack Abendshan, the all-star headed out of the tunnel. Alan Ford described what happened next.

"Abendshan slipped and fell during the introductions. The track was muddy, so when he got up and ran out, he had this big brown spot on his rear end. Of course, the guys would never let him forget that. When you get down to that game, it's pretty emotional in the locker room. So that did certainly loosen us up."

"He fell in the mud," Lancaster said. "We all laughed. That was good. You always think of things that can relax you. He was going across some boards through that mud and his cleats went out from under him and he landed in the mud. Everybody just laughed."

Said Eagle Keys: "I think it had a lot to do with setting the mood. It helped us relax a bit. Still, I think we jumped offside the first two or three plays."

They did indeed.

"I went off once and Ed McQuarters went off another time," Atchison confessed. "I'd say that you could look at that as a pretty good indication of how ready we were."

Abendshan kicked off at 2:00 PM under an overcast sky, with a temperature of about 10°C. Assisted by those offsides, Russ Jackson marched Ottawa in five plays to their own 49. Making those who predicted an eastern rout look like geniuses, Jackson combined with Whit Tucker on a 61-yard pass and run for a touchdown. Moe Racine missed the convert. The victim on the play was Dale West. He explained what happened.

"On that first one, I don't know if I had not been paying attention to the films or what, but I saw Ronnie Stewart going through a three back and I came up and supported which I never did for six or seven years of my career, so I don't know why I would do it then. Tucker ran by me and got a touchdown. Larry Dumelie got blamed on television, which was fine with me, but I knew it was me."

West soon atoned for his sin by intercepting a Jackson pass at the Ottawa 43.

"The end came out and got tangled up with Dushinski and went down. The ball came to me and I took it to the nine-yard line. Then Ronnie threw one to Jim Worden for the touchdown."

"Jim Worden was telling Ronnie all the time that he could beat Gene Gaines," recalled Ford. "Worden said he could beat him deep. Ronnie hit him at the back of the end zone. I remember Worden coming back saying, 'I told you I could beat him deep.'"

Gaines grimaced and agreed:

Ronnie Lancaster was such a great actor. He ran the play action pass on us, and we stuck our noses in places where we shouldn't have. We were a very aggressive team and so we wanted to get up because he had the great runner in George Reed. So we thought he was going to give the ball to George most of the time. He stuck the ball in George's gut, pulled it out and the next thing you know Jim Worden is wide open and bang, touchdown. Worden was the big boy. We all took a bite out of it, we all took the bait.

The underdogs led after 15 minutes 7–6, even though Ottawa had eight first downs to Saskatchewan's two, Jackson was good on three of five for 85 yards and Lancaster three of five for 42 yards. Ottawa even out-rushed the Green Riders 62 yards to three. Saskatchewan went offside five times in the first quarter, probably a record.

In the second stanza, linebacker Wally Dempsey snuffed out an Ottawa drive at the 33 by wrestling the ball away from Jay Roberts. Lancaster kept a drive alive with a third-down gamble at the Ottawa 50. He marched down to the 19, aided by a spectacular Buchanan catch. He then threw to Al Ford in the end zone. The ball sailed right through defensive back Bob O'Billovich's hands into Ford's waiting arms.

"Right through!" exclaimed Ford. "It took a little speed off it, made it like it was a knuckleball landing in my lap. It was probably the easiest reception I ever made, the one I'll remember the longest."

O'Billovich felt the same way:

I'll tell you exactly what happened on that play. We were in a three deep zone and I was playing deep third to my side. Hugh Campbell ran an out on my side.

The inside guy ran what we call a corner where he went in and then came back out to the flag on the corner and I reacted to the throw. If I make the play and could hold on to the ball, I'm a big hero because that wasn't even my responsibility.

I don't think Al Ford could have got the ball if it hadn't been deflected right into his lap because he slipped and fell in the end zone. When he was cutting and I cut in front, he started to stop and come back to the ball and he fell down.

So it was just the luck of the draw that when I wasn't able to squeeze the ball to hold on to it, that it would fall right in his lap. I mean, it could have gone in any direction.

But it didn't. Saskatchewan 14, Ottawa 6.

Ron Lancaster was sympathetic. "Many times you'll see one guy in the secondary chasing another guy for a touchdown and everybody automatically assumes that's the guy that was beaten. Many times it isn't. If they're in a zone defence, it's somebody probably altogether different. These are things you never know about."

On Ottawa's first play from scrimmage after returning the kickoff to their 25, Jackson was flushed out of the pocket, running for his life. He rifled the ball down field to a streaking Whit Tucker who caught up to it at the Saskatchewan 39 and kept going to the end zone. Once again, Dale West was the culprit.

"I had Tucker man to man and was okay with him down the field. Jackson came up towards the line of scrimmage and I thought he was going to run, so

I came up. He threw it over my head. For five or six years CTV had that picture of me chasing Tucker to the end zone in their lead-in to every CFL game."

So Dale West messed up big time?

"Nah, he didn't," said Russ Jackson. "We just found a little extra time, and when you do that with receivers like Tucker, they're going to find some open space."

George Reed wasn't pointing the finger at West. "They were broken plays. I think a lot of times when people feel bad about a play, you also have to give somebody credit. Obviously sometimes the offence makes a great play.

"Jackson must have had time to deliver the ball so the offensive line must have blocked not bad and Tucker made a great catch, so, hey, there's six points." Seven with Racine's convert. Bill Kline kicked a single, making the score at halftime, 14–14.

Although the stats still favoured Ottawa, momentum was beginning to shift.

The punters were paramount in quarter number three with Ottawa spending most of the time hemmed in their own end. The Green Riders began to exert themselves on the ground after an anemic two yards rushing in the first half. Near the end of the quarter, Garner Ekstran threw Jim Dillard for a loss and Don Gerhardt sacked Jackson, forcing Bill Cline to punt from his end zone. Gene Wlasiuk returned it to Ottawa's 32-yard line, setting up the *coup de grace*. As the quarter ended, the game remained tied at 14.

At the beginning of the final frame, Reed picked up a first down on three carries. Lancaster threw to Hugh Campbell at the five. On the next play, Campbell out-duelled Joe Poirier for the touchdown. Abendshan converted, giving the good guys a seven-point lead.

Ottawa went three and out on their ensuing possession. Starting at the Ottawa 47-yard line, Buchanan ran for six and Reed for 10 down to the 31. Reed then blazed his way to the end zone. The convert made it 28–14. Three minutes later, Ford completed the scoring with a single.

Final score, Saskatchewan 29, Ottawa 14. The Roughriders had won their first Grey Cup!

The Riders had picked up 169 yards on the ground in the second half. Once Campbell gave them the lead, their ball control offence finished Ottawa off. The beginning of the end came earlier, however. The Eastern Riders had only one first down in each of the second and third quarters and two in the fourth, both coming near the end of the game.

"We never got away from our ground game," Reed explained. "We were able to keep pounding away. Lancaster threw a couple of passes that put us in a position to deliver the knock-out punch. I happened to be the knock-out punch."

The victory was all the sweeter because no one gave them a chance. "Oh, yeah," said Reed, "we had no chance of winning. They had already given the Grey Cup to Ottawa, so it was quite a thrill to show them we belonged on the same field with Ottawa and we won the game, and then watch everybody's disbelief that we won it."

Russ Jackson said they hadn't taken Saskatchewan lightly. "I don't think they did," Reed agreed. "I think they knew we had a good team. Russ had played with Ron for a couple of years so he knew what type of competitor he was. They respected us, the other teams in the league respected us. The media was the one that didn't respect us."

Dale West: "The television cameras were in the Ottawa dressing room, so if anybody wanted to get interviewed they had to walk across to the Ottawa side. So maybe only three or four of us got interviewed."

Eagle Keys: "We never should have been six-point underdogs. But the publicity sure didn't hurt. The way folks were writing about the game, you'd have thought we didn't belong on the same field as Ottawa. That got to our fellows a bit. They have pride in themselves, and they didn't enjoy being downgraded so much. We had beaten some pretty good teams to get there."

Why did they win?

Defence.

"Oh, absolutely," affirmed Dale West. "They couldn't do anything. They couldn't run against us, and their passing game was marginal at best. We were getting a real good rush out of the front, and the defensive backs were doing a wonderful job. We were really swarming. We could have had three or four more interceptions. Kosid and I lost one because we fought over it in the air.

"George Reed was just amazing. He just ran over, through and around people, and Ronnie was right on his game."

"We put a lot of pressure on Jackson," recalled Wayne Shaw. "Our defence probably played way over its heads. Russ Jackson was one helluva athlete. He could throw the ball; he could run. He was a really great quarterback. We had to play over our heads or he would have beaten us."

Ron Atchison:

> I would say in the Grey Cup, and maybe with a lot of Grey Cups, the game is won one way or another before you ever get on the field. We were six-point underdogs, but we had a real good feeling.
>
> You have the feeling. It's an inner feeling that you have. I noticed it lots of times. After four or five minutes into the game, I could tell you whether we were going to win or lose lots of times. If the guys weren't up for it, you could just get the heebie-jeebies. I can remember saying lots of times, "Hey man, this is going to be a long day."
>
> By the time you get to the Grey Cup, the teams are pretty evenly matched. You've got good men everywhere. So it's a matter of who is really going to take charge. That's an inner thing.

Eagle Keys:

> We were so well prepared in that Grey Cup that we scored on things that we thought we could do. It was as good a game as we could ever call.
>
> On our first touchdown, we faked the play into the line and threw deep. It was a perfect play. It was set up by preparation and it worked. You prepare a team

a lot of times to do things and they never work. But in that Grey Cup game I thought what we did was great.

Sure we had some great defensive plays. Dale West intercepted a pass but he got beat early in the game. We were lucky when Al Ford scored a touchdown when it bounced off somebody's hands.

Defensively, Keys singled out Garner Ekstran, Don Gerhardt and Wayne Shaw for special praise.

Ron Lancaster:

We always felt that we were a pretty good fourth-quarter team because of the style of offence we ran. We ran a lot of running plays. There were actually times in those years with Eagle where our offence was split 50-50 running and throwing.

So we were the type of offence that we needed to build, get momentum and stay on the field. The longer we stayed on the field, the better we were going to be late in the game. That's exactly how that game went. It was close at the half. We got our ground game established in the second half and we controlled it. But that's exactly how we played all year.

Why did Ottawa lose?

"We were a team that was emotionally drained because Bill Smyth, our assistant coach, had died suddenly in Ottawa during the semifinal week," said Russ Jackson. "We had won first place. We then had to go and play Hamilton, a two-game total point series in which we played terrifically. There was an air strike and we had to go by Chicago and Seattle and bus up from Seattle to Vancouver. That's not an excuse because certainly the Saskatchewan Roughriders were full value for the win.

"At half-time, it was 14–14, and our whole offence was scrambling, sort of broken plays where Whit Tucker got in behind the defence and I happened to catch him for two touchdowns. But they controlled the game, controlled the ball."

Bob O'Billovich:

> In the second half, George Reed ran the ball right up our butts. We lost coach Smyth who had run the defence and coached both lines.
>
> During the game, we had to make adjustments with our defensive line. They were taking wide line splits. The reason I know all this is I was playing behind them as a DB and I could see what was going on. Our defensive line was splitting out with them instead of closing the gap. Nobody really got the word to our players for adjustments. We never could get that word down in the second half, and that's why George ran the ball up our rear ends.

"We had shot our bolt against Hamilton," said Ronnie Stewart. "The Grey Cup was kind of anti-climactic."

Ottawa coach Frank Clair:

> While we were playing one of our poorer games, Saskatchewan was playing an extremely good game. Football is largely a psychological game, and I'm afraid subconsciously we lost our edge somewhere. We reached our peak when we absolutely humiliated Hamilton. That was the game our players and the city of Ottawa had been waiting for through a good

many disappointing seasons. It was like winning the Grey Cup right there.

When we left the locker room at the start, I thought they were going to be all right but they lost it very quickly. Once Regina got a touchdown in front, I knew they could go for ball control which we couldn't prevent. In Reed they had a fullback who could carry the ball for any pro team in the world and they used him to full advantage. There's not a team in the country except Regina that keeps both ends in tight and runs the ball right at you.

That was one of Eagle Keys' innovations, another was the extensive use of audibles. He always liked to catch the opposition by surprise.

"On the first play of the ball game," recounted Keys, "we always tried to do something different. I always tried to go deep or something like that. Fake a run and throw off it. We were innovative that way."

To win a championship, physical adversity must be overcome. Sophomore linebacker Wally Dempsey tore his knee ligaments in the season opener against Edmonton, made it back at the end of the regular season and starred in the playoffs, despite excruciating pain. Whitehouse should have been in the hospital, Atchison on the bench. Both had sustained serious knee injuries. They played. Nursing an aggravating shoulder injury, the Grey Cup was Dale West's first full game since September. And Reed was always nursing deep bruises in his thighs.

Why was that Roughrider team so good?

Jack Gotta:

The guys we had were as good as any guys who ever played in the league. Eagle was the perfect guy to bring it all together. He was such a dedicated, hard-working, intense guy. He was up early, stayed late. He left nothing to chance. All the players had the greatest respect for Eagle, and the feeling was mutual.

We had some bright guys on that club. I don't think George Reed ever blew an assignment. Ronnie was a student of the game. I admired him from the standpoint of the stature of the guy. He was really tough mentally. Much tougher than people would recognize such a nice person to be. He would never be intimidated by anybody or anything. He was the leader. When he called something in the huddle, everyone had the confidence that this is what you should be doing.

Alan Ford:

We had a pretty good crew. We were pretty close in those days. 1966 wasn't an easy year. We worked real hard to get where we were. We had a quiet confidence about us that we were going to win.

As far as being a close-knit group, the coach can't do that, the general manager can't do that. It's got to be the guys in the locker room. You need to have guys that are leaders. There was no "I" in George, there was no "I" in Ron. Those were the guys who carried the team in terms of the "we" stuff. George worked harder than anybody else at practice. Ron would never miss practice. Both would play hurt. All those little things, if you've got your leaders, it really makes a difference. As the quarterback of the team, Ron would do what he felt was necessary to get ready to play, and other people would notice that and follow along with him.

The victory was especially meaningful to Regina-boy Ford. "As a kid growing up, I watched the Riders. I never thought I'd be playing in a Grey Cup, let alone with the Roughriders. I was in the band, marching all the time. I remember telling Atch when I joined the team in '65 that I used to march out to play the national anthem. I'd look over and there was Ron standing there. That shows you how old he was."

Hugh Campbell, who coached Edmonton to five straight Grey Cup championships, relished the whole experience.

I remember a lot of it vividly. I remember staying outside of town in a motel. I remember the excitement of the challenge of playing Ottawa and Eagle Keys telling us that we may never get this opportunity again and we'd better take advantage of it.

I remember a few of the practices leading into the game and how the team was up awfully high, awfully quick and then we seemed to relax after awhile, and I really felt confident going into the game.

And then in the game, I remember Garner Ekstran going offside the first couple of plays because we were so keyed up. Ottawa scored a quick seven points and it looked like we were doomed. Then Dale West intercepted a pass and we got some confidence and momentum going.

I remember Ed Buchanan catching a long pass on a pick play we had worked out to take advantage of Ottawa's man defence. And, of course, George Reed just romping through them.

I remember afterwards the great satisfaction. We could hardly live with ourselves we were so proud to have beaten Ottawa because they were heavily favoured, and Saskatchewan had never won. I remember Reggie Whitehouse stealing the Grey Cup and we all went downtown with it to Trader Vic's. My parents were there. It was a pretty proud night.

Campbell compared Grey Cups won as a coach and a player. "None of them are much above winning as a player in Saskatchewan. That was a very special time. I was 24 years old at the time and everything was ahead of me."

Ed McQuarters had no idea what a Grey Cup would mean to the people of the Wheat Province.

I didn't because that was my first year in Saskatchewan. To me, quite honestly, it was just another championship game. Not until after I got back to Regina and was here about a week did I start to realize the significance of it and the importance of it to the Saskatchewan people. The folks just went wild, my phone never quit ringing.

Every time you turned the TV on, they were replaying the Grey Cup. Then I started to realize how fanatical Saskatchewan people are about their football.

The following year we were playing Winnipeg. I couldn't believe they allowed the fans to sit down

*around the field. I mean they were no more than
three yards from the out-of-bound markers all around
the field. I thought these folks are going to get hurt, but
it was allowed. But that's how fanatical they were....
Going through it was something to behold.*

The moment the Grey Cup game ended, pandemo-
nium broke out all over the province. Strangers, weep-
ing tears of joy, hugged each other on 11th Avenue.
The sounds of church bells ringing and car horns
honking could be heard all over the city. Green beer
flowed freely at every hotel.

Cars crammed the downtown area in the thousands,
causing massive traffic jams that didn't ease up until
10 o'clock at night. There were 26 traffic accidents, but
only one person was hurt, even though inebriated
fans were hanging out of car windows as far as they
could go.

There were only two acts of vandalism reported.
A store window was broken and a mirror was ripped
off a car. Police inspector Fred Heinzig said he didn't
believe either incident had anything to do with the
Grey Cup celebration. So good-natured and fun-loving
was the crowd that no extra police were called in.

City officials had asked citizens to put up their
Christmas lights early so they could be turned on with
other lights to create as brilliant and welcoming sight
as possible for the team when their plane approached
Regina. The Roughriders arrived back in Regina at
9:30 Sunday night to a welcome and celebration that
long-time residents said was greater than V-E Day in
1945. Eight thousand people had filled the Armoury by

7:30 PM, packed shoulder to shoulder in every square inch of the 20,000-square-foot auditorium. They almost took the roof off with their mighty, sustained, three-minute cheer when the Grey Cup was brought to the stage.

Eagle Keys introduced all the players, saying something about each. Premier Thatcher gave a short speech to a chorus of boos, Mayor Baker to thunderous applause. Ron Lancaster, Hugh Campbell, Ed Buchanan, George Reed and Ron Atchison responded to chants from the crowd and came forward to speak. Big Atch summed up the feelings of the team when he said, "Ever since I've been here, we've had great fans. This year we had a great team."

A great feeling of euphoria enveloped the province. No longer second best, no longer the butt of jokes, the people of Saskatchewan felt a tremendous sense of almost unutterable pride in their team. True, the eastern media refused to credit Saskatchewan with a win, preferring instead to find 100 reasons why the superior Ottawa Rough Riders had lost. But Rider fans didn't care. Being the most knowledgeable fans in the country, they knew the truth. Their team had dominated Russ Jackson and company that day, leaving no doubt which was the better team.

Chapter Eight

Frustration

After winning the Grey Cup for the first time in 1966, it was assumed that the powerful Roughriders would win many more. "I thought," said Alan Ford, "since we had a fairly young team, we were going to win the thing another five or six times."

They would dominate Canadian football for the next 10 years, but the words of Eagle Keys would come back to haunt them: "You may never get this opportunity again, so you'd better take advantage of it."

The Riders would get to the Grey Cup four more times and come away emptied handed. Twice a better team beat them; twice they shot themselves in the foot. In and around those Grey Cup disappointments, the team had a winning percentage of .675, the best in the league.

The most notable retirement after the 1966 season was Reggie Whitehouse, calling it a day after 15 seasons. Never formally recognized as an all-star, he played like one for most of his career. His leadership in the dressing room, his good humour and sense of camaraderie were sorely missed. He was inducted onto the Plaza of Honour in 1992.

The most impressive new arrival in 1967 was Gary Brandt, a local boy who attended the University of Washington and became a mainstay on the offensive line for 11 seasons.

For the defending Grey Cup champions, a rivalry was about to begin with the Calgary Stampeders, a rivalry that endures to this day because of the large number of Saskatchewan people who moved to the Foothills city over the years.

Ron Lancaster reminisced:

> *We had a rivalry with every team. When I first got here, it was BC, then Winnipeg, then it was Calgary and in the '70s, Edmonton.*
>
> *But during that time, it seemed we played Calgary every other week. We played them one pre-season game, three times during the regular season and a couple of times in the playoffs. They were good games.*
>
> *We had some great battles with those guys. They always had a heckuva football team to compete against. Wayne Harris I thought was in another world. He was as good a football player as you were ever going to meet. And playing him so many times, you got to know him as a person. He was an awfully good guy, too.*

The feeling was mutual. Middle linebacker Wayne Harris:

> *I really enjoyed those games. Saskatchewan probably had the best team in the CFL during that time.*

We always gave them a battle. I never did go back and see how man games we won. [Including playoffs, Calgary was 12–13–1.]

It seemed like they would win the close ones, we'd then come back and kick the heck out of them the next game. They had a great offensive line and, of course, George Reed, Ron Lancaster, Hugh Campbell. They were a very balanced team, very strong.

We had a good team, too. You always want to beat the best. They offered that challenge to us.

Stamp punter and end Jim Furlong agreed: "They had a tremendous football team. They were always hard hitting. We used to go out there and try to beat each other's heads in. But strangely enough, they were always clean games. No cheap shots."

Saskatchewan and Calgary battled all the way down to the wire in Canada's centennial year, each finishing with a record of 12–4. Even though it was their finest showing in modern team history, the Riders finished in second place by virtue of losing the season series to Calgary.

The Roughriders eliminated the Eskimos 21–5 in the semifinal and headed to Calgary for the first game of the Western final.

Coached by the cerebral Jerry Williams, the Stampeders had a great passing attack with quarterback Pete Liske and receivers Terry Evanshen, Herm Harrison, Gerry Shaw, Bob McCarthy and Ted Woods. Lovell Coleman was in the backfield. The greatest middle linebacker to ever play the Canadian game, Wayne Harris, anchored the defence.

In game one, the Riders led 11–8 late in the fourth quarter. Driving into field-goal range, the Stamps faked the three points, and Liske threw to Coleman for a touchdown and a 15–11 win.

Back in Regina , the playing surface was a sheet of ice. Said Wayne Harris, "That was one of the coldest games I can recall playing. There was a lot of snow on the field. It got warm during the day and it melted and started freezing at night. It was kind of a skating rink out there, but there was still a lot of moisture, so when you got completely wet, with the wind factor, it was like 40 below."

Saskatchewan won 11–9. The turning point in the game and in the series came when Terry Evanshen broke his leg. Given the fact the Rider margin of victory was two, the Stampeders could make a strong case that the loss of their receiver was a fatal blow.

"Terry could go deep," said Herm Harrison. "Without him, we didn't have that deep threat. He was so elusive. When he got hurt, it seemed like the morale of the team went down. You could just see heads dropping."

Harris said, "We lost Terry. I wouldn't say that was the key to it. They had a good football team. I can't take anything away from them."

In game three back in Calgary, Lancaster threw two touchdown passes, the defence sacked Liske five times and George Reed went on a rampage, carrying 37 times for 204 yards, both records, as the Riders won 17–13.

They would defend their Grey Cup title against Hamilton, a team they had defeated 22–21 during the season in Regina.

In honour of Canada's 100th birthday, the Grey Cup would be contested in the nation's capital at Lansdowne Park.

The Roughriders had played four post-season games in a week and a half, all on frozen fields. Their bruises were deep, and they were tired. Hamilton was on a roll, having finished first for the ninth time in 11 years. They had not allowed a touchdown in the last six games of the regular season. Their opponents scored but 17 points in the last three games of the season, the Eastern final and the Grey Cup. The Tiger-Cats had one of the greatest defensive teams in CFL history. They could score, too.

For Balfour Tech grad Gary Brandt, a dream had come true. "In 1967, I was a rookie. I think I was more awestruck than anything else, just the event. The Grey Cup week itself was spectacular. I recall the practices out there and the game itself. I only played on special teams in that game. Being in my first year, it was something special to be playing in a Grey Cup."

Things started to go wrong when the Riders arrived in Ottawa. "We had no facilities whatsoever," growled Keys. "The weather conditions were bad, but had we stayed in Regina where we could have had a cleared field to practice on, we would have been far better prepared. They put us on a practice field, but it was just like a skating rink. Hamilton, though, stayed home until the last moment."

December 2, the big day arrived; it was freezing cold but dry. Hamilton opened the scoring with a touchdown. Saskatchewan replied with an Alan Ford 87-yard single, a Grey Cup record that still stands. Was it a cherished Grey Cup memory? "No, it just means I had a good wind, I guess. I happened to hit it, it bounced and away it went," said Ford.

The final score, Hamilton 24, Saskatchewan 1.

What most Rider fans remember is a wide-open Ed Buchanan in the second quarter dropping a long bomb that would have scored a touchdown. A hero in 1966, Buchanan became a scapegoat in 1967 and soon after left town.

"There was a turning point in the game," said Dale West. "Ronnie lays one up for Eddie, hits him right in the hands, he's wide open. He drops it. That was a chance maybe to get some momentum going. But we were never in it after that. They were a tough opponent. They'd dare you to come at them. We tried but we weren't very successful."

Was it just a bad day? "I don't know whether it was such a bad day. I think there was a turning point in that game. Ed Buchanan was wide open. Lancaster laid the ball perfectly into his hands. It would have been about a 70-yard touchdown. He dropped the ball and that seemed to deflate us," said George Reed.

Ron Atchison had had a good feeling before the 1966 Grey Cup, but "I knew within two minutes into the 1967 game we were going to lose. The first time that Hamilton had to kick the ball, the kicker ran between Ken Reed and I, and we could have killed him.

I made the attempt to hit him, and Ken Reed didn't, so he went between us.

"I said, 'Why the hell didn't you hit him, Ken?' He said, 'I didn't want to cause a penalty.' So I said, 'Look, if we're going to worry about causing penalties, we're in big trouble. We could have killed that son-of-a-bitch. He might not have kicked the rest of the game.' I thought that was a bad omen. [That "son-of-a-bitch" was Joe Zuger, also Hamilton's quarterback.]

"George Reed was slipping around and he wouldn't change his cleats. The field was very bad, and, of course, Buchanan dropped that pass. It was really just a disaster. We didn't play like a good team. They just steam-rolled us."

Hugh Campbell had a different perspective. "In that game we were beaten so thoroughly that I didn't feel robbed. I suspect they had better players than us."

Ed McQuarters was frustrated that day:

No matter how hard we tried, nothing worked. They kicked us, they whipped us. I guess the game-winning touchdown was scored over me. I mean, there I am. I'm dug in. I had the feeling they were going to come right at me, and sure enough they did. No matter how hard I fired out and stopped the offensive linemen, they still just bowled me over and scored the touchdown right over top. I felt kind of silly, but you have those days.

I think we were probably tired. This time they let us stay downtown where all the functions were. There were just too many distractions.

Wayne Shaw mentioned the unmentionable. "We should have had another quarterback in there for a little while. Ronnie was all shook up when he threw that pass to Buchanan and he dropped it. It's not the end of the world, but Ronnie couldn't get going. Someone should have gone in for once."

Lancaster said, "I was disappointed to be shut down that way. We just didn't think anyone could beat us that easily. They did a great job on us."

Was Buchanan the goat? "Anytime you lose, somebody wears the goat horns. I didn't play very well. But people who did all the criticizing never got to a Grey Cup. Ed Buchanan did. He dropped that pass which may or may not have been a key play. Someone asked me after the game what the importance of it was. I said that had he caught that pass, we would have lost 24–8," said Lancaster.

Eagle Keys was blunt. "We had a bad game. I know that. The game was a lot closer than the score indicated. But there were a variety of reasons. Dropped passes that would have been touchdowns, we were called for interference on the one yard line. Basically, though, all our pass receivers were being tackled at the line of scrimmage, and Hamilton was never called for interference."

Buchanan retired after that game. It was rumoured that Keys told him not to come back because he dropped that pass. "No, that's not true," Keys angrily replied. "I didn't say that. But Ed didn't like the cold weather. On a warm day, he would have caught it."

Lancaster concurred. "Eagle didn't do that. He wasn't that kind of guy."

Ed Buchanan passed away in 1993, suffering from Lou Gehrig's disease.

When you're hot you're hot, when you're not, you're not. "I was a salesman in Regina," said Wayne Shaw. "After the '66 Grey Cup, I couldn't do many sales because I partied all winter. After the '67 Cup, I'd go make sales calls. Now, Regina's a great football city. When I was a young, shy guy, it helped me overcome my shyness and helped me with stuff. I know guys bought from me because I played football. But after '67 in the wintertime, I'd go make a sales call, guys would give me a half-hour spiel about why we lost the game. Then he'd say, 'I'm too busy, I've got to do something else,' and I wouldn't make a sale. They were mad at me. Same thing happened in '69. After '72, I couldn't stand it anymore, so I went to Winnipeg."

Ed McQuarters had a great year in 1967. In addition to his All-Canadian selection, he won the Schenley Award for Most Outstanding Lineman.

The Undertaker Cometh

At the end of the 1967 campaign, Buchanan, Larry Dumelie, Garner Ekstran and Gene Wlasiuk retired. Campbell left for two years. New on the scene were DB Larry DeGraw from Utah, Iowa running back Silas McKinnie and a man who would become a larger-than-life legend in Saskatchewan and one of the greatest ever to play the game. Bill "The Undertaker" Baker was a Notre Dame, Wilcox, and Scott Collegiate boy who attended Otterbein in Ohio. He was born in Sheridan, Manitoba, and raised in Kindersley, Saskatchewan. His grandfathers were Kindersley pioneers.

"I graduated in 1968," recalled Baker. "I was on the Riders' protected list. [Argo coach] Leo Cahill called me at Otterbein and said, 'Bill, if you go to the Riders' training camp and flop around and do whatever to get cut, Toronto wants you, and we'll pay you a couple thousand dollars more.' That was my first experience with the whole pro thing.

"At that time I had to decide whether I should stay in the States—I had some opportunities in the NFL— or go to Canada. The whole Vietnam thing was on, so instead of taking a chance and staying in the States, I signed with Saskatchewan.

"It was a great period. It was the Riders in their best years, 1968–71. We had great teams, we had a tremendous amount of fun. Those were truly wonderful years. I had opportunities to go to the NFL, but between working and the team, it was just a great situation. Eagle was there and it was great playing for Eagle."

The 1968 Riders returned to first place with a sparkling record of 12–3–1. Their first game on the road was in Calgary, a thrilling 25–24 victory. The opener was typical of the regular-season battles between two magnificent football teams.

Liske and Lancaster filled the air with footballs, running up over 800 yards in total offence between them. It was the first game that the Stampeders wore the horse on their helmets, an innovation of GM Rogers Lehew.

On a beautiful Sunday afternoon, September 29 at McMahon Stadium, the teams met again. George Reed ran 78 yards before collapsing at the Calgary one-yard line. The fans booed the referee for not awarding the visiting warrior a touchdown. Reed picked up 149 yards that day. Stampeder Herm Harrison established a still-standing team mark of 237 yards receiving. Saskatchewan led 35–24 with five minutes left when Calgary responded with two touchdowns, the last a beautiful throw down the middle to Gerry Shaw who had 102 yards on only four completions. The final score was 38–35, Calgary.

In the final regular-season match-up, the Riders beat the Stamps 19–15 in Regina. The total point differential for the three games was eight.

The 10–6 Stampeders bombed the Eskimos 29–13 in the semifinal. Everybody expected a hammer-and-tong battle to determine the Western champion. It was not to be. In the opener at Calgary, the locals destroyed the Riders 32–0.

The second game was more typical of play between the two teams. At the end of regulation, they were dead-locked at 12. In overtime, Larry Robinson intercepted Lancaster and returned it to the Rider 17. Two plays later, Liske hit Evanshen in the end zone for the touch-down. Art Froese recovered a fumble for another touchdown, making the final score 25–12, sending the superior Stamps to the Grey Cup for the first time since 1949. The Roughrider dynasty had died a sudden death.

George Reed was runner-up to Toronto's Bill Symons for the Schenley Most Outstanding Player Award even though he had 1222 yards and 16 touchdowns, compared to Symon's 1107 and nine majors. Eagle Keys won the Coach of the Year Award.

At the end of the 1968 season, Galen Wahlmeier and Dale West retired. Al Benecick was traded to Edmonton after 10 seasons in green and white, a career that propelled him into the CFL Hall of Fame in 1996.

Big Atch

Living legend Ron Atchison also called it a day. The Saskatoon Hilltopper had arrived in Regina in 1952.

> *I started at $1000 and a job. The job was more important than the money made playing football. You played football for the fun of it. I finished at $15,000. There was $1100 for the 1966 Grey Cup, but we spent it all going and coming. There never was very much money in it. It was good for me because I was a carpenter by trade. I used my football money to buy up houses. I had a little rental business. It was a real good life, the best part of my life.*

When Atchison first arrived, he became the victim of a veteran's prank. The rookie took on one of the most feared men in the league.

> *Martin Ruby told me that if I went up and socked [Blue Bomber] Buddy Tinsley a couple of good ones, he'd quit. He talked me into giving Tinsley the best forearm shot I could. "He'll just die," Ruby said.*

> *So I started out to do what I was advised. I caught Tinsley a couple of times looking the other way and I gave him the forearm across the side of the head. He couldn't believe what was happening. I saw him in*

the line asking some of the guys. He was pointing at me.

At the end of the half, he grabbed me under the front of the shoulder pads and lifted me right off the ground and said, "Look, Ollie, I'm going to get you in the second half."

I wondered where he got the Ollie from. I looked down at my helmet and here I was wearing a helmet with "Ollie" on it. I went into the dressing room and took off the "Ollie" and put on "Atch." In the second half, he was still looking for Ollie.

Atchison learned some tricks of the trade. "We were playing Edmonton and Gene Kiniski kept punching me in the stomach. I taped a thigh pad on my stomach and he darn near broke his hand."

Despite two artificial hips and a bad knee, Atchison loved being a Roughrider. "It gave me a way of life. If you didn't have football you were just another one of the masses. Football makes you a bit of a hero." Atchison was inducted into the CFL Hall of fame in 1978.

Ottawa defeated Calgary 24–21 to win the 1968 Grey Cup.

Destiny's Darlings

In 1969, Saskatchewan finished 13–3 in first place and swept the Stampeders in the Western final, setting up a rematch with Ottawa and one of the greatest performances in Grey Cup history, Russ Jackson's swan song. It was also an opportunity for them to avenge their Grey Cup loss to Saskatchewan three years earlier.

The Rough Riders of Jackson and Stewart were destiny's darlings. You didn't have to convince Eagle Keys. "There are some games you get the feeling you're not going to be allowed to win," he drawled. "That was one of them."

The Western Riders didn't win. With snipers stationed in the light turrets of Montréal's Autostad to protect against an FLQ terrorist threat, Jackson and Stewart put on a dazzling performance. But it didn't start out that way.

Saskatchewan took a 9–0 lead on a 27-yard Lancaster to Ford touchdown pass, plus a safety touch conceded by Billy Van Burkleo. The Westerners added two singles in the third quarter but that was it. The day belonged to the Red Riders.

First of all, Jackson finished a long drive by completing a 12-yard pass to Jay Roberts for a touchdown. Soon after, Jackson tossed a short pass to Ronnie Stewart who ran 80 yards for the score, putting Ottawa into a 14–9 lead at halftime.

Their third touchdown came when Jackson eluded a fierce pass rush at the Saskatchewan's 12-yard line and found Jim Mankins alone in the end zone. Jackson admitted it was a broken play.

"Yep. We were rolling right and McQuarters had me right in his grasp and I happened to get lucky and get away from him. I came back across the grain and Mankins was standing there just over the goal line."

Ottawa's last touchdown was similar. Cliff Shaw had Jackson in his grasp, but he somehow got the ball to Stewart who ran 32 yards for the score. The final, Ottawa 29, Saskatchewan 11.

Alan Ford starred for Saskatchewan. "I scored a touchdown on a 12- or 13-yard reception. And I had a single. I dropped a long pass in the end zone that I should have caught." He also set a Grey Cup record with a 78-yard kickoff return, eclipsed in 1991 by Toronto's Rocket Ismail against Calgary.

Bill Baker blamed the icy field for their defeat, believing it nullified their strength, the pass rush.

"Exactly. I thought it hurt us. I thought we had a better team than they did. It does neutralize a team because on ice, you're all the same. We had a heckuva defensive line, but we didn't do a very good job that day. We took it to them earlier in the season and really laid a beating on them. It was a completely different game in the Grey Cup."

Ford wasn't buying it. "Your pass rush is somewhat nullified in those conditions, no question, but they could say the same thing. They wanted to get to Lancaster, too. I don't think it makes a hill of beans of difference, really."

Lancaster agreed with Ford. "I don't really think the field conditions on that day would favour anybody. I mean you're there all week practicing, and you sort of know what to expect. That was just one of those days where it went almost the way it was written, that Russ was going to retire and he was going to win. Ronnie Stewart had a great game.

"It was one of those days when it seemed like they were destined to win the game."

George Reed: "That was a bad field, but it was Ottawa's year to win. Their defence played well. They shut us down completely after we went up 9–0. I think they adapted to the condition of the field faster and better than we did, and more power to them."

Hugh Campbell: "In 1969, I felt like it was a movie where we were supposed to be the victims—or like a wrestling match where it was decided ahead of time the other guy was going to win. There was a big sensational thing over the fact Russ Jackson was retiring. It was his last game. It just seemed like everyone got on his bandwagon.

"I only had that feeling one other time when Ron Lancaster played his last game here in Edmonton. I felt that no matter what we did, it was meant to be that Lancaster would win his last game."

After the 1969 Grey Cup, the trophy was stolen. The CFL Commissioner was Jake Gaudaur.

"What I did along the way was take the original Grey Cup and put it safely in the Hall of Fame where nobody could touch it and had a replica produced. I did that the year after it was stolen and recovered by the Ottawa police early in 1970. At that time, I decided that we shouldn't lose the symbol of what we were supposed to be all about and decided to protect it in that way.

"Traditionally what happened back then, the team that won the Grey Cup took it back to their place and used it for promotions or whatever they wanted. There was high potential for it being stolen and lost forever."

Retiring at the end of the decade were Plaza of Honour members Hugh Campbell, Wally Dempsey and Jim Worden, as well as Don Gerhardt and Lance Fletcher. Arriving were tight end Nolan Bailey, the versatile Bob Pearce from Stephen Austin College and quarterback Gary Lane from Missouri, now a respected major league umpire.

The Second Worst Day in Rider History

After the disappointing Grey Cup loss to Ottawa, the Roughriders came back in 1970 more determined than ever to win another championship. Eagle's teams kept improving. In 1970 they had the best record in Roughrider history before or since, 14–2. Ron Lancaster won his first Schenley for Most Outstanding Player.

The Riders accomplished their incredible record despite the fact George Reed played with a serious leg injury for eight games and then was out of action for three more after it was diagnosed. It was the only season other than his rookie year that he didn't gain 1000 yards. He picked up a mere 821 on one good leg!

Said Reed: "I cracked a bone in my leg. I played up until we clinched first place and then they found the crack in my leg and I took three games off. I probably could have played. I had played eight games on it. If that hadn't happened, I probably would have had 12 straight years of 1000 yards."

The team's only two defeats came in Alberta, losing 10–6 in Edmonton and, ominously, 30–0 to Calgary. They beat the Stamps 21–17 and 21–14 in Regina. The Alberta teams finished with 9–7 records, the Eskimos taking second place by winning the season series with Calgary. In the semifinal at Clarke Stadium, Calgary won 16–9.

The Stampeders then rolled into Regina and over the Roughriders 28–11. In the second game in Calgary, the 9–7 Stampeders had the 14–2 Roughriders on the ropes, ready for the knockout punch with 39 seconds left on the clock. Trailing 4–3, Calgary had the ball at the Rider 23. Jerry Keeling went back to pass and was hit by defensive tackle Ken Frith. The ball fell to the turf where for the second time in his illustrious career, Ed McQuarters scooped it up and ran 80 yards for the touchdown and an 11–3 Saskatchewan victory.

The Riders returned to Taylor Field for game three and what would turn out to be the second blackest moment in the history of Saskatchewan sports.

There had been ominous signs. Calgary had been 3–6 at home but 8–2 on the road, including the playoffs so far. And the King of the Quarterbacks wouldn't be playing. Ron Lancaster was out with broken ribs. Bill Baker described what happened.

"I remember Ronnie got kneed badly by [Dick] Suderman in Calgary and broke his ribs down by his kidney, and so, Ronnie wasn't playing. That was a terribly flagrant play. That was one of the cheapest shots I've ever seen. I can remember so clearly the hit he had on him. He led with the knee and broke some ribs."

"He jumped on me with his knees," recalled Lancaster. "It was a little bit late."

Gary Lane was his replacement.

For the Sunday afternoon showdown, the weather was simply frightful. In what was one of the worst days imaginable in Canadian football history, the two teams battled through a blizzard and arctic cold, until it looked like the Roughriders would finally put the stubborn third-place Stampeders away.

Calgary took full advantage of the wind in the first quarter, jumping into a 9–0 lead, the big play a 63-yard punt return by Jim Silye. The Riders answered with 11 points in the second quarter to lead by two at the half. The teams traded field goals in the second half and with less than two minutes to go, moving in for the kill, Calgary's Hugh McKinnis fumbled on the Rider four-yard line.

The Roughriders were deep in their own end. After two running plays, they punted. The coverage team slipped and slid on the icy surface, Calgary got a good return to the Saskatchewan 42-yard line. Keeling threw to Hugh McKinnis who was knocked out of bounds at the 26 with three seconds left.

If the Riders had let him run a little more and then hit him, the clock would have run out. Larry Robinson came on to kick a 33-yard field goal into the teeth of a gale-force wind. He made it. Calgary won 15–14 and were off to the Grey Cup. The cold hand of despair gripped Saskatchewan by the throat.

Even Larry Robinson was surprised he had made the field goal:

"It was a low and wobbly snap from centre. Basil [Bark] could hardly hold on to the ball. His hands were frozen.

I don't know how Keeling could hold on to the ball, but he placed it just right. I kicked it deliberately off to the side. I was trying to play the wind, and man, when I saw that wind take the ball and hook it back inside the goal posts, I just couldn't believe it."

Nor could the Roughriders.

Asked if Robinson was lucky, Eagle Keys replied, "I don't know, but I'd like to bet a $1000 even money every time he tried one under similar circumstances.

"I'm not taking anything away from the Stampeders. They never gave up, but when Ron Lancaster couldn't play, we had to throw out our game plan today and make changes from the bench."

As far as the Roughriders were concerned, the final score should have been 21–12. George Reed had scored one touchdown, Gary Lane another. In both cases, the official ruled that the ball carrier hadn't made it over the goal line. Lane squeezed in by the out-of-bounds marker. Everyone but the referee could see the footprints in the snow.

"Both Gary Lane and I were in the end zone," Reed stated emphatically. "In those days I guess they didn't clean the goal line off, and the officials didn't give us the touchdowns. When you're in the end zone from the waist up, it is a touchdown. I don't know what the officials were looking at or thinking about, but it is just one of those things.

"Then Larry Robinson kicked the field goal and knocked us out. That was probably our best team.

That was the one game that hurt the most in my whole career. It's still bitter, it still sits there in my stomach."

A review of game film showed both men made it to pay dirt. Calgary great John Helton didn't need film. "If George Reed said it, it's true. He's an honourable man."

Wayne Harris disagreed. "They had the ball on our three-yard line. George thought he got in, but we didn't think so, and the referees didn't think so."

Bill Baker talked about the Gary Lane touchdown that wasn't.

I was on the field. I was a tight end blocking for him, and to this day, I have no doubt in my mind that he scored. I thought George scored, too. I've never been surer of anything in my life, but that we scored on both those occasions.

With our great bouts with Calgary, it was anybody's game a lot of the time, and it was always whoever made the big play, won. That's the way it should be. The thing is, we were 14–2, we were clearly the dominant team in the CFL, and then we blew it in the playoffs that cold game.

Larry kicked that miracle field goal. We've all got the same story. We looked around and it was missing the posts and it blew back in, and I think it was Kosid who said at the end, it just fell over the bar in the corner.

I fell to the ground and I said, "I'm quitting. I'm never playing again." I was so disappointed. To have gone 14–2 and to be out there when it was 30 below or whatever it was.

*That truly was an amazing kick. I mean into the
wind, the ball was frozen. It was an amazing kick,
a kick of a lifetime.*

Eagle Keys summed it up. "That was a tough loss.
We'd had such a good year and we were expecting to
go back to the Grey Cup. I didn't even think they were
going to try the field goal because I didn't think they
had a chance in the world of making it. But he made
it. With the wind blowing the way it was, nobody ever
made a bigger field goal than that one."

At the end of the 1970 campaign, Larry DeGraw,
Chuck Kyle, Gary Lane, Ken Reed, Cliff Shaw and Ted
Urness retired. Urness had been the All-Canadian
centre six straight seasons, from 1965 through 1970.

Acknowledged as the greatest centre of all time,
Urness never won a Schenley Award, a reflection of
the voters' lack of knowledge about the most difficult
position to play on the offensive line. He was inducted
into the CFL Hall of Fame on June 3, 1989.

Also leaving was the Big Bird from Turkey Neck Bend,
Eagle Keys, who flew off to BC to coach the Lions. He
explained why he left.

"At the particular time, I was a real good friend of
Jackie Parker's. They made Jackie general manager
out there. I felt we had gone as far as we could go in
Regina. Sometimes you just have to make a coaching
change. Sometimes you feel you're not improving
yourself. BC was having a tough run at the time. Every
coach figures he can come in and win, so I thought we
could come in and win."

Keys made the playoffs twice in BC. His best record on the coast was 8–8 in 1974. The following year he was fired.

Eagle Keys was inducted into the CFL Hall of Fame, on April 28, 1990. His replacement in Saskatchewan was former BC Lion head coach Dave Skrein.

George Reed compared the two:

> *Skrein and Keys were two different coaches. Eagle expected a lot of you. Skrein was more laid back but a very good coach in his way, too. Everyone respected Dave Skrein.*

> *If you played poorly, Eagle would let you know. One thing about Eagle, he would never single you out. He'd never argue with you, he'd never say anything bad about his team in the paper. But on Monday after the game, he certainly let us know if we played poorly or if he expected more from us. Then you got both barrels.*

Ted Urness' position was taken by Larry Bird. Other newcomers were Bill Manchuk, a linebacker, defensive back Gig Perez, lineman Archie McCord, linebacker Charlie Collins and defensive tackle Tim Roth.

In 1971, it was the Year of the Horse. Calgary and Saskatchewan tied for first place with 9–6–1 records, the bye going to the Stampeders because of a better points differential.

Winnipeg made the playoffs for the first time in five years but lost the semifinal in Regina 34–23. Calgary swept the Western final and moved on to Vancouver where they defeated Toronto 14–11 to win their second Grey Cup.

Bill Baker made the Western All-Star team for the first time, along with Wayne Shaw and Bruce Bennett. George Reed and Jack Abendshan made both dream teams. Reed ran for 1146 yards and 12 touchdowns, passing Johnny Bright to become the CFL's all-time leading rusher.

Chapter Nine

Gabriel, Blow Your Horn

The worst year for the Green and White since 1965
was in 1972, when they also finished third. The
Blue Bombers finished in a 10–6 tie with Edmonton
for first, awarded to Winnipeg because they won the
regular-season series. The great rivalry between
the Stamps and Riders came to an end as the Horsemen
missed the playoffs for the first of six straight seasons.
The new rival was Edmonton.

The Eskimos won the first and third games of the
season, 31–29 and 25–23, respectively. The Riders took
the other tilt 14–12. Saskatchewan won the semifinal
in Edmonton 8–6, making the margin of victory in
each game two points.

For the first time since 1949, the Western final
would be a single game. For the first 30 minutes,
everything went Winnipeg's way as they ran up a lead
of 21–0. Saskatchewan responded early in the third
quarter with a touchdown; the Bombers responded
with a field goal. The Riders stormed back with two
touchdowns and a field goal and, with time running

out on the clock, found themselves in field-goal range.
Ron Lancaster remembered it well.

> *We were down 14 late in the third quarter. Don*
> *Jonas threw a pass to a fullback somewhere around our*
> *10-yard line. If he catches the ball, he walks in. But he*
> *drops it. They kicked a field goal and made it 24–7.*

> *They missed that touchdown and had a chance to*
> *put it away, and for some reason, we got rolling after*
> *that. We came back and tied it, and we had the ball*
> *and were moving down to kick the winning field goal.*

> *We get into field-goal range. On the last play, Jack*
> *[Abendshan] missed it. Paul Williams kicked it back*
> *out of the end zone. I caught it and kicked it back in.*
> *Williams got it and kicked it out, and they got called*
> *for no yards. We got another shot. Jack kicked it*
> *through and we won.*

The final score was 27–24.

Chortled Gary Brandt:

> *Winnipeg was supposed to have been better than*
> *we were. Their head coach was Jim Spavital—I hated*
> *him. But they had a really good defensive line. They*
> *were kicking our ass. They were yapping the whole*
> *game. They were feeling pretty confident, as well they*
> *should have.*

> *At halftime we went into the locker room and*
> *nobody said anything. We just all had a Coke and some*
> *guys had a cigarette. We just thought about it.*

> *The second half we got a few breaks, and George*
> *[Reed] started running the ball real well off tackle,*

*and all of a sudden, things changed. Those guys who
were yapping in the first half stopped talking. At the
end we weren't surprised we won. The second half
we just dominated them.*

Off to their fourth Grey Cup appearance in seven
years, the Riders would play the Tiger-Cats in Hamilton
at Ivor Wynne Stadium.

"That was another tough, football game," Ron Lancaster
recalled. "Tough, tough defence and they played it that
way." Since interlocking play began in 1961, the Roughriders had won but once in Hamilton, 23–22 in 1970.

The 1972 Grey Cup was special to Hamilton because
it was the first time since 1944 they had hosted the
event. It would be the fifth meeting between the teams,
the fourth in Steeltown. On the down side, a home
team had not won the Grey Cup since 1952 when
Toronto turned the trick against Edmonton.

General manager Ralph Sazio had hired Jerry Williams who had enjoyed considerable success in Calgary.
Fired in Philadelphia, Williams got to the Grey Cup
with Hamilton in his first year.

The King versus The Kids

The Ti-Cats had rookie quarterback Chuck Ealey,
straight out of college, and an 18-year-old rookie place
kicker, Ian Sunter, as well as seven newcomers on
defence. They faced a Roughrider squad loaded with
grizzled Grey Cup veterans.

In the first quarter, Al Brenner picked off a Lancaster
pass, and Ealey directed his team 52 yards for the

opening touchdown, a 16-yard pass to Dave Fleming in the end zone. The Riders argued vehemently that Fleming, after leaping up for the ball, had come down out of bounds. The film confirmed that.

"Isn't that too bad?" sneered Angelo Mosca.

Saskatchewan responded with a 75-yard drive, capped off with an eight-yard TD pass to Ohio State rookie Tom Campana. The Ti-Cats argued to no avail that defensive back Gerry Sternberg had been the victim of an illegal Bob Pearce pick.

"Isn't that too bad!" said Wayne Shaw.

The teams exchanged field goals, after which the game settled into a tight defensive struggle until the dying moments of the fourth quarter. Deadlocked at 10, Chuck Ealey went to work.

With 1:51 left in regulation time, Hamilton scrimmaged on their own 15-yard line. Although he had done nothing throughout the game, second-year homebrew and All-Canadian tight end Tony Gabriel caught three consecutive passes of 27, 12 and 15 yards, bringing the ball to the Rider 41. Ealey ran for two yards and threw to Garney Henley who made a circus catch at the 27. Ian Sunter trotted onto the field. "Keep your head down, kid," Henley advised. He did, kicking it right down the middle. Final score, Rookies 13, Grizzled Veterans 10.

The loss was the result of more than the Riders running out of luck.

In the first place, they didn't help their cause on special teams. Although Sunter was named Player of the Game, Bob Krouse blocked a Saskatchewan punt, partially blocked another and fell on the ball when John Williams blocked a third. And Dave Skrein made at least two coaching errors that cost his team their second Grey Cup.

George Reed described his day:

> It was a good day. I thought the game was going along quite well. I thought we should have won the game. Probably that's the second-most bitter defeat because I thought we were controlling the ball, controlling the tempo of the game, and I thought the referees gave them a touchdown. Fleming was clearly out of bounds, and everybody sees that now, so he got a touchdown he shouldn't have got.

> We had a turning point in that game. We punted the football when we shouldn't have. We were on about our 35-yard line. We had a third and two. We went for it and made it with ease. We got close to mid-field and we had the same situation, a third and one or two, and the coach elected to punt. We could always get one or two yards when we wanted to get them. If we had gone for it, they wouldn't have had a chance to come back and win the game.

Bill Baker: "I think that's the kind of play that really hurts you because it sucks away your energy. Instead of being aggressive, you're being passive. In the CFL, boy, you've got to keep that ball. It's so easy to score at the end of the game."

"The thing we never understood as players," said Lancaster, "late in the game we gambled on third and one at our 35-yard line and made it. On the very next series, we came up third and one farther up and we didn't gamble. We kicked, giving it back to them, and they moved it down and scored the field goal and won. We didn't understand why we gambled at one spot and not farther up the field."

Skrein's second major mistake was listening to assistant coach John Payne.

Gary Brandt explained: "Wayne Shaw was playing the right outside linebacker position the whole game. Wayne Shaw was an all-star. Dave Skrein knew they were going to try and pass all the way down the field. For some reason, he decided to pull Wayne and put Bill Manchuk in. Manchuk was a backup.

"They exploited that move and passed all the way down the field and kicked the winning field goal. Wayne Shaw was so mad—and rightly so—that he wouldn't even come back with us from Hamilton. Dave thought he was going to get someone in there who was a little quicker who could cover the pass."

Shaw was still seething 25 years later.

> *In the 1972 Grey Cup I was an outside linebacker. Canadians were not given the opportunity to play middle linebacker. They had to be Americans. We had a middle linebacker by the name of Steve Svitak who was a big tough American kid, but he was a rookie. He was good against the run, completely lost on the pass.*
>
> *When we were in a zone defence, he'd drop back 10 to 12 yards in the middle of the zone. He had that problem all year. I used to room with him, I used to tell him, "Don't drop so deep."*

All day long, I'm playing on that big Canadian tight end Tony Gabriel. He never caught a ball on me until the fourth quarter.

When it was late in the game and Hamilton needed some action, they took Garney Henley who was a great defensive back and put him in at flanker and I'm worried.

Late in the game, Gabriel had not caught one pass. I can handle him. I'm hitting him off the line all day and I'm with him. My job was to play on him, hit him right off the line and cover him to the curl zone, 10 or 12 yards deep.

Steve Svitak would keep dropping deep. I kept telling him not to. No way he was fast enough to cover Henley or Gabriel deep and, besides, deep coverage was not our responsibility.

Now what happened, I hit Gabriel. I stopped in the curl zone, I'm with him. I see Ealey looking inside at Garney Henley. He had lined up outside and came into the hook zone. I'm in the curl zone with Tony Gabriel.

I look, no sign of Svitak. I made a step inside. Ealey threw to my guy. I made a mistake trying to cover up for Svitak. We stopped them, they don't score. I go on the bench. The offence goes out, doesn't do anything. Skrein sends in Manchuk.

Chuck Ealey drops back and throws the ball to Gabriel. I said, "Skrein, let me in there, I'll hit him. This is my last year, my fourth Grey Cup. Skrein, let me in there! I'll hit him. I won't let him off the line."

Three times in a row Ealey hits Gabriel, and Skrein won't say a word to me. I've never been so pissed off in my life. There is no way I'd have let Gabriel catch those passes on me. I was hitting him off the line. Manchuk was faster than I was but he couldn't cover him.

Skrein quit and never coached again, as far as I know.

I almost wish I had ignored Skrein and ran on the field and told Manchuk to get off. I don't know what the hell would have happened, but I'm sure they wouldn't have stopped the game, and Manchuk would have come off.

The trouble was, I was a shy young Canadian, and for 12 years they convinced me the coach was God. But it was my 12th year, what the hell could they have done with me?

The opposition saw it the same way as Shaw. Ti-Cat linebacker Mark Kosmos observed, "Tony Gabriel came into the league in 1971. I remember him having the great press coming up. I played against him when I was in Montréal.

"I found Tony very easy to keep on the line of scrimmage. Here was a guy who was very gangly. He wasn't a big, strong guy but he had great speed. I don't think he ever experienced people that would get him up in front and not let him off the line. But Tony was the kind of guy whenever he was on the field he was dangerous. If somebody gave him a break like they did in '72 and '76 and gave him some room, he was going to kill you."

George Reed praised the other receiver Shaw had worried about. "Tony made some big catches, but the guy who made the biggest catch was Garney Henley. He made the catch standing on top of his head and put them into position for Ian Sunter to kick a field goal.

"That was a bitter defeat. The 1969 Grey Cup we got beat, and so after the game you go and have a beer and forget about it. But it was tough to forget 1972."

During the last minute of the game, Alan Ford could sense the panic.

"Oh, yeah! When you see the clock going and they're moving, holy cow! We've got to stop them. The tendency there is let's change the defence. Let's fool them or at least get out of the defence that's been causing the problems. Usually there's another reason for it. It's not the defence. Someone's not playing the defence the way it is supposed to be played."

Often, teams go from aggressive defence to the "prevent" defence, so-called, it has been suggested by some cynics, because it prevents you from winning. That was Ed McQuarter's view.

"The prevent defence, I don't know who invented the darn thing, but it's useless. You may as well just play your regular game because you've got a better chance instead of just sitting back. But there wasn't a whole lot we could do about it. That's what was called. That's what we had to do."

Bill Baker summed up that wretched day in Hamilton. "That was not a good game to be part of. We didn't seem to be in sync, the coaches and the players. There were too many different agendas on the sidelines. Instead of worrying about the other team, there was too much going on. We were over-coached."

Roughrider veterans marvelled at the thorough preparation of Eagle Keys. It is hard to imagine Keys making the mistakes Skrein made in 1972 and Payne made in '72 and '76. They didn't do their homework, costing the Green and White two Grey Cups.

Tom Campana was runner up to Chuck Ealey for the Schenley Outstanding Rookie Award. George Reed, Jack Abendshan and Bill Baker were All-Canadian.

Eight veterans called it a day, including Barry Aldag, Nolan Bailey, Bruce Bennett, Wally Dempsey, Bob Kosid, Gig Perez, Don Seaman and Wayne Shaw. Bennett was an all-star in six of the seven seasons he played. Shaw had been an all-star on seven occasions. Shaw, Kosid, Bennett and Dempsey are on the Plaza of Honour.

Donning the green and white for 1973 were guard Jim Hopson, now the team president and CEO; Regina Ram fullback Steve Mazurak, now director of marketing; local boy Frank Landy, a defensive tackle; safety Ted Provost; DB Lorne Richardson; and linebacker Pete Wysocki.

John Payne took over as head coach.

Bill Baker Wrecks Esks

Over the course of the next 10 seasons, the Edmonton Eskimos would go to the Grey Cup nine times, winning six, including a record five in a row, 1978–82, under former Rider Hugh Campbell. For the first three years of this remarkable run, the Esks' only real opposition was Saskatchewan because Calgary, BC and Winnipeg all struggled. In 1973, the teams tied for first, Edmonton 9–5–2, Saskatchewan 10–6 with the Esks getting first for the usual reason. After dispensing with BC 33–13 in the semifinal, the Roughriders lost a thriller in Edmonton 25–23.

A fierce rivalry developed between the teams, fuelled by the activities of Bill Baker. In back-to-back games during the regular season, Baker put all three quarterbacks out of commission, earning him the sobriquet "The Undertaker."

Baker said, "I had hurt a lot of quarterbacks that year. Every team in the league I seemed to knock out a quarterback. In one game [against Edmonton] I knocked Bruce Lemmerman out, he broke his shoulder, and the next game they brought in Dave Syme andWilkie [Tom Wilkinson]. I knocked Wilkie out, then they brought Syme in and I knocked him out, they brought Wilkie back in and I knocked him out again."

Were they late hits perchance? "I got no penalty at all. But then I got a letter that I wish I had kept. I got a letter from [CFL commissioner] Jake Gaudaur after the Edmonton game here in Regina and it said, 'You are hereby fined a hundred dollars for excessive roughness throughout the game.' For a defensive end, you couldn't be paid a higher complement.

"Actually, I had a great relationship with the Eskimos. I used to go to their team parties."

And the nickname "The Undertaker"?

"It was that game in Regina. That's when my friend Norm Kimball [Eskimo GM] tried to get me thrown out of the league. I found that distressing, upsetting. In hindsight, it was pretty rough play. At the time, I just thought I was doing my job. But when I look at the play, I think I'm lucky I didn't kill somebody. In those days you could clothesline and head slap with no penalties. I know it resulted in a change of rules."

In a game against Toronto, Eric "The Flea" Allen was in motion coming down the line. Baker reached over and clotheslined him. Allen couldn't speak for a week.

Never regarded as a dirty player, Baker forged lasting friendships with players from every team in the league. Even the referees liked him.

At the end of the season, Bill Baker played out his option to sign with BC, coached by Eagle Keys.

"It was great to be playing for Eagle," said Baker. "Once he left, the team changed quite a bit, and it wasn't nearly as much fun to be there.

"I played my option out three different times there because I was still getting the old line, 'You're not bad for a Canadian.' That was the line they used on you all the time, and it kind of irked me after a while.

"So in '73, I played out my option. It was not money, it was the 'You're not bad for a Canadian' that stuck in my craw. I just felt degraded all the time."

The man degrading him was a fellow Canadian, General Manager Ken Preston.

"Exactly," replied Baker. "That was the sad part about it."

The Riders did an outstanding recruiting job for 1974. They signed the veteran George Wells to replace Baker. Wide receiver Rhett Dawson arrived from the NFL. Others included tight end Laurie Skolrood; receiver Leif Petterson from Otterbein; Penn State, All-American linebacker Steve Smear from the Alouettes; and Ken McEachern who would star in the defensive backfield.

The 1975 Riders' edition ran into one of the worst rash of injuries in team history. At one time or another, they lost McQuarters, Landy, Abendshan and Reed. At one stretch they lost six of eight games, before finishing 9–7 in second place. They got stronger as the year wore on, winning their final three games and the semifinal.

In the Western final, Saskatchewan and Edmonton battled down to the wire before the Eskimos came from behind in the dying minutes to win 31–27.

George Reed played through several serious injuries to lead the league for the sixth and last time with 1447 yards. Reed, Wells and Richardson made All-Canadian.

At season's end, Pete Wysocki left for the NFL. Also gone were Don Bahnuick, Archie McCord, Marion Latimore, Bob Pearce and Ed McQuarters. Bobby Thompson was released because he dated a white woman.

McQuarters Calls it a Day

The great Ed McQuarters had lost an eye in a household accident in 1971, and he had knee operations in each of the next two seasons. In 1973, he spent most of the year on the injury list. In 1974, he signed a new contract but was on injured reserve for six weeks. When he came back, Ken Preston asked him to retire but McQuarters refused. When he cleared waivers, the team cut him.

McQuarters reviewed his career: "The 1967 Roughrider team was the best I ever played on, as far as togetherness and camaraderie, the closeness. After all the home games there was a party at some player's house. Matter of fact, after I left the game that's what I miss the most—the togetherness."

He discussed leadership: "Wayne Shaw was one of those on our team, a quiet leader. Wally Dempsey was that, Al Ford was a leader. Bill Baker, I tried to follow his example. He was just a mean, tough, hard football player. I tried to do that. Without either of us realizing it, I was trying to do what he was doing, and he was trying to do what I was doing. It made both of us better.

"You have to be unselfish. You have to park your ego at the door."

What's the downside of being a professional football player?

All of my fingers have been broken except for four. The rest have been broken or dislocated. I've got a bad wrist, it's really bad, sometimes it's so tender I can't do anything. I've got two bad knees, bad neck, bad shoulder and a bad right foot. That's all part of the game. When I get up in the morning, I can tell you whether or not it's going to rain or snow or there's going to be a lightning storm.

Have you noticed with the players these days when they get the slightest injury how they lay down on the field and stop? The Players' Association has told these guys, "Look, don't try to be heroes like we did back in the old days because most of us can't walk anymore, have bad nights sleeping, bad backs. Better you stop, don't be a hero."

It is the right thing to do because when they get through with their careers, they'll be in a lot better shape than us old guys. I don't know of any guy in my era who is not banged up. I have to always crawl into my car because of the way my knees are banged up. I can't fit. I've got to crawl in and out. There is not a day that goes by that something doesn't hurt.

How good was Ed McQuarters? So good that even though he played only six full, relatively injury-free, seasons, he was inducted into the CFL Hall of Fame on March 5, 1988.

Two major rule changes came into effect for 1975. Blocking on punt returns was permitted, and the two-point conversion was adopted.

Despite another rash of injuries, the Riders finished second to the 12–4 Eskimos with a mark of 10–5–1. Reed rushed for 1454 yards, his second-best season ever but second to Calgary's Willie Burden who set a new record with 1898 yards. The star in the Rider firmament was Rhett Dawson, who was second in the league in receiving. Ron Lancaster was the leading passer.

Saskatchewan beat Winnipeg 42–24 in the semifinal and headed to Clarke Stadium for the third straight year.

At the beginning of the 1975 season, Ray Jauch said, "No matter what kind of season we have, even if we go undefeated, it will all likely come down to a cold day in November and Lancaster and Reed."

In addition to the cold, it was foggy in Edmonton, not a problem for the players, but the spectators could not see what was going on for most of the game.

Because half of Edmonton's losses had come at the hands of the Roughriders, Jauch thought drastic measures were called for. He significantly changed his defences.

The "experts" commented that Ron Lancaster just wasn't sharp that afternoon, throwing his passes two feet off the ground or over the receiver's head. In fact, stymied as he was by Edmonton's new look, those were the only places he could throw without being intercepted. He was brilliant in a losing cause.

Jauch explained what happened: "We did some things quite differently. We did some different rotations in the secondary, we used different coverages than we used before. We only rushed three guys sometimes in order to cover everybody. Ronnie would take his normal reads and he'd go to dump the ball off, and we would have a guy right there in his face. That kind of fouled him up a bit. It might have been the first time a three-man rush was used."

It worked. Edmonton won 30–18 and went on to win their first Grey Cup since 1956, defeating Montréal in Calgary, 9–8.

Lancaster and Lorne Richardson made All-Canadian.

At the end of the season, two wonderful workhorses, Jack Abendshan and Clyde Brock called it a day. Other tandems have been as good as those two, but none better. Abendshan will be inducted into the CFL Hall of Fame in 2012. Brock deserves entry as well.

Also retiring was defensive back Ted Dushinski. "The Hilltopper" wore the green and white for 11 years. Always reliable, he was one of Sandy Archer's 100-percenters.

In January 1976, George Reed signed a two-year contract with the Riders. In May, at age 36, he announced his retirement, leaving a hole in the line-up as wide as the prairie he played on.

Over his illustrious 13-year career, the greatest Roughrider of them all, set every professional football rushing record, except yards gained in a single season.

Perhaps his most remarkable statistic was the 11 seasons with over 1000 yards gained. The average life of a running back in professional football is five years. The fact that Reed was able to perform consistently at such a high level over 13 seasons made him one of the most remarkable athletes of all time, in the same category as Gordie Howe.

When a panel of experts selected the Top 50 CFL players of all time for TSN in 2006, George Reed was second only to Doug Flutie.

Asked if he was healthy for his Grey Cups, Reed replied, "No, I was never healthy at the end of the season because I took such a pounding. I carried the ball a lot, and, in a lot of those games, I was basically the only one running the football. Everyone took their shots at me.

"But I was always of the opinion when I got up on a game day, if I put the uniform on and I felt pretty good, I could play. I could play with a great deal of pain so that's what carried me through. Normally by the end of the year, I had a couple of bad shoulders, but it was just time to play, and you went out and played."

He emerged from his career relatively unscathed. "Yeah," he replied in 1997, "outside of the cracked bone in my knee which has lingered on with me, and that's probably because medical techniques back then weren't what they are today, I have a little twinge in my knee once in a while, but outside of that I feel good and healthy."

Reed went out in style. "I think my last year before I retired [1975] was probably as good a year as I had. I wound up with almost 1500 yards and I thought I played very well."

George Reed was inducted in the CFL Hall of Fame on June 30, 1979. We shall never see his like again.

Once More into the Breach

The 1976 Roughriders were long in the tooth, ready for their last hurrah. Significant additions included cornerback Paul Williams, middle linebacker Cleveland Vann, kicker Bob Macoritti and rookie guard and future Hall-of-Famer Roger Aldag from the Regina Rams. Later in the season, running back Molly McGee came aboard.

Although Saskatchewan looked good during the pre-season, they displayed an old weakness in their win over Edmonton in July, a weakness that would come back to haunt them. With less than two minutes left in the game and protecting a five-point lead, they gave up the ball three times. Great defensive play saved the day. In their two 1975 losses to the Eskimos, they failed to pick up a first down in the late going. Coach John Payne admitted his concern.

"That situation has bothered me. That is a situation we need to avoid."

The Riders were 10–5 going into the last game of the season against the 2–11–2 Calgary Stampeders. A win would give them first place and a bye into the Western final.

So far they had handled the Stamps with ease. But new Calgary coach Joe Tiller, who went on to fame and fortune at Purdue, had his team playing with determination. They also had a new quarterback in John Hufnagel. And, of course, they were playing the Roughriders who have always disdained doing things the easy way.

At less than two minutes on the clock and with darkness falling and the lights on at McMahon Stadium, Calgary was leading 31–26. Then Ron Lancaster went to work, leading his charges down the field. On the last play of the game, he found Rhett Dawson in the end zone. Final score, Saskatchewan 33, Calgary 31. After the game, wearing only a gold cigarette holder, Ron Lancaster met the press. "Gentlemen," he said, "it was never in doubt."

The Roughriders finished on top for the first time since the beginning of the decade. They would be playing in their 11th straight Western final, a record that still stands.

Because the Bombers had swept the season series with Saskatchewan, there was a collective sigh of relief in the valley of the Jolly Green Giants when Edmonton upset Winnipeg in a thriller, 14–12. Rider dominance over the defending Grey Cup champion Eskimos continued as they won the Western final 23–13.

Saskatchewan's Grey Cup opponent would again be the Ottawa Rough Riders and Tony Gabriel.

On Thursday, November 25, Lancaster won his second Schenley Most Outstanding Player Award. Tony Gabriel won for Most Outstanding Canadian.

The Worst Day in Saskatchewan Sports History

Grey Cup day in Toronto was windy and cold.

As in the Riders' last Cup appearance, it was the veteran King of the Quarterbacks versus a downy-cheeked youngster, this time Tom Clements from the Fighting Irish of Notre Dame. Saskatchewan was favoured by seven. As in 1972, the villain was Tony Gabriel. And once again, Coach John Payne made critical errors.

The darkest day in the history of Saskatchewan sports was about to begin.

Saskatchewan's first drive began on their 40-yard line. Steve Molnar ran 20 yards and fumbled. Wonderful Monds picked it up and ran 60 yards to the end zone, but the play was ruled dead. On the next play, Molly McGee fumbled, Ottawa recovering at their 45. After Gerry

Organ missed a 57-yard field goal, the Westerners scrimmaged at their own seven. On the second down, Lancaster went back into the end zone to pass, scrambled to elude linebacker Mark Kosmos and slipped and fell at the one. Footing on the slick field was a problem all day for Saskatchewan, the third Grey Cup where they couldn't find the right footwear. Their opponents didn't seem to have a problem.

Bob Macoritti kicked from 14 yards deep in his end zone. The Green defence came up big, forcing Ottawa to settle for a three-yard field goal at 9:27. Ottawa 3, Saskatchewan 0.

The Roughriders scrimmaged at the 35. After two incomplete passes, Macoritti got away a 40-yard punt into the wind. The stiff breeze held the ball up for a second or two. Rookie Bill Hatanaka fielded the ball on the run. Ted Provost lunged desperately at him. The rookie brushed him aside and out-raced Lou Clare and Macoritti to the end zone. It was the longest punt return in Grey Cup history to that point. In 68 seconds, Ottawa had scored twice to jump into a 10–0 lead.

Ottawa's head coach didn't consider the return a broken play.

"No," said George Brancato. "It's a good special teams play. There has to be some good blocking and certainly some good running by the returner. It's a big special teams play, like a blocked kick. You work on those things every week and you just hope that one day you'll break one."

The second quarter belonged to Saskatchewan. Starting out at their 48, Lancaster alternated hits and misses: to McGee for 23, Leif Petterson for 14 and 12; first down at the Ottawa 13; incomplete, nine yards to Dawson, third and a foot at the four.

For 13 years, whenever the Riders needed a yard, George Reed was "Mr. Automatic." It was second nature to Lancaster to call the fullback's number in this situation rather than his own, although twice in the Western final he kept crucial drives alive with quarterback sneaks. Not this time. Fullback Steve Molnar piled into the line and didn't gain an inch.

The Green defence came up big again, forcing Ottawa to punt. Although the Riders took advantage of good field position to put three points on the board, a golden opportunity had been lost. Saskatchewan had to rely on Ron Lancaster's arm, and he had a magnificent day, as did his primary receivers Leif Petterson and Bob Richardson. However, their inability to pick up short yardage on the ground was their undoing.

Their next possession was set up by Steve Mazurak's 24-yard punt return. From the 45, Molnar picked up eight yards, McGee one. Faced with another crucial third down, Lancaster kept it, and Ottawa was offside. It was a 16-yard toss to Mazurak at the 15. Lancaster then threw left to Mazurak across the middle. He got a great block from Rhett Dawson to make it to the end zone. Tie ball game.

Three plays later, Ted Provost, who contrary to myth, played a great game for Saskatchewan, intercepted Clements at the 51, returning it 26 yards to the Ottawa 25. Lancaster promptly hit Bob Richardson at the 10. The big tight end shook off Ron Woodward like a dog flicking a flea and thundered into the end zone. Saskatchewan 17, Ottawa 10 at the half. Lancaster completed 15 of 21 passes for 170 yards and two touchdowns. Clements was having a miserable afternoon with only 25 yards through the air. The football universe was unfolding as it should.

The Roughies opened the second half with a 51-yard Bob Macoritti field goal. Gerry Organ replied on their next possession with a 40 yarder into the wind.

With about a minute left in the third quarter, Ottawa was third and 10 at their own 37. Organ went back to punt, but to everyone's surprise, he ran for 52 yards. He did it entirely on his own, according to Brancato.

Ottawa couldn't cash in. With a first down at the Saskatchewan 21, Clements was picked off by Cleveland Vann. The quarter ended with the good guys holding a seven-point lead. But the Eastern champions had outplayed the Westerners in the third quarter and had the wind for the final 15 minutes.

Things started to go wrong immediately. Punting from the enemy 52, Gary Brandt snapped the ball high. Macoritti jumped up and pulled it down but was almost tackled by Kosmos. The punt dribbled away. Ottawa took over on their 54, only two yards beyond the Saskatchewan line of scrimmage.

Neither offence could do much, but the Roughriders were being punted into poor field position because of the cold, wet wind blowing in off Lake Ontario. Halfway through the fourth quarter, Ottawa capitalized on field position and narrowed the score to 20–16 with a 32-yard field goal.

From his 35, Lancaster and Leif Peterson moved the ball to the 55-yard line. On second and one, Lancaster again eschewed the quarterback sneak and gave it to Molnar. He slipped and fell a good yard short. Macoritti punted, Ottawa started out at their 26.

Tom Clements only had two good drives in the entire game. They came exactly at the right time. Behind almost perfect protection, he threw to Jeff Avery for 13 yards. After an incompletion, he hit Art Green for 16. Green then took the hand-off to the Saskatchewan 51.

On the next play, Tony Gabriel got off the line, cut across the middle, cradled Clement's picture-perfect pass and ran 41 yards to the Roughrider 10. The young quarterback, cool as a cucumber, had the best secondary in the CFL back on its heels. As Yogi Berra said, it was déjà vu all over again.

Or was it? Perhaps lightning wouldn't strike twice. Green picked up two yards. On second down, Clements carried down to the one where he fumbled, but the ball was ruled dead. On third and goal, the magnificent seven of Frank Landry, Tim Roth, George Wells, Jesse O'Neal, Cleveland Vann, Bill Manchuk and Roger Goree held firm. Saskatchewan took over on their one-yard line with 1:32 left to play.

On first down, Tom Campana sliced off tackle for five yards. Lancaster called the same play again. Campana got a yard. Macoritti punted. Ottawa took over at the Saskatchewan 35.

Art Green picked up a yard on first down. With 40 seconds left, Tony Gabriel got off the line, cut across the middle and caught one for 10. With 20 seconds left,

Gabriel faked inside and ran to the end zone where he got behind the secondary and broke a million Saskatchewan hearts. His touchdown gave the Ottawa Rough Riders their ninth Grey Cup victory by a score of 23–20. Compared with the depression that settled over the land of the Roughriders, Mudville would have seemed positively euphoric.

Tom Clements had 151 yards passing in the second half, 104 of them on his last two possessions.

Throughout his career, Ron Lancaster was the best comeback quarterback in CFL history, his trademark a top hat and rabbit. Trailing late in a game, he could always be relied on to reach into his bag of tricks and snatch victory from the jaws of defeat. He always did it by passing, and in the '76 Grey Cup he was picking Ottawa's secondary part.

For Lancaster, protecting a lead late in the game was another matter. Then he became conservative and went into a shell.

"You're probably right," he admitted. "That's the hardest place on the field for me—deep down in my own end. That is the hardest place to operate from when you're protecting a lead late in the game, especially. You don't want to give them a cheap touchdown."

As far as that Grey Cup was concerned, Lancaster said, "When you have the ball on your own eight-yard line and you've got a minute and a half left, you play percentages. You don't take chances." He paused. "You know, since I've had a chance to think back on it, we should have thrown the football. But if I was put in the same situation again, I'd probably do the same thing. That's what's crazy about it."

Mark Kosmos was more than surprised at Saskatchewan's conservative strategy. "I was shocked. I'm calling the defensive plays. I remember us getting in the huddle and I said 'GAP defence.' That's almost like a goal-line stand defence. I'm basically saying we're going to stop the run because that's all they were going to do. If Ronnie would have thrown the ball, the guy would still be running. None of our guys were playing the pass. We knew they were going to run. They had to know that we were going to play the run."

George Brancato: "What I thought would happen was that they'd give up two points and kick off and get us out of field position because there was less than a minute left in the game. They surprised me when they punted the ball and we took over in good field position at their 35."

Playing conservatively was the Riders' first mistake. Not surrendering a safety was the second error. In the process of conceding a safety, Macoritti could have run all over the end zone before stepping out, taking at least another 20 seconds off the clock. Ottawa would likely have got the ball on the ensuing kickoff about their own 45-yard line with under 50 seconds left.

John Payne's third mistake was his strategy against Tony Gabriel. Everyone in the ballpark knew Clements would go to Gabriel, but they couldn't stop it from happening. Remember 1972 when Wayne Shaw kept Gabriel in check by hitting him on the line of scrimmage? This was the same John Payne who was the Rider defensive coach four years earlier and made the decision to pull Shaw and get somebody with more speed on the big tight end. Didn't work then, didn't work now.

Said Mark Kosmos: "If the situation had been reversed and I had been playing against that team, Gabriel would never have left the line of scrimmage. In those days you could hit people coming off the line. You could hit him coming across the middle, you could clothesline him. I mean, receivers were fair game.

"Tony came out on that play, nobody touches him at the line, he goes in, he goes out, just like he was running a play on a street in Hamilton [Gabriel's hometown] and he gets this beautiful pass from Tommy. That was it. Everybody knew the ball was going to Tony. Tony was running free as a bird. I don't remember much of a pass rush, either."

Gabriel described the dramatic moment. "I'd been hit hard on the previous play by Cleveland Vann and I was dazed and seeing stars. I got back into the huddle, and Tom Dimitroff had sent in Gary Kuzyk, the wide receiver with a play from the bench. Time was counting down, and Tom Clements shouted, 'No!' and called the play that won the Grey Cup.

"It was a Fake 324, fullback through the four hole and a tight-end slash. Ironically, the set they were in defensively, [linebacker] Roger Goree was off the line of scrimmage and they had a defensive end lined up over me. That allowed me to escape the line. Ray Odums followed our wide receiver and left my area empty.

"When the ball was coming, my heart was pounding and my eyes were open wide. If I had dropped that pass, I may as well have retired right then."

Because Gabriel was seen running away from him, Ted Provost has been wearing the goat horns ever since, unfairly according to George Brancato.

"It was the corner, the outside guy, Ray Odums. He jumped on the underneath guy. It was a three-deep defence and the corner didn't get back. Tony broke for the corner. Provost was actually in a good position, taking the middle away. But he had no help on the outside. You usually blame the guy closest to the ball. The fan does and probably most of the press do, too. In this case, it just so happened that the guy closest to the ball was not responsible. He was just chasing."

But as Kosmos pointed out, Gabriel shouldn't have got off the line in the first place.

Ron Lancaster felt it should never have come down to the last minute. "Special teams played a big part. They faked a punt on us and ran for a first down. We punted the ball and Bill Hatanaka ran it back for a touchdown.

"We had a chance to score when we had a first and goal at the four and didn't get it. If we had taken advantage of our opportunities, the last minute wouldn't have mattered." He paused and then emphasized, "Would not have mattered. No question. It wouldn't have mattered a bit. But we didn't get it done. We had chances to put that game away and we didn't do it."

Why didn't you throw a pass on your last series?

"I really don't know. The coach made the decision."

Of the four Grey Cups Lancaster lost, 1976 was the hardest one to take.

Yes, it was. In 1972, during that last series, you could see it going by you. In '76, we thought we were good enough to beat anybody. We weren't overconfident but we did have confidence, where as in '67 and '69, you could see at the start of the game we were going to get dominated.

The 1976 Grey Cup meant more to me than any of them because I was in the twilight of my career and I thought it was about high time we won a Grey Cup. That game was the last-play-of-the-game thing again. I thought we were supposed to win that game. In our minds we thought we should have had that game.

1976 was the beginning of the end of an era. I think people sensed that. A lot of us had played a long time together and the team was starting to disband. People probably felt like I did. That was the year. If we were going to win it, that had to be the year to do it.

It was a sad way for Alan Ford to end his career.

When I came back to Regina from College of Pacific in 1965, after the pre-season I started the second game playing in Edmonton and hurt my knee. I missed the rest of the season except for the last game and the one playoff game we had. From then on I was a starter until my last year in '76. I played in 179 straight games.

In 1976, I injured my neck in training camp and I just couldn't function by the last game of the season, so that was my retirement bell. I didn't play in the Grey Cup. I watched it from the press box.

*1976 and 1972 were the real disappointing ones.
I thought we were the better team in both cases, and
we lost both of them on essentially the last play of the
game. That's what's so great about our game. It's
never over until it's over, but sometimes it's heart-
breaking.*

Another player who didn't see action that Grey
Cup day was a raw-boned rookie from Gull Lake,
Saskatchewan, by the name of Roger Aldag.

"My first year was 1976, the year we went to the
Grey Cup," Aldag recalled. "I played a couple of
games. I hurt my ankle and I went on the injury list.
I was on the sideline at the Grey Cup and I thought,
'Gosh, this is great. I should be here next year, too.'"

How little did he know.

Chapter Ten

The Agony

> *Joseph said to Pharaoh: "Both of Pharaoh's dreams*
> *have the same meaning. God has thus foretold to*
> *Pharaoh what he is about to do. The seven healthy*
> *cows are seven years, and the seven healthy ears are*
> *seven years.... So also, the seven, thin ugly cows that*
> *came up after them are seven years, as are the seven*
> *thin, wind-blasted ears; they are seven years of famine.*
>
> *Seven years of great abundance...will be followed*
> *by seven years of famine...when all the abundance in*
> *the land...will be forgotten."*
>
> —Genesis 41:25–30

Joseph was a piker. Try 11 years of feast and famine. Children grew into adults wondering why their team could never win. Little heads began to wonder if contrary to the bedtime stories their mothers told them, Ron Lancaster, George Reed and the Big Bird from Turkey Neck Bend ever existed.

Grey Cup? Finding the Holy Grail would have been easier.

First the feast. From the 1966 season through to 1976, the Roughriders won more games than any team in the country, 117 out of 176 for a winning percentage of .665. They lost 55 and tied four. They appeared in five Grey Cups, winning one. They garnered 48 All-Canadian selections, three Schenleys and one Coach of the Year Award. They appeared in the Western final 11 straight years. There are 11 Roughriders in the CFL Hall of Fame from that era.

After one of the most incredible periods of success in Canadian football history, the Riders authored a new, likely never to be broken, record for futility, missing the playoffs 11 years in row.

It was an amazing stretch. One would have thought that between 1977 and 1987, a team might come down with injuries and allow the Roughriders to slip into third place. One would think a team would manage at least one lucky break or two in such a long period of time.

It wasn't meant to be. Adding to the despair of the people of the Wheat Province, Saskatchewan in the 1980s suffered through the worst economic downturn and the poorest crop yields since the Dirty Thirties, as well as a government that sank into the depths of incompetence and corruption.

There is a little bit of Job in everyone from Saskatchewan. A farmer plants his crop, hope etched deeply in his furrowed brow, only to see 40 bushels to the acre pummelled into the ground by that cruel twist of fate, a hailstorm in late June or early July. Not many Canadians live with the prospect that Mother Nature can destroy their life's work in a 15-minute rampage. If you are from Saskatchewan, you get the feeling that if the fickle finger of fate isn't inserting itself into your left ear, it is only because a flood in Manitoba has caused the gods to be momentarily distracted. Still, that 11-year span was almost too much to bear, even for Saskatchewanians.

The end of greatness came with a whimper rather than a bang. The Roughriders slid slowly into football hell.

Gone was John Payne, replaced by his defensive coordinator Jim Eddy. Also leaving were DBs Lorne Richardson, Ray Odums and Jim Marshall; defensive linemen Jesse O'Neal and Frank Landry; guard Jim Hopson; and receivers Alan Ford and Rhett Dawson. Richardson, a four time All-Canadian and one of the best defensive backs to ever play the game, and Marshall were traded to Toronto for Steve Dennis and Dave Hadden, a bad trade if there ever was one. Landy and O'Neal were the price paid to bring Bill Baker back to Saskatchewan. Upon his release, Odums went to Calgary for seven years, earning Western All-Star honours four times and all-Canadian recognition three times. It seems some of those hailstones hit Rider management square in the head.

Baker had won the 1976 Most Outstanding Defensive Player Award, but coming back to Regina to continue his career with Interprovincial Steel Co. proved to be a mistake. "I probably should have stayed retired or stayed with BC one more year. I came back and the coach was Jim Eddy. Well, Jim Eddy and I had nothing in common whatsoever."

If integrating several new players wasn't enough of a challenge, the Riders were savaged by the injury bug come September 1977. Still, they were 7–5 at the three-quarter poll. However, the fans were extremely unhappy, especially when they lost 11–1 to the 2–8 Stampeders. The object of their disaffection was Ron Lancaster. He was not amused.

"So many changes. When you make as many changes as we've made, both before the season started, and as the season's gone along because of injuries, it is frustrating to a quarterback because you never really get to be familiar with your pass receivers. You're spending so much time teaching new guys the basic offence that you can't refine and change things. We've made a lot of mistakes because of that."

Still, Lancaster was leading the league in passing and was having as good a year as 1976 when he was named the CFL's Most Outstanding Player. "Yeah," he agreed. "I think I've played better football this year than last, but the results aren't the same and therefore it is not as noticeable this year."

Because of the relentless criticism, Lancaster wasn't enjoying 1977 very much:

> People around here aren't used to losing. They haven't seen a team struggle as much as we have recently. They can't quite understand it.
>
> I get the impression that a lot of people believe you can dress 32 dummies up in green and white and expect them to win. With the calibre of teams in the Western Conference this year, that just isn't possible, and it isn't true at the best of times. It's a year where

you have to execute and you have to have the horses to do that. We had the horses but we've had to change them so often that it's just about impossible to get things going the way we want to.

And another thing: I get so much heat all the time about not having a running game. But if we run the ball all the game, then they say we don't have a passing game. I do what I think we have to do to win the football game, and I don't care if people like it or not.

But Lancaster did care. A proud man, a good person, a great athlete and competitor, he was hurt that the faithful had turned against him at the first sign of adversity.

Although the Riders finished second in total offence, only Calgary gave up more points. The Riders missed the playoffs with a record of 8–8.

How did the Roughriders go from Western champion to also-ran in one season?

"Oh, very simple," replied Lancaster. "I think that 1976 was kind of our last hurrah. A whole lot of guys were getting up there. They probably needed to make some changes each year leading up to '76, but we didn't do it because we had a good nucleus of players.

"We had reached the plateau and we would have started down the other side. They decided that 1976 was going to be our last shot at this thing, we were going to try to win it all and, if we won it, there were going to be a whole lot of guys going out on top as champions.

"We didn't win it. It was time to change the personnel. We'd gotten old in a lot of positions. The guys decided they'd had enough. There were so many changes that had to be made that we couldn't make them all and maintain any continuity from the year before."

At season's end, Leif Petterson was traded to Hamilton where he made all-star. Ted Provost, Tom Campana, Gary Brandt and Tim Roth retired. All four are on the Plaza of Honour.

The End of an Era

The biggest change going into the 1978 season was the retirement of long-time general manager Ken Preston, who was inducted into the CFL Hall of fame on April 28, 1990. Widely regarded as one of the best in the business, he was replaced by former player and hospital administrator Hank Dorsch, a man with no front-office football experience whatsoever. Perhaps the Riders thought his work at the Regina General Hospital would help with their chronic injury problem. Dorsch lacked the knowledge and respect needed to rebuild a once-proud franchise.

The dressing room was deeply divided with coach Jim Eddy on one side and most of the players on the other side. After losing their first six games, he was fired.

Lancaster was blamed for the team's sorry record, even though he was playing well.

When asked if he wished he had retired after the 1976 Grey Cup, he replied, "Sometimes I wish I had never played. So, yeah, I think so. But I made the decision to play.

"A quarterback is always judged by winning and losing. The consensus of opinion around here is that

I'm not playing well. I can throw the ball now as well as I ever did. It's just that we're not playing well and someone has to take the blame.

"I knew it was going to be a tough year when we started because the fans expected Larry Dick to start right away and that was encouraged by people in the organization. I was put in a position where no matter what I did, I couldn't win."

After being turned down by Eagle Keys to succeed Jim Eddy, the executive asked Lancaster to take over. He said no.

"They still wanted me to play quarterback. I don't feel you can be the head coach, the offensive coordinator and the quarterback all at the same time."

Eddy was replaced by his assistant Walt Posadowski, whose record the rest of the way was 4–5–1.

"It was a funny situation," said Posadowski. "We lost the day before and we were all in the office looking at film and Dorsch is on the phone. Hank said, 'I've just released Jim Eddy and he said to talk to you about taking over as head coach on an interim basis.' I asked, 'If I do a good enough job, will I get any consideration for the head coaching position?' He said, 'Yes.' I knew that was not an accurate statement because as long as Ronnie was there, he would get the job."

The team played well over the rest of the season because Posadowski simplified the defence, shortened practices and "I tried to put the onus more on the players than on anyone else. I just didn't feel we were getting the most out of our players, that they weren't as committed as maybe they should be. Putting pressure on them to perform helped."

On October 14, Lancaster celebrated his 40th birthday. He had already announced that the 1978 season was his last. The next day they lost to Jack Gotta's revitalized Stampeders 32–13, and Lancaster received a standing ovation from the good folks at McMahon. A week later, the Riders closed out their home schedule by losing a close one to Winnipeg, 13–7. In his final appearance at Taylor Field, Lancaster was booed.

The last game of the season in Edmonton, Lancaster relieved Larry Dick in the fourth quarter and engineered two touchdowns and a win over the mighty Eskimos. The Edmonton fans gave him a standing ovation.

His final year was a good one. He finished third in passing in the CFL. Lancaster retired as the greatest quarterback in league history and was inducted into the CFL Hall of fame on May 28, 1982.

Although finished with the Roughriders as a player, he came back in 1979 as the head coach, a disastrous experience for him, losing 12 games to start the season. Their first win came on Thanksgiving, 26–25, over the visiting Eskimos. They had one more win to finish 2–14, their worst finish since 1959 and second worst since 1910 when they were winless.

Because of Lancaster's legendary status in Saskatchewan, fans were patient with him, although many felt he would have been better off learning the coaching ropes as an assistant with either one of his buddies, Jack Gotta or Hugh Campbell. Resurrecting the Roughriders would have been a challenge for the most experienced coach, let alone a rookie who, overnight, had become the boss of his former teammates. One of the hardest lessons for him to learn was that not all players approached the game with the same dedication he did as a player.

"I know I prepared for a game," he said in 1979. "I'd take the game plan and make sure I knew my assignment. I assumed other players did the same thing. I found out differently."

At the end of the season, Dorsch was fired, replaced by Jim Spavital, formerly an assistant in Saskatchewan and Calgary and the head coach of the Blue Bombers. He was hired by Rider president Gord Staseson, who stressed marketing for the first time in the club's history. Staseson introduced the team fight song, "Green Is the Colour" and began selling the idea of Rider Pride.

A legendary tightwad, Spavital's first victim was Walt Posadowski, who Dorsch had promised extra pay for adding player personnel director to his offensive line coaching duties. Spavital told him the team owed him nothing, take it or leave it. He left it, signing with the Stampeders. When Jack Gotta left in 1983, Posadowski retired to the oil patch and resides in Calgary to this day.

The Riders entered the new decade with a rookie general manager, a head coach with one year's experience and 16 new faces in the line-up, including quarterback John Hufnagel who Posadowski had enticed from Calgary before leaving Saskatchewan's employ. Later in the season, QB Joe Barnes from Montréal came aboard.

The Rider faithful were optimistic, but Hufnagel was struck down in the first game of the regular season.

"1980 was a very tough luck year," Hufnagel recalled. "A lot of players were injured. A lot of progress was made but without visible signs for the fans to see.

"Everyone's optimistic in training camp. The Roughriders got some offseason additions, myself included. But it was a very difficult year. I tore the ligaments in my thumb the first game out in BC. We just didn't play well."

They finished at 2–14. Despite a coaching record of 4–28, Lancaster was offered a new contract. Angered by media implications that he was only offered another contract because his name was Lancaster, he said no. The decision wasn't announced, but Jim Spavital went to work immediately to find a head coach, and a few days later came to terms with Eskimo assistant Joe Faragalli.

Gord Staseson continued the story: "We went to the Grey Cup the next week and we took Ronnie with us because we didn't fire him, he quit. We still had his airline ticket and his reservation and we all loved him. So he went along.

"By Thursday of Grey Cup week, Ronnie had changed his mind. I met with him on the Saturday night and he wanted to be reconsidered. Well, it was too late. Jim had already made a deal with Faragalli."

Lancaster refused to talk about those events. "That was a very unhappy time," is all he ever said.

The Lancaster era was over. He won the Grey Cup as head coach of both Edmonton and Hamilton. He passed away at age 69 in 2008.

Joe Faragalli explained how he got the job: "Spavital talked to Cal Murphy, and Cal mentioned George Dyer who we had worked with in Winnipeg. Jim called George who was with Arizona State and he said you should talk to Joe Faragalli.

"Spavital came to Edmonton. We met at a motel and talked. He offered me a cheap cigar. He wanted me to talk to the directors. I went down and talked to them. They offered me the job. I said I had to go back and talk to my wife. They wanted the answer right away but I said no, not until I go back and talk to my wife. They phoned me the next morning and I became the head coach."

Nicknamed the "Happy Warrior" or "Papa Joe," Faragalli was a wonderful man, upbeat and friendly, even though he was always overlooked for the top job until the Riders came calling when he was 54 years of age.

He made a lot of changes, saying goodbye to a dozen veterans, including Bob Macoritti and Cleveland Vann. By using Canadian Greg Fieger at fullback, he was able to go with newcomer Joey Walters in the slot, along with another fresh face, Chris DeFrance. Walters caught 91 passes for 1715 yards, the most in team history. DeFrance had 64 receptions for 1195 yards.

A major reason for the rebirth of the offence was Faragalli's use of the two-quarterback system, John Hufnagel and Joe Barnes, dubbed "J.J. Barnagel."

"They got along real well," said Papa Joe. "It really depended on what we wanted to do. If we wanted to break containment and roll out, then I went with Joe. If I thought we could beat these guys by throwing the ball down the field, I went with John. After a while, we had each one play a half."

Any quarterback worth his salt wants to be number one, and Hufnagel and Barnes were no exceptions. Still, Faragalli got the most out of them with a minimum of unhappiness.

Faragalli also shored up the defence, bringing in linebackers Frank Robinson, Carl Crennel and rookie Vince Goldsmith. His punter, Ken Clark, was the best in Rider history.

The coach's biggest challenge was creating a winning attitude, a sense of team.

"Prior to my arrival, the players weren't allowed to hang in the locker room. A lot of them had time on their hands. In Edmonton, they all came in early. They played cards or rolled up a ball of tape and played basketball or soccer with it.

"When I went to Regina, those guys never came in until it was time to get paid. I preferred players to come in early, sit around, chit chat, do what they want to do. I wanted them to be together and become teammates."

Hufnagel appreciated Faragalli's approach. "Joe was a fun coach. He realized he was coming to a team where the players had been beat up the last couple of years. He wanted to give us back our self-esteem. The players responded to it."

Did they ever! And soon an entire province was believing.

Halloween Nightmare

By Labour Day 1981, the Eskimos and Lions were 7–1, Winnipeg 5–3, with Calgary and Saskatchewan two points behind at 4–4. Papa Joe was being hailed as Saint Joe. Not only was the team playing .500 ball, but they also were exciting to watch. Taylor Field rocked to "Green is the Colour!"

Things only got better for the Happy Warrior. The Riders had their best September since World War II, going undefeated, moving them into third place. J.J. Barnagel continued to excite the multitudes.

With the last game of the season on Halloween in BC, they were tied with the Lions for the final playoff spot, each at 9–6. It was the first meaningful game they had played in five years.

To say it was raining that afternoon would be an understatement. "General Joe" addressed the troops before the kickoff.

"This game is going to be won or lost on a miscue. It's not going to be a shoot-out. I bring this up because I want you to think when you field the punts, don't worry about running, make sure you secure the ball. When we throw, catch the ball. I don't care if you catch it and fall down. I want you to secure the ball."

He particularly stressed caution to Stewart Fraser and Greg Fieger. But it was in one ear and out the other.

The teams battled through the rain until, late in the fourth quarter, with BC leading 6–5 and the Riders pinned deep in their own end, the fickle finger of fate intruded as Roughrider fans instinctively knew it would.

Twenty years later, the Happy Warrior, retired to Narragansett, Rhode Island, was still haunted by the events of that Halloween afternoon on the opposite shore. With a rain-laden squall rolling in from the grey Atlantic, Faragalli, like Samuel Coleridge's Ancient Mariner, looked back on a dreadful day so many years ago.

"That was one I'll never forget. I think about it constantly, over and over again. Fieger was the fullback and we put this play in where it was a reverse to Dwight Edwards. I thought this is the time we run the reverse, we're going to whip them.

"The field was awful. Terrible rain, unbelievable rain.

"We ran the play with Fieger getting the ball and handing off to Edwards, but Fieger just dropped the ball before he handed it off. If Edwards got the hand-off, he could have sashayed down the field. BC recovered the fumble and scored a touchdown."

Earlier in the game, continued Faragalli, "Fraser tried to run with the ball on a punt, fumbled and fell on it. When he came off the field, I said, 'Give me your hand.' He didn't know what I was going to do, but he knew I was upset. I said, *'Give me your hand.'*

"I unbuttoned my shirt and stuck his hand on my chest and said, 'Do you feel that thing? Do you know I had a heart attack once, do you want me to die?' I was trying to make a point—hold on to the damn ball."

Near the end of the game, Lui Passaglia punted from his goal line. Fraser fumbled it on the run at the BC

40-yard line, the Lions recovered, game over. BC 13, Saskatchewan 5. The playoff drought continued.

Joey Walters made All-Canadian and Vince Goldsmith with 18.5 sacks won the Schenley for Most Outstanding Rookie.

Joe Faragalli received the Coach of the Year Award in Edmonton in January 1982. Resplendent in a green tuxedo, dubbed the "Green Zucchini," the old warrior was never happier than he was that night. Everybody was happy for him, including Hugh Campbell, whose 14–1–1 Eskimos had won their fourth straight Grey Cup.

Well, not everyone was happy. Key additions to the 1981 Riders had been brought in by Jim Spavital. Given the talent on the field, Spavital thought the team should have done better. Believing the team lacked discipline, he had privately decided to fire Faragalli, but when the media made Faragalli Coach of the Year, his hands were tied.

Certainly there would have been a huge public outcry if Saint Joe had been sent packing after coming so close to the playoffs.

But Spavital's worst fears were confirmed. In 1982, it all fell apart.

Bye-bye, Barnagel

The first mistake Joe Faragalli made was breaking up the dynamic duo of J.J. Barnagel. Deciding Hufnagel would be number one, he traded Barnes to Toronto for defensive back Marcellus Greene.

During the offseason, place kicker Paul Watson injured his Achilles' tendon and retired. Spavital signed a kid named Dave Ridgway.

He also signed quarterback Joey "747" Adams from Tennessee State. Adams had an arm like a cannon. Unfortunately, he was about as smart as a cannon and would prove to be his coach's undoing.

Faragalli was optimistic about his second season. "There are times when you are whistling in the dark, saying you are getting better when you're not. Last year the players dispelled the notion that they couldn't win. Now they know they can win. They've come closer together as a team. We're going to play 16 games and see if we can get in the playoffs."

They couldn't.

Four and four at Labour Day, the Riders went winless for September. Despite the fact their beloved Roughriders had lost four straight games, 28,245 pom-pom waving fanatics filled Taylor Field on October 3 to give their heroes a chance to redeem themselves. Stung by a media barrage of criticism directed at the erstwhile Saint Joseph Faragalli, the Green and White unleashed all their frustration on the Calgary Stampeders, thrashing the visitors 53–8. The love affair between the province and football team continued.

Not for long. They finished last at 6–9–1.

There were highlights. Joey Walters set a new receiving record with 102 catches for 1692 yards. His total of 193 catches for 3407 yards was the greatest two-year performance in CFL history to that point.

Five Riders made All-Canadian, including Fran McDermott, Ken Clark, Dave Ridgway, Mike Samples and Walters.

The rap on the Riders was that Faragalli was too soft on his players and that a country club atmosphere prevailed. They were first in fumbles, interceptions, penalties and losing the ball on downs. Defensively, they were the worst in the league.

The case of Joey Adams was instructive of Faragalli's weakness as a coach. Papa Joe said he repeatedly urged Adams, a college track star, to run more, but he refused. What made Joey run? Certainly not his head coach.

Said Faragalli, "He never took to coaching. He wasn't a bad kid, it's just that he was never disciplined."

In May 1983, Spavital was offered big money by Detroit of the upstart World Football League. Going blind and worried about his future, he jumped at the chance. The Rider executive named John Herrera as GM. Faragalli tried to quit after his contacts told him Herrera was trouble.

The executive, thinking Faragalli wanted out of his contract to join Spavital in Detroit, refused.

Herrera was a disaster, and matters soon came to a head. With the team 1–3, Faragalli was fired, replaced by assistant Reuben Berry. The first thing he did was cut 747 Adams.

The losses under the new regime continued to pile up. They didn't win again until the Labour Day weekend, 32–30 over the Bombers, followed by a 29–28 victory over Ottawa. After Hufnagel played well in both games,

Berry traded him to Winnipeg. The team won two more games at the end of the season, finishing fifth at 5–11. They surrendered 526 points. The last team to give up that many points was the 1959 Roughriders, legendary for their ineptitude.

Reuben Berry was a hardnosed individual who declared the country club closed. He traded for veterans, saying, "Rookies get you beat." He promised an aggressive team that would battle all the way.

His biggest acquisition was quarterback Joe Paopao, released by BC in favour of Roy Dewalt. Berry's most important newcomer was Canadian rookie receiver Ray Elgaard.

Despite a veteran quarterback and Berry's tough talk, the team had their worst first half in 25 years, losing six of eight. The only bright spot was Dave Ridgway's record eight field goals at Ottawa on July 29. The second half was better, 4–3–1, but they still finished out of the playoffs. The Rider executive cleaned house, hiring Bill Quinter as general manager. In a move that delighted the populace, Quinter hired his long-time associate Jack Gotta to coach.

Popular as a player and assistant to Eagle Keys, Jocko had won a Grey Cup in Ottawa and restored Stampeder fortunes in Calgary. He had won three Coach of the Year awards. If anyone could lead the Roughriders to the Promised Land, it was Gotta.

He approached his job with infectious enthusiasm. "I couldn't be happier," he said before the season opener. "This is a good group of guys."

Optimism reigned supreme when they walloped the eastern Riders 46–22 in their home opener at Taylor Field. After losses to Toronto and Montréal, Saskatchewan won three of four, going into Labour Day with a record of 7–3, two points up on Edmonton for third place. The Riders were playing exciting, entertaining football, and they were winning. Happy days were there again. Then as Gotta said, "Lightning hit the outhouse."

His team recorded only one more win, missing the playoffs for the ninth straight year.

Nine straight years! Nobody else had ever come close to that kind of football futility. Fan fury was felt at the gate. The 1985 average attendance of 23,117 was the lowest in six years. It was the third straight season to record a drop in attendance. In 1985, the team lost $940,000. The provincial economy was as bad as the team, also reflected at the gate.

With the future existence of the Saskatchewan Roughriders in doubt, the lieutenant-governor, Honourable F.W. Johnson, appealed to the people of the province to buy season tickets and save the team. Where else but Saskatchewan would the Queen's representative make a public appeal on behalf of a professional football team? It worked. The team soldiered on into 1986.

Again, Jocko was optimistic. "I feel this is the year. We're going to have a great crop!"

The schedule expanded to 18 games in 1986. For the Riders, it was just two more opportunities to lose. And lose they did, finishing up the track once again with a record of 6–11–1 in last place.

When a team is losing, small matters are magnified. Gotta was accused of heading home to Cochrane, Alberta, at every opportunity, leaving preparation to his assistants. Bald Bill Quinter wore a trademark white cowboy hat at all times, even with formal wear. It seemed he never took it off. As the losses mounted, so did irritation with his hat.

President Tom Shepherd and his executive cleaned house. With attendance down, the treasury empty and the team lying at death's door, the Riders turned to the man they called The Undertaker to restore the football corpse to life.

Chapter Eleven

The Ecstasy

Why did Bill Baker leave a successful corporation to assume command of the *Titanic*?

"The club was really floundering," he explained, "and I couldn't turn down a challenge. I thought I knew what to do. I thought I knew what the answers were. I didn't know if I could go back and run a small company. It was a heckuva challenge to go from a fat-cat corporate job where you worked your butt off but you were really taken care of, to running a small-time football club where you have to do everything."

He took over a virtually bankrupt team. They began 1987 with a season-ticket base of 12,756. Besides missing the playoffs 10 years in a row, confidence in the league was at a new low because of the collapse of the Montréal Alouettes. All Baker had going for him was his reputation as a man who got things done. It would be enough.

In his first few months, he cut $700,000 from the budget by getting players to take salary cuts. He then hired as head coach John Gregory from Cal Murphy's

Winnipeg Blue Bomber staff. Only football insiders had ever heard of him.

Baker explained his choice: "Coach Gregory is a man of character. He is an unusual guy with a lot of personality and enthusiasm. We get along well and we also argue sometimes and have some good debates."

An old friend was back.

"John Hufnagel is doing a player coach's job," said Baker. "Tom Burgess is looking good at quarterback and so is rookie Jeff Bentrim."

The Riders opened the season at home by blowing a 21-point fourth-quarter lead to Calgary. They followed that up by losing to Toronto, coming up empty three times within the Argos five-yard line. Trying to mount a comeback at home against Edmonton, various Riders were called for spearing, objectionable conduct and roughing the passer in the third quarter. Gregory ranted and raved up and down the sideline and threw a piece of chalk at a reporter after the game. Even worse, John Hufnagel's career came to an end that night. He described what happened.

"I was really looking forward to playing. It was my first game. When I went in I was pleased with what I was able to do. I lasted two quarters. Then I planted my foot, maybe the cleats stuck in the artificial surface and I tore my Achilles tendon. That was very discouraging, very disappointing." He never played again.

It was all downhill from there. The Riders finished fifth, nine points out of a playoff spot with a record of 5–12–1. The playoff drought had reached an amazing 11 years.

For the 1988 season, Bill Baker had a beautiful new surface called Omniturf installed at Taylor Field. This was no small matter given the horrendous number of injuries the team sustained during the 1980s. John Gregory shook his head sadly.

"Last year we lost 13 people to the injury list, including four quarterbacks, John Hufnagel, Tom Burgess, Jeff Bentrim and Kent Austin. That is devastating to a young team. A lot of the injuries were because of the turf. With the new turf, a lot of that will end."

In addition to getting the new turf, Baker re-priced the stadium, established the idea of the Labour Day Classic and put in a souvenir store.

"I knew the first year we were going to have a real tough time being competitive. We had to make enough changes that people knew how much we cared and how committed we were to the team and to the province. That was our mission—to make people proud of being part of the Roughriders."

Baker also had to improve the product on the field.

"I was fortunate," he said. "I give credit to Dan Rambo because without Dan, no way. He was the key guy. He brought in Kent Austin, Don Narcisse, Jeff Fairholm.

"We did a series of trades very quickly. We completely changed our defence. We brought in James Curry, Rick Klassen and the guys from Calgary, Richie Hall and Vince Goldsmith. We went from a shaky defence to the toughest, most physical defence in the league. We had Austin and Burgess. I was determined to have two quarterbacks after seeing as a player how dependent on

Ron Lancaster we had been. The first year we struggled, but by year number two, we were a helluva team."

Indeed they were.

Defence led the way. Bobby Jurasin and Vince Gold-smith had 31 sacks between them. Dave Albright and Eddie Lowe had 187 tackles. The secondary, anchored by Richie Hall and Glen Suitor, was a good one, severely tested in an era of fire-wagon football.

The Roughriders hadn't scored more points than they had given up since 1976! All that changed with Gregory at the helm. The offence was powerful with Ray Elgaard, rookie Jeff Fairholm and Don Narcisse. They had a running game with Tim McCray and Milson Jones.

The offensive line was solid with Roger Aldag, Ken Moore, Mike Anderson, Bryan Illerbrun and Vic Stevenson. The big question mark was quarterback. Could Tom Burgess and Kent Austin get the job done?

In summing up Rider prospects for 1988, John Gregory was cautious. "We're going to be a very solid football team. It will take us longer to be a dominant force in the league but we will be adequate."

With the team running out of money and the fans running out of patience, would adequate be good enough? To end the post-season drought, the Riders would need some luck. They were long overdue, luck being a lady who did not reside in Regina.

The Riders started the season as fast as prairie fire, winning their first three games, over Ottawa and Edmonton and hammering Winnipeg 46–18.

The rookie Fairholm had five catches for 160 yards and a touchdown.

The joint was jumping, the stands were full with fans chanting "We're number one." The faithful didn't want to leave. Half an hour after the players left the field, 15000 fans lingered, savouring the moment.

For the first time in years, the Jolly Green Giants were playing with confidence. Said middle linebacker Dave Albright, "Winning is contagious. Teams that continually lose always find ways to lose. We've brought in some veteran players from winning programs. We now have a winning attitude instead of expecting to lose."

The bubble burst in August, losing 43–27 in Edmonton and 48–10 in Calgary. They beat the Stamps back home, 24–21 but then lost heartbreakers to Toronto and Winnipeg. "Here we go again," the consensus seemed to be.

But it wasn't. Saskatchewan won four straight in September to move into a first-place tie with Edmonton. They split their final six games to finish at 11–7, the same as the Eskimos who were awarded first place because of the points differential in the games between the two teams. Not only was the playoff drought over, but the semifinal against the BC Lions, who finished two points back, would be played at Taylor Field.

Things were looking good since they had won both regular-season games against the Lions. What the Roughriders didn't have was post-season experience.

It showed. The Lions roared in and out of Taylor Field with a 42–18 victory.

"BC came into town and whipped our ass," recalled Baker. "We were too up, too high and made all sorts of mental errors. We were too emotional. The locker room was crazy before the game."

Roger Aldag, Ray Elgaard, Bobby Jurasin and Dave Ridgway made All-Canadian. For the only time in team history, the Roughriders had two Schenley Award winners, Elgaard for Outstanding Canadian and Aldag for Outstanding Offensive Lineman.

The biggest loss in the offseason was Bill Baker who left for Toronto to become the Chief Operating Officer and President of the Canadian Football League. It was a mistake. Going through a divorce, Baker realized he needed to be there for his children in Regina and so asked the league if he could operate from the Queen City. They said no, so he resigned in 1989. After running Sask Energy, he moved to Calgary and became a successful entrepreneur in the oil patch.

Quarterback Controversy

The Rider nation approached 1989 with confidence based on the fact that not since the days of Ron Lancaster was the team as strong at quarterback with Kent Austin and Tom Burgess.

New York native Tom Burgess began his pro career with Ottawa in 1986. They traded him to Saskatchewan in 1987 for Joe Paopao. Because of a shoulder injury, Burgess only played 10 games, but the following year he played them all, finishing with 159 completions out of

331 attempts for 2575 yards. Probably the most under-appreciated quarterback in Rider history, he would start half the games in 1989 and play an important role in the Western final.

Kent Austin attended Ole Miss. He explained how he ended up in green and white: "Saskatchewan got in touch with me out of college my senior year. Dan Rambo wanted me to come down for a free agent camp in Shreveport, Louisiana. I decided not to because I'd been working out with the NFL and I got drafted by St. Louis in 1986 and made the team.

"I was released in my second year, and Saskatche-wan brought me in a week later. I came up here in 1987 with eight games to go and played the last five." He won his first two starts.

In 1988, Austin started the seventh game and contin-ued in that role until he was injured in game 14. Burgess took over and led the Riders to the playoffs.

John Gregory thought the two quarterbacks comple-mented each other: "Each has special things he does. I like Austin, I like Tommy. Burgess threw 19 touch-down passes, Austin 8. Austin completed 58 percent of his passes, Burgess 48 percent. Burgess throws the hot routes fantastically. Anytime you blitz Tom, you've got a chance to get beat badly. But he doesn't throw well against zone coverages. Austin throws very well against zone coverages but has trouble with the blitz."

Austin didn't like sharing the duties with Burgess and disagreed with Gregory's assessment.

"I don't feel like I have any problem with the blitz. I can read coverages as well as anybody in the league, better than most.

"Coach Gregory feels that he has to have two guys ready to play, but I feel at times if the team is struggling, everyone looks at the quarterback and says he's the cause when he might not be.

"You've always got that in the back of your mind, that if you don't make it on the next series, you might get pulled. If you can't handle that, you put more pressure on yourself to get things done and you try to do things you can't do. But that's the way it goes. I guess Matt Dunigan's the only one who can play miserably and not get pulled."

In the season opener against Calgary, Austin played miserably and was pulled. Burgess engineered a brilliant comeback win and held the starter's job thereafter with mixed success. Halfway through that season of optimism, the Roughriders were tied with the Lions for third place, each with marks of 4–5. Their next game was in Toronto.

Trailing the Argos 24–10 at the end of the third quarter, Gregory pulled Burgess in favour of Austin. Saskatchewan won 29–24. The following Sunday, Austin got his first start since opening day, leading the team to a 48–35 win over Edmonton. He was the starter the rest of his career in Saskatchewan.

Two steps forward, two back, a 36–27 loss in Ottawa and then a soul-searing defeat at home, losing to the Lions after time expired.

"There were seven seconds left and we were up by five points," said Gregory.

All we had to do was let BC catch the ball and tackle them and the game was over. They were going into a very strong wind. Dunigan threw a Hail Mary up there and Glen Suitor was called for extremely obvious pass interference. By then the clock was out. The next play they threw the ball into the end zone, and Suitor was called for pass interference again, which gave them the ball on the one-yard line. They ran a quarterback sneak. Dunigan fumbled, but someone else fell on it and that's how we lost the game.

A lot of the fans thought that game was the end of the season for us. But we hadn't lost heart because we felt we had a good team. We pulled up our bootstraps and went from there.

If I was ever proud of myself for accomplishing something as a coach, I was proud of the fact that we were able to hold everybody together. That loss could have been disastrous, but we were able to keep together and keep working.

The Riders were 3–2 the rest of the way, losing the last game in Edmonton 49–17. They finished third—nine wins, nine losses. The future looked bleak.

So many players were injured that they had to start third-string quarterback Jeff Bentrim at slotback in the semifinal at Calgary. The Stampeders were prohibitive favourites.

But the Roughriders had beaten Calgary three out of four times during the season, outscoring them 122–97.

Home-field advantage? Give the edge to the Green and White who felt comfortable in McMahon Stadium, enjoying the warm support of so many loyal fans. With the local TV blackout lifted and it being a cold day, only 16,286 fans showed up, most of them wearing green and white. Nothing messes with the heads of the home team like having the crowd solidly behind the opposition.

The Roughriders ran up a 23–9 lead at the half on the basis of two Tim McCray touchdowns and three Dave Ridgway field goals. Mark McLoughlin kicked all of Calgary's points. The Rider offence dominated time of possession with one long drive after another.

The Stampeders tallied the only score in the third quarter, a Kennard Martin touchdown. The good guys carried a seven-point lead into the final frame. Never a team to do things the easy way, it wasn't enough.

Calgary stormed ahead with a 32-yard McLoughlin field goal and a 36-yard TD strike to Daric Zeno. With their season ticking away, the Roughriders were trailing 26–23.

After the kickoff, Austin led his team into Stampeder territory. With second down and long at the 46-yard line, Gregory called a draw play to little-used Canadian fullback Brian Walling. Expecting a pass, the Stamps launched an all-out blitz. After clearing the line of scrimmage, Walling waltzed to the end zone. Ridgway wrapped it up with a field goal. The final score was Saskatchewan 33, Calgary 26.

The Riders were off to Edmonton to face the mighty Eskimos who had a record-setting 16–2 season and had defeated Saskatchewan twice by a combined score of 94–36. Edmonton was well rested and ready.

But one of Edmonton's losses was to Saskatchewan. Again, many of the 35,112 fans at Commonwealth Stadium were cheering for the Riders. And, according to John Gregory, the Riders were lying in the stubble.

"The last game of the year, we played Edmonton with a skeleton crew because we had lots and lots of injuries, and we knew we were already in the playoffs. They beat us pretty good, but we were stronger than we looked.

"Then, when we went over to play Calgary, we were still really banged up. We had to play Brian Walling in the backfield, Ray Elgaard was still out. But I knew if we could get by Calgary, we'd have all our horses back for the Edmonton game. I really felt we could beat Calgary but about Edmonton, I wasn't so sure."

There was no need to worry. The Eskimos would beat themselves.

Edmonton jumped into an early 10-point lead. Ridgway replied with three. Halfway through the second quarter, a blitz caused Eskie quarterback Tracy Ham to fumble. Dave Albright picked up the ball and ran 62 yards for a touchdown. Shortly after, Austin converted another turnover and a penalty into a touchdown pass to Ray Elgaard. The Riders led 17–13 at the half.

Ham put the Eskimos into a three-point lead with a 10-yard TD pass in the third quarter. Hearts then sank all over Saskatchewan when Kent Austin went down with a knee injury. The clock was ready to strike midnight. But no! On came Tom Burgess in magnificent relief, completing nine of 12 passes for 120 yards and two touchdowns, the first to Jeff Fairholm, the second to Elgaard. Saskatchewan outscored Edmonton 14–7 in the third quarter. Both defences came up big in the final frame, allowing just an exchange of singles. The Roughriders had pulled off the most improbable upset in their history since the miracle at Taylor Field in 1963. It was David 32, Goliath 21.

Don Narcisse observed, "After beating Calgary, we said, 'We can do it, we're only one game away.' We weren't that good a team, but we were together as a team."

The Kick

The Roughriders headed for Toronto to meet Hamilton in the inaugural Grey Cup at the Sky Dome. The Ti-Cats had defeated Saskatchewan 34–17 on a stormy July night in Regina. Hamilton won the rematch at Ivor Wynne 46–40. Still, Tiger-Cat coach Al Bruno said his team would have preferred to play Edmonton. Maybe he knew something nobody else did.

Saskatchewan had led the league in passing yardage an d touchdown passes. The Ti-Cats were second in passing yardage and completions. Neither team had a good pass defence. Everything pointed to a shoot-out of epic proportions.

Kent Austin would start. John Gregory explained why: "I knew we were going to play Tommy Burgess against a blitzing team and Kent Austin against a zone team. Hamilton was a zone team. They were in all kinds of different zones and coverages.

"A lot of people questioned me. In fact, they even had a pick-the-quarterback contest in the newspaper and everybody called in which I was very upset about. My thought was with the guys on the field. I really felt Kent would give us the best chance to win."

Although Burgess played magnificently against Edmonton, he had been the quarterback in both regular-season losses to Hamilton.

Said John Gregory, "I felt good about the game before it ever started. I was positive we were going to win. I think our players did, too. At the press conference the day before, I said the game will probably come down to a last-second kick, and there isn't anybody I'd rather have kicking the ball than Dave Ridgway."

Despite Gregory's confidence, the early going wasn't promising. On Hamilton's second possession they kicked a 42-yard field goal. Four plays later, a Kent Austin pass was deflected into the arms of defender Frank Robinson. The Tabbies kicked their second three-pointer to lead 6–0. Saskatchewan replied with a single.

Starting at the 35, Ti-Cat quarterback Mike Kerrigan led his team to pay dirt in six plays. He threw 15 yards to Tony Champion for the TD. At the end of the first quarter, Hamilton led 13–1.

Austin was unconcerned. "I felt we had a good offence. We certainly had enough weapons to put points on the board. Offensive football in the Canadian league is a matter of tempo. The sporadic start didn't allow us to get into a groove. Once we put a couple of first downs together, we ended up having an unbelievable second quarter."

The fun began on the second possession of the quarter. Starting at his own 48, Austin hit Fairholm for 22 yards. Testing the secondary, Austin missed on a long bomb to the end zone but connected with Ray Elgaard for 16. After an incompletion at the 24-yard line, it was a strike to Don Narcisse at the five. Ray Elgaard then caught the touchdown pass. Hamilton 13, Saskatchewan 8.

Elgaard was more impressed with the 16-yarder at the Hamilton 24. "I scored a touchdown, but that wasn't a particularly memorable catch. But I did catch another pass that was a pretty big play for us. We were down at the time and we weren't really rolling. Kent threw me a ball that I had to extend forward on, and I snagged it. It seemed that after we scored on that drive, we were just playing pitch and catch."

So was Hamilton. After taking the Rider kickoff to their 53, the Ti-Cats replied with a TD of their own in three plays. Hamilton 20, Saskatchewan 8.

The Riders were not to be outdone. Scrimmaging from their 35, Austin found Jeff Fairholm streaking down the left side. At the moment he caught the ball, a flag came down, but the second-year sensation broke through the interference and ran 75 yards for the touchdown. Hamilton 20, Saskatchewan 15. That was the signature play of the 1989 Grey Cup.

Fairholm was a study in concentration. "On the catch I made for the touchdown, I didn't even know I had been interfered with even though the guy was on my back. I just caught the ball, ran for a touchdown, looked back and saw the flag and thought, 'Oh, my God, somebody held.' I had no idea that the guy was all over my back until I saw the film the next day."

That was the big moment of his professional career. "It will always be in my memory. Every day I look at that football I caught."

Don Narcisse felt the Fairholm touchdown gave the team a big lift. "When Jeff made that long touchdown, everybody got excited. I think everybody was sitting back, waiting for a big play, and once that big play came, it was just like, 'Hey, it's not that bad after all.' Everybody contributed to it and it was just wonderful."

Hamilton was not impressed. With contributions from Tony Champion, Bob McAdoo and Rocky Dipietro, Kerrigan marched his team 71 yards for a major. Hamilton 27, Saskatchewan 15.

"So what?" said Saskatchewan. Three passes to James Ellington plus completions to Narcisse and Elgaard brought the Riders to the five where Austin found Narcisse alone in the end zone. At halftime, the scoreboard read, Hamilton 27, Saskatchewan 22.

Saskatchewan had launched an all-out aerial attack. Austin was 11 for 16 and three touchdowns in the second quarter. He went exclusively to the air, he said, "because we got down and Hamilton kept scoring. We didn't run the ball once in the second quarter. We couldn't afford to. We had to keep scoring to keep pace with those guys. We got on a roll with the passing game and we didn't get away from it."

In the third quarter, the teams traded field goals on their first possessions. Pinned at their three-yard line by a Terry Baker punt, Hamilton conceded a safety touch and kicked off. From the Rider 33, Austin threw to Narcisse for 47 yards. An interference penalty brought the ball to the one, from where Tim McCray crashed into the end zone. After three quarters, the Roughriders had their first lead of the game, 34–30. A minute into the final frame, Ridgway made it 37–30.

Ball at his 35, Kerrigan was intercepted by Glen Suitor at the Cat 51. Austin, in turn, drove the Riders toward the enemy goal line, where Ray Elgaard threw an interception.

"We ran a reverse pass," explained Gregory. "It was a run-pass option. He should have run. It was kind of a trick play that didn't work. It was too bad because we probably could have gotten a field goal out of it."

Added Austin: "That was a big turnaround for Hamilton because if we had gone in to score, we may have pulled way from them."

The teams twice exchanged punts. At the 8:39 mark, Paul Osbaldiston kicked a 47-yard field goal. Ten plays later, Ridgway replied with a 20-yarder. With 1:58 left in regulation time, it was Saskatchewan 40, Hamilton 33.

Austin thought that drive was critical. "It helped us maintain the atmosphere and tempo. It helped us show Hamilton they were going to have to keep scoring to stay with us."

Can do, said Kerrigan. From the 35, he drove his team down to the Rider 11. On third down, Kerrigan threw to the right side of the end zone. Tony Champion made a dazzling over-the-shoulder catch while falling backward. The convert was good. With 44 seconds left, Hamilton 40, Saskatchewan 40.

Tim McCray returned the ensuing kickoff to his 36. There was no thought of playing conservatively, hoping for a win in overtime. For once, in the last minute of a Grey Cup, the Riders attacked.

"When Kent went out there," recalled Gregory, "we told him to use the clock wisely, which he always did. They were probably going to play zone, so we told him to read the coverage and hit the spots. That's exactly what he did."

"On the first play of that drive," said Austin, "I went to Narcisse on a stop-and-go and overthrew everybody, but that was really more to send a signal to Hamilton that they weren't going to squat on a route. There were three more passes. Elgaard caught one, Mark Guy, two.

"I didn't feel like they could stop us. There was plenty of time to get into scoring range for the best kicker I've ever played with. Before that, Elgaard made a big second-down catch on the sideline that kept the drive alive, and then Mark Guy came through with a big catch. On the first one over the middle, he took a good hit but held on to the ball."

With the ball on Hamilton's 26, Austin went down on one knee to stop the clock. The teams exchanged time-outs. Then at 14:58 of the fourth quarter, before 54,088 anxious fans, the greatest moment in the history of Saskatchewan sports took place. The Kick.

The snap went back. Suitor placed the ball, Ridgway moved toward it. For a split second, the great domed stadium was silent. Then as the ball flew toward the goal posts, the crowd roared. When it split the uprights, all Saskatchewan fans followed the ball onto cloud nine.

The final score of the greatest Grey Cup ever played, Saskatchewan 43, Hamilton 40.

Dave Ridgway talked about the kick.

> *There was no doubt there was a tremendous amount of pressure. If there's one thing that really helped me it's the thing athletes call the zone. It is a psychological outlook in which you get tunnel vision and you become very focused on what you are doing.*
>
> *I was totally oblivious to the meaning of what that kick was until after the fact. Then I sat down and said, "Holy Cow! That was a big kick."*
>
> *We got out on the field, there were two time-outs and I asked my holder Glen Suitor to talk to me about something other than football. I've never been camping so he told me he was going to take me camping before training camp next spring and get me eaten up by a bear. That got me laughing and before I knew it, it was time to attempt the kick. I get a strange kick out of doing it. I like walking on the field in that situation, and I expect to make it.*
>
> *Still, I would rather that game hadn't come down to a field goal because that's an awful lot of pressure on one person's shoulders. I just don't see living in this province if I had missed.*

Kent Austin was sensational, completing 26 of 41 passes for 474 yards and three touchdowns, winning him the Grey Cup MVP Award.

Back in Saskatchewan as soon as The Kick cleared the crossbar, the party began wherever there were Roughrider fans.

Assistant coach Dick Adams saluted the fans. "We went to the playoff game in Calgary and a bunch of Green Riders showed up. We went into Edmonton and all the people came in singing 'Green is the Colour.' And we walked out of there a winner. It was unbelievable. We thought that was probably the best we could hope to see until we walked into the Sky Dome and the place was green. There isn't any place like Saskatchewan to go as a player or a coach because the fans get into it, the province is behind you."

Alan Ford was part of every Saskatchewan Grey Cup in the modern era except 1951. He compared his experiences. "It's never the same if you're not a player. I think there are four levels of enjoyment: player, coach, manager and fan. Obviously the closest to it is the player. I think I enjoyed 1989 more because it was for our fans.

"You can't get any lower than after the BC game when we lost with no time left on the clock. It looked like we weren't going to make the playoffs. And then to keep battling back. Everybody in Saskatchewan identified with the team—that's the way this province is. Nothing can ever match the way things went in 1989."

Said John Gregory, "The thing I always appreciated about the players in Saskatchewan was that they played hard. A lot of times I think they played over their heads. And the fans, although they liked to pick the quarterback for you, they were great. I was really proud for the Saskatchewan people who supported that team so strongly. It was interesting how it affected everybody, from the farmers to the meat cutters, to the presidents of banks."

Indeed. What a magical, enchanted evening. After 10 years of low wheat prices, rural depopulation, crop failures and losing football teams, winning the Grey Cup was just what a beleaguered people needed to carry them into the last decade of the century with confidence. Winners at last. The 23-year Grey Cup drought was over.

Chapter Twelve

The Fickle Finger of Fate

For the next 18 years, the Roughriders often fielded good teams but always came up short, for the usual reasons of bad luck or bad management, often both. They were certainly well coached through the '90s, but those coaches didn't last long—fired, moved elsewhere or quit.

For the first time, the Roughriders began a decade as Grey Cup Champions, brimming with confidence. They had a host of all-stars, and John Gregory was Coach of the Year. He was also a realist.

"I think we approach everything a bit differently this year. We're the team to beat now. Previously, other teams may have overlooked us."

Both Tom Burgess and Kent Austin wanted to start so Gregory traded Burgess to Winnipeg, making Jeff Bentrim Austin's backup.

Defence was Gregory's main concern. By the middle of August 1990, the Riders were second in team defence but were surrendering 40 points a game. Still, they were 5–4 after Labour Day, 4–5 the rest of the way, finishing at 9–9 in third place. Edmonton was ready for them this time, winning the semifinal 43–27.

Ray Elgaard won his second Outstanding Canadian Award but didn't make All-Canadian. That honour went to Kent Austin, Don Narcisse, Roger Aldag and Dave Ridgway.

Vince Goldsmith was traded to Hamilton and Jeff Bentrim, Mark Guy and Tim McCray were released. Chuck Klingbeil, defensive MVP in the 1989 Grey Cup, signed with Miami.

Things started to go wrong right away in 1991. The team blew a 20-point lead in the home opener, losing to the Eskimos 34–25, a triumphant return for new Edmonton coach Ron Lancaster. Kent Austin got hurt and didn't return to form until it was too late. When his backup Rick Worman proved ineffective, Austin was forced back into action too soon.

On August 21 at home, the Riders were leading BC 47–36 with a minute left to play. Doug Flutie engineered two touchdowns to win 50–47. A chorus of boos accompanied the Riders to their dressing room.

The next day, John Gregory was fired. Why?

"We were 1–6," explained GM Alan Ford. While acknowledging that Kent Austin had been hurt, Ford said, "Don Matthews became available. It was better to make the switch at that time rather than gambling and waiting until the season was over when other opportunities might have presented themselves to Don."

Only two coaches had won a Grey Cup in Saskatch-ewan. Gregory was one of them. Throwing him under the bus was terribly unfair. But attendance had been dropping, and the fans were angry. Having won five Grey Cup rings as an assistant in Edmonton and one as head coach of the BC Lions, Matthews was a big name who could sell tickets and win.

When Ford became general manager in 1989, the Roughriders lost money every year, despite winning a Grey Cup and finishing third. Ford knew John Gregory wasn't the reason the team was 1–6, but in Saskatche-wan, when the paying public wants somebody's head, they get it.

Cal Murphy was Winnipeg general manager then. "I remember saying to Al at the time, 'Al, are you going to fire John?' And he said, 'I may have to.' And I said, 'Don't do that, Al. It's not his fault, you know that yourself. Let's face it, your quarterback's down, you've had all those injuries, who are you kidding?'

"So they fired him. It was the yuppie guy who did that basically, Phil Kershaw [team president]."

Don Matthews, who would end up second in career wins to Wally Buono, explained what happened.

"I was with the Orlando Thunder. Saskatchewan got off to a poor start and so they called me and asked me. It was Phil Kershaw. They said they wanted to make a coaching change and would I be interested? My first reaction was 'no.' And then they had another bad game and he called me again. I had a week to think about it. I was in the middle of a football season, not doing any football. [The World League of American

Football played in the spring.] To be honest, I missed it. When we talked again, I decided I would be interested. They were 1–6 at the time I accepted."

Matthews got off to a good start, winning two straight. His optimism was restrained.

"There was a lot of work to be done. The usual reason I'm hired is that the team has done badly. Somebody has to come in and make a lot of changes. A lot of coaches get attached to their players, and when the players get past their prime, they have a difficult time replacing them.

"My opening statement to the team was, 'John Gregory is a good football coach. The reason I'm here is because you players are not winning, not because John Gregory is a bad coach. My job is to, one, try to make you play better, and, two, find players who will play better.'"

Matthews was considered a defensive genius, a good thing considering the Riders were surrendering an average of 43 points a game. He left the offence to Ray Jauch and Kent Austin, and he implemented an attacking, gambling, "living on the edge" defence, a Matthews' trademark.

Matthews arrived in August 1991, a survival year—the team finished 6–12 and was in the cellar, surrendering a horrendous 710 points, a league record that may never be broken.

During the offseason, Matthews signed several free agents, including Jerald Baylis, Tyrone Jones, James King, Charles Anthony and Ventson Donelson, all defenders. In October, the coach picked up running back Mike Saunders from Pittsburgh. He brought in Brent Matich from Calgary to handle the punting.

Before the 1992 campaign began, Matthews proclaimed, "Anything less than first place and hosting the Western final is unacceptable."

Burned by lofty statements too often, the faithful stayed away in droves, with only 20,416 showing up for the home opener, a 44–26 loss to the Stampeders. Game two was an overtime loss in Edmonton. Their first win came before 20,117 fans at Taylor Field over Ottawa 23–13, followed by a 38–24 loss at Hamilton.

But 1–3 was the worst it got. The Riders went 8–6 the rest of the way, finished third and prepared for the semifinal in Edmonton.

It was a ding-dong battle from the first quarter on. Henry "Gizmo" Williams electrified the crowd with a 103-yard punt return for a touchdown. In the last minute, trailing 22–20, Kent Austin marched his team to the Eskimo 40. On the last play of the game, the most reliable man in CFL history would win it for Saskatchewan. "Robokicker" took the field.

The signals were called, Bob Poley fired the ball back and Glen Suitor put the pigskin on the tee. Ridgway advanced to the ball and slipped and fell on his duff. Edmonton 22, Saskatchewan 20. The curse was back.

"I've attempted over 700 field goals in my career," said Ridgway two years after that game. "Nobody goes through an athletic career unscathed. I've got more on the plus side than the negative side. That one was tough to handle. The next year I came back and made 90 percent of my field goals, which is something I had to do."

Roger Aldag and Bob Poley retired after the 1992 season, and Vic Stevenson and Chris Gioskos left because of salary disputes. Matthews released Milson Jones and made Mike Saunders his starting running back. For 1992, Matthews made a dozen roster changes, six more in 1993. Was he close to having the team he wanted?

"Very close. Right now I'm not concerned about putting this team up against anybody," said Matthews

The Riders opened the 1993 season in BC with a loss. Just 17,566 fans turned up for their home opener against Edmonton, especially disappointing since the team was saluting the career of Roger Aldag by retiring his number 44, only one of eight players in Rider history to be so honoured.

Despite lousy attendance and other problems, the Roughriders had their best season since 1988, finishing 11–7 but once again in third place. If they hadn't allowed the expansion Sacramento Gold Miners to record their first victory in franchise history against them, they would have finished second. The Riders were off to Edmonton again for the semifinal where they were trounced 51–7.

Jerald Baylis won the Most Outstanding Defensive Player Award. Once again, Kent Austin led the league in passing. Austin should have been the toast of the town in Regina. Instead he was vilified and booed regularly. Fans heaped abuse on his wife in the stands. He wanted out.

Alan Ford was skeptical when Austin stated he wanted to play closer to his home in Nashville.

"That's the reason he gave.… He was under contract to us for a very good salary. But it came down to the point where he said he wasn't going to play at all.

"Kent wasn't easily liked as far as the fans were concerned. And anybody that doesn't want to be here, the fans don't take very kindly to."

Austin was traded to Ottawa for four players, including former Blue Bomber Tom Burgess. Ottawa immediately sent Austin to BC for Danny Barrett. In the end, Austin's desire to leave had little or nothing to do with fans booing his wife or being closer to home, it was all about money.

In 1994, the CFL expanded big time into the U.S., adding teams in Las Vegas (their quarterback was a rookie named Anthony Calvillo), Baltimore and Shreveport.

As Alan Ford explained, league expansion's impact on Saskatchewan was immediate.

"We lost Don Matthews, our personnel guy Jim Popp, a couple of assistant coaches and a number of players to Baltimore. We couldn't compete because most of the Americans wanted to play in the States and there was no salary cap involved. They could make U.S. dollars and pay fewer taxes."

Baltimore owner James Speros made "the Don" an offer he couldn't refuse. "It was strictly a business decision," said Matthews.

Matthews' successor was Ray Jauch, one of the architects of the great Eskimo dynasty. He was asked what veterans wouldn't be back for 1994.

"Who did we lose? Holy smoke!" he laughed. "We lost Charles Anthony, Barry Wilburn, Jerald Baylis, Jeff Fairholm, Kent Austin, Craig Hendrickson and Stewart Hill."

Up until 1994, Jauch's 110 wins as a head coach in Edmonton and Winnipeg represented the third best record in CFL history. He had two Grey Cup rings and two Coach of the Year awards. Because of his experience, he approached his newest challenge cautiously.

"Everything could work out eventually. Team strengths? I don't know. We've lost so many players on both sides of the ball."

In a topsy-turvy 1995 season, the Riders rode the arms of Warren Jones and Tom Burgess to an 11–7, fourth-place finish. They lost the semifinal 36–3 in Calgary.

The highlight of the year for the fans was the opportunity to vent their displeasure at Kent Austin when the Lions visited Taylor Field on October 15. The month before in a newspaper poll, readers overwhelmingly picked Austin as the most disliked sports personality. A radio announcer urged fans on the east side to take eggs to the game to throw at him.

Hell hath no fury like a Roughrider fan scorned.

Earlier in the year, the fans booed Jeff Fairholm mercilessly when he returned home with the Argonauts. Austin received an even ruder reception. Saskatchewan beat BC 38–27.

No matter what happened to the Roughriders on the field, 1995 was memorable because, for the first time, Regina and Saskatchewan would play host to the Grey Cup. The slogan was "Huddle Up in Saskatchewan."

Billed as the greatest homecoming in provincial history, the good people of the smallest centre in the CFL would stage the greatest Grey Cup ever.

Again Jauch had holes to fill. Star running back Mike Saunders signed with San Antonio, nee Sacramento. Gary Lewis and Glen Suitor retired.

The league was divided into North and South Divisions, with the Canadian teams north, U.S. teams south. Saskatchewan finished sixth with a mark of 6–12 and out of the playoffs.

In 1995, Dave Ridgway struggled through his worst year since 1986. For the last two games of the season, Jauch decided to give Paul McCallum a chance. He was good on 11 of 15 field-goal attempts. But typical of the Queen City, the change created an ugly situation. Again the media got involved in a "Name that Kicker" contest. Ridgway came out on top. A group Jauch openly despised, the media antics neither surprised nor bothered him.

What did bother him was Ridgway's public reaction to his benching and his request that Alan Ford intervene with Jauch on his behalf. Ford did so. Determined not to allow the inmates to run the asylum and believing that both the kicker and GM should know better, Jauch refused to budge. At the end of the season, Jauch resigned.

Jauch was vindicated when Ridgway retired. Robo-kicker's career was over. But Ford's mishandling of the situation cost the Riders the services of one of the best coaches in the history of the CFL.

Thus began 10 long years of futility and mediocrity with an odd blip in 1997.

From Bad to Worse

Ray Jauch's replacement was his defensive coordinator Jim Daley, an Ottawa native with five years experience as a CFL assistant. As honest and fine a man as anyone would want to meet, Daley experienced the best and worst of football in Saskatchewan during his three-year stewardship with the Roughriders.

U.S. expansion was put to rest in 1996. The Baltimore entry was reborn in Montréal as the Alouettes.

Because you were guaranteed Grey Cup tickets if you were a season-ticket holder, Saskatchewan set an attendance record in 1995, averaging 28,490. That enthusiasm didn't carry over, though, and once again the team faced financial disaster. They really needed a winner on the field.

They didn't get it.

Because of the dispersal draft after the collapse of the Southern division, a lot of imports were in camp, the most impressive being receiver Curtis Mayfield, who became part of an outstanding pass-catching corps that included Ray Elgaard, Don Narcisse and Dan Farthing.

But Daley didn't have anyone to throw to them. He was counting on Warren Jones, but when it became clear he couldn't find the end zone with a seeing-eye dog, Jones was released in August. From there it was quarterback-by-committee with Jimmy Kemp, Heath Rylance and Kevin Mason.

Daley wasn't worried about the other side of the ball. "The defence has been pretty sound for the last two years. We have 11 of our 12 starters back, and we've added some veterans."

But the new coach's confidence was misplaced. The Riders were good at stopping the run only because their pass defence was so bad that the opposition seldom ran the ball. All in all, it was a disaster, with the team finishing with a mark of 5–13, their worst record in 12 years.

Saskatchewan was dead last in passing in 1996. How bad was it? Their leading passer was the Jones boy whom they cut in August. The Lions with Damon Allen, and Ottawa with David Archer, did much better. Saskatchewan tried to sign them but could afford neither one.

Later in the season, the Roughriders had to forego their television revenue in order to prop up failing franchises in Ottawa and BC, facing bankruptcy because they spent too much money on quarterbacks! The Riders lost four games to teams they were supporting financially while facing insolvency themselves. Alan Ford didn't know whether to laugh or cry.

"We tried to sign Damon Allen and he ends up making huge money in BC, and the owner, Bill Comrie [also owner of The Brick stores] leaves and we have to give money to BC because his salary wasn't paid."

The bright spot that year was running back Robert Mimbs who led the league in rushing and was runner up to Argo Doug Flutie for the Outstanding Player Award.

Averaging 22,393 fans per home game, the Riders were at death's door. President Fred Wagman laid it on the line, telling the populace that if they didn't step up now, the team would fold. The message was received, the faithful dug deeper and the team increased attendance by more than 5000 per game.

It was an interesting beginning to a strange year.

During the offseason, Daley signed former Winnipeg quarterback Reggie Slack. Throughout the year, the coaches wanted and started Slack, the media and fans wanted Mason. Only in Saskatchewan.

Daley added perceived troublemaker and linebacker K.D. Williams, run out of Winnipeg, and Lamar McGriggs.

In early September 1997, the Riders were 4–6, the quarterback controversy continued to rage, with Daley denounced from Duck Lake to Davidson. The fun was just beginning.

On September 2, an article appeared in *The Globe and Mail* in which Williams and McGriggs accused the coaches of racism. Although he desperately needed both players, Daley traded them to Hamilton because, "During the course of a year, there are a lot of things said in a locker room, but there is a line you cross.

Those comments made it impossible for them to function with our players."

As for needing them, Daley said, "You don't make a decision based on needs, you make it based on right and wrong."

The result? On September 7 the Riders hammered the Lions 46–12! Daley's action so galvanized the team that they won three more games and made the playoffs with a record of 8–10.

Smoke and Mirrors

With shades of 1989, the Green and White headed for Calgary. Nobody gave them a chance against the powerful Stampeders, even though Saskatchewan had beaten the Horsemen earlier in the year on the strength of Reggie Slack's running.

The Riders drew first blood with a Paul McCallum field goal. Early in the second quarter, running back Shawn Daniels finished off a 39-yard-drive set up when Bobby Jurasin recovered a fumble.

Late in the half, Calgary finally picked up a first down and drove to the Rider 14, but the defence held the Stamps to a field goal. After the ensuing kickoff, Slack marched his team 80 yards for a major. At half-time, the underdogs were leading 17–3.

After trading field goals in the third quarter, Dave Dickenson found Vince Danielson in the end zone. When the quarter ended, the Riders were at the Calgary four. Mike Saunders scored 17 seconds later.

Calgary roared back. With under three minutes to go, they led 30–27.

First down at the 35, Slack screened to Saunders for 29 yards. Slack ran for 12, Daniels, 11 and 6. First down at the 17, Slack ran it into the end zone. Saskatchewan won 33–30 and headed to Edmonton. Surely, it couldn't be happening again!

The Eskimos finished first and were hosting the Western final and the Grey Cup. But they hadn't won a final at home since 1986, and the Riders had played them tough all year.

Saskatchewan jumped into a 24-point lead before Edmonton could get on the board. At halftime, the Riders led 24–14. Four times in the second half, Edmonton drove deep into Roughrider territory, but the defence was magnificent, holding the Esks to a brace of field goals and a single.

With less than two minutes remaining, Slack ran 14 yards for the clinching score. The final was Saskatchewan 31, Edmonton 30. The Riders moved into the Eskimo dressing room to await Don Matthews, Doug Flutie and the Toronto Argonauts.

Crusty Cal Murphy, coaxed out of retirement by Jim Daley to coach the special teams and be Daley's mentor, was impressed. "After we lost Williams and McGriggs, I said to our defensive coordinator Greg Marshall, 'You guys are doing it with smoke and mirrors.'"

Daley was unconcerned about their underdog status.

"Any team going into the Grey Cup against Doug Flutie would be the underdog. But we beat Toronto earlier in the year. We're on a bit of a roll and feel we can compete with them."

Grey Cup day got under way with an ominous sign for Saskatchewan. The PA announcer began the introduction of the Roughrider offence by calling out the name of centre Carl Coulter. Nothing happened. No one appeared. Sensing what lay ahead, had the Roughriders decided to stay in their dressing room? Au contraire. After what seemed like an eternity, Coulter emerged from the tunnel, prepared to meet his doom.

And doom it was. Toronto 47, Saskatchewan 23. When the score had reached 41–9, Greg Marshall said to Murphy, "The smoke machine is clogged."

Why did they lose? "Too much Flutie," Murphy replied. Matthews had won his third straight Grey Cup.

From the verge of extinction to Grey Cup finalist. For the Saskatchewan Roughriders, 1997 was a wonderful year.

Same Old, Same Old

The success didn't last. The Riders finished fifth in 1998, Jim Daley was fired and another Hall of Famer, Cal Murphy, took over as head coach. Although he brought in better talent, Murphy's efforts went for naught when it was revealed that Reggie Slack had a substance abuse problem and would enter rehab. When he came back, he wasn't the same.

The team was 3–6 after Labour Day but didn't win another game. As the losses mounted, so did public discontent. Alan Ford said he would resign if the team didn't make the playoffs, so his fate was sealed.

Murphy wanted out as soon as possible. He described coaching in Saskatchewan: "When it was time to make decisions about players in this city, they get so ingrained in the people and the people get so close to them, they don't understand why anybody has to go and yet they want you to win."

Near season's end, Murphy said, "We were in Edmonton, and Hugh Campbell and I got talking on the sidelines before the game and I told him, 'Hugh, it's over. Nobody's talked to me but it's finished. I have no intentions of coming back. Halfway through the season I said to Joyce [Mrs. Murphy], 'I feel like I'm beating my head against the wall. If it weren't for the other coaches, I'd resign.'

"There is no question we upgraded the talent. We would have been a pretty good team except for the Slack situation. That cost a lot of people their jobs."

So, John Gregory and Jim Daley were fired, Don Matthews left town, Ray Jauch quit and Cal Murphy jumped before he was pushed. Why would anyone want the job? To prove that African Americans could manage and coach a professional football team as well or better than whites.

Believing their problem was lack of talent, the Roughriders hired the best bird-dog in the business, Calgary Stampeder assistant GM and personnel director Roy Shivers. A man who fought against racial inequality all his life, he was determined to make his mark in the executive suite and give his brothers a leg up.

His empathy with black players was legendary; he had brought some of the greatest players to the CFL, such as Allen Pitts.

It was no surprise when Shivers introduced Danny Barrett as his head coach on January 29, 2000. Barrett, a black quarterback with Toronto, BC and Calgary, had been an assistant for three years with the Stampeders and Lions. His race is worth mentioning because he was only the second black head coach in CFL history. Roy Shivers was the first black GM.

Theirs would be the second longest tenure at their positions in Roughrider history, seven years. They were given every opportunity to succeed, but in the end they fell short.

The biggest offseason 1999 acquisitions were receivers Curtis Marsh and Demetris Bendross; D-linemen Demetrious Maxie and Sheldon Napastuk; DBs Omarr Morgan and Ladouphyous McCalla; and quarterback Henry Burris. Tired of backing up Jeff Garcia and Dave Dickenson in Calgary, Burris signed with the Riders as a free agent and became an immediate fan favourite.

Offensively, the Roughriders were competitive the first year of the Barrett regime. Behind an excellent line of Jeremy O'Day, Andrew Greene, Dan Comiskey, John Terry and Gene Makowsky, Burris ranked second in passing, Curtis Marsh led the league with 102 receptions for 1560 yards and 10 touchdowns. Eric Guliford had 1084 receiving yards, Darren Davis had 1024 yards rushing.

Saskatchewan finished out of the playoffs with record of 5–12–1 because their defence couldn't stop the

Sweet Sisters of Charity. They gave up the most points and yards and had the fewest interceptions. Prima donnas and frustration infected the dressing room.

In October, with the club at 4–10–1, Demetrious Maxie publicly called out his teammates. Two days later, Curtis Marsh had a practice field altercation with a DB. When rebuked by Barrett, he stormed off the field and was suspended.

Shortly thereafter, the 253-pound R-Kal Truluck took the chair from nose tackle Colin Scrivener's cubicle and smashed the team ping-pong table. While fixing it, carpenter Colin asked to be moved since this was the third time Truluck had destroyed his chair.

The big improvement on offence gave Rider Nation reason to hope. But then, come February 2001, a major setback occurred when Henry Burris exercised his NFL clause and signed with the Green Bay Packers.

His replacement was Marvin Graves.

Roy Shivers moved to strengthen his defence. He raided the Stampeders for DB Eddie Davis and All-Canadian rush end Shont' Peoples. When Shivers added Omar Evans and Jackie Mitchell to the secondary, it was the best in the land. Now the offence was the worst.

By August 2001, it was obvious Graves couldn't do the job, so Barrett turned to rookie Kevin Glenn. The team finished last at 6–12. During the offseason, Shivers acquired quarterback Nealon Greene from Edmonton. He was unpopular in Saskatchewan from the start. Still, he was a five-year veteran.

On defence, Shivers revamped the linebacking corps with Reggie Hunt, Trevis Smith and Davin Bush and added Ray Jacobs and Nate Davis to the line. He was assembling a defence that would rank with the league's best for years to come.

In 2002, the Riders ended their four-year playoff drought and made the playoffs. They wouldn't miss post-season play the rest of the decade. They still finished last with a mark of 8–10. But their better record was better than eastern teams and therefore crossed over for the semifinal in that division against Toronto, losing 24–14.

To win more games, Shivers knew he had to bolster his offence. He signed the great veteran receiver Travis Moore, as well as sensational rookie receivers Matt Dominguez and Jamel Richardson and running back Kenton Keith.

In the 2003 season opener at Toronto, Nealon Greene threw two touchdown passes to Corey Grant in the final 48 seconds to pull out a 20–18 win. The Riders followed that up with a 32–20 win in Regina versus the Lions. Next came narrow losses to Montréal and Winnipeg.

Kenton Keith made his debut against Hamilton, rushing for 86 yards as the Riders won at home 42–9. Returning from an injury, Greene moved the Riders into a three-way tie for first with a 32–14 win in Edmonton. The good times rolled into August when Saskatchewan won their first regular season game in Calgary in 14 years, 27–11. After splitting back-to-back games with Ottawa, the Roughriders lost three in a row, including both games to the Bombers during Labour Day week.

Aerial view of Taylor Field in Regina at the 2003 Grey Cup game between the Edmonton Eskimos and the Montréal Alouettes. The Esks won the game by a score of 34–22.

Amid all the summer excitement, with Greene playing well, prodigal son Henry Burris returned to the fold, his sojourns with Green Bay and Chicago at an end. Greene continued to start for the rest of the season, with Smilin' Hank listed third on the depth chart behind Kevin Glenn.

With Greene at the helm, the Riders won five of their last six games to finish third. On to Winnipeg for the semifinal, dubbed the "Banjo Bowl" after Bomber kicker Troy Westwood referred to Saskatchewan folk as "banjo-pickin' in-breds." The Riders plucked the Bombers 37–21 and got ready to appear in their first Western final since 1997, the venue once again Commonwealth Stadium in Edmonton.

The bubble burst with Tom Higgin's Eskimos advancing to the Grey Cup with a 30–23 win. The Riders were behind 30–2 before the stubborn Danny Barrett replaced Greene with Kevin Glenn who mounted a furious comeback, scoring three touchdowns. It seemed to the faithful fans that no matter how badly Greene played, he would always be Danny's boy.

The Eskimos went on to win the 2003 Grey Cup in Regina over Montréal, 34–22.

Omarr Morgan, Reggie Hunt, Jackie Mitchell and Andrew Greene made All-Canadian. Nate Davis, Jeremy O'Day and Paul McCallum were Western All-Stars.

The Shivers-Barrett regime was bearing fruit.

The 2004 Roughriders had Kenton Keith and Corey Holmes in the backfield and returning kicks. Matt Dominguez left for an NFL tryout but returned later in the year. Moose Jaw boy Scott Schultz teamed up with Daved Benefield, Nate Davis, Scott Schultz and Lamont Bryant. Come the fall, the great Alondra Johnson, released by Calgary, donned Rider livery. Elijah Thurman was added to the receiving corps. This was one powerful football team.

In January 2004, Shivers and Barrett declared Nealon Greene as the starting quarterback, angering Burris and Glenn, who demanded and was granted a trade. Handling quarterbacks would ultimately be Danny Barrett's undoing.

When their season opened in Toronto with a loss, no team had greater depth at quarterback than Saskatchewan. Then Nealon Greene broke his leg, and Henry Burris had a bad shoulder. Rocky Butler was at the controls in the home-opening loss to Calgary, 33–10. Burris started game three.

The Riders lost four of their first five games and were 4–8 after losing twice to Winnipeg. They split their last six to finish 9–9 in third place. Once again it was off to Edmonton for the playoffs.

In May, when Danny Barrett was asked what the team had to do to take the next step and get to the Grey Cup, he replied, "We've got to go into Edmonton and win."

They did just that. Combining ferocious defence with the running of Kenton Keith, the Riders ground it out to win 14–6, advancing to a second straight Western final.

The Roughriders' opponent in the 2004 Western final was the BC Lions with whom they had split during the season, the Riders winning at home 42–19 and losing in Vancouver 40–38 the last game of the season, a loss that deprived them of the opportunity to host a playoff game for the first time in 16 years.

The final featured an entertaining display of offence. The Riders had the Lions on the ropes but gave up a late fourth-quarter touchdown that tied the score at 24. In overtime, Saskatchewan drove down to the BC 11. Paul McCallum came out for an easy 18-yard field goal to take the lead and force BC to score to stay alive. He missed, picking up a single. Minutes later,

Duncan O'Mahoney put it through the uprights, BC winning 27–25.

Angry fans threatened McCallum's wife and children, and one tried to dump manure on McCallum's driveway, but the fan got the address wrong and fertilized the asphalt of McCallum's neighbour instead. It was a disgraceful way to treat a fine man and the second most prolific kicker in Roughrider history. After enduring another season of abuse, he signed with BC in 2006.

The big story during the offseason was the Henry Burris saga. Shivers signed Nealon Greene to a three-year deal and then turned his attention to "Smilin' Hank" who was also considering an offer from Calgary. In the end, Burris signed with the Stampeders because, according to Shivers, they offered more money. Burris disputed that, indicating the reason he left Saskatchewan was because Barrett refused to designate him as the starter. Barrett replied, "When you offer a guy $300,000, to me that says you're the guy. The fact is, he didn't want us to bring Nealon Greene back. That's very selfish."

Jilted a second time, Burris was thereafter in for a rough ride when the Stamps came to Regina. In fact, he never beat the Roughriders in a playoff game.

Although the 2005 season started with a bang when Corey Holmes ran the home-opening kickoff 81 yards for a major against Winnipeg, after winning their second contest, the Riders lost five in row, including 44–18 in Calgary to a red-hot Burris and were 3–6 at the halfway point. They then proceeded to win five in a row, finishing the regular season at 9–9, in fourth place, good enough for the crossover playoff position against Montréal, who won 30–14.

Gene Makowsky won his second consecutive Most Outstanding Offensive Lineman Award (Andrew Greene was so honoured in 2003), and Corey Holmes picked up his second Most Outstanding Special Teams Player Award. While the 2005 Riders led the league in rushing with Kenton Keith, they were dead last in passing, despite a talented receiving corps and an offensive line that gave up the fewest sacks. The problem was quarterbacking. Marcus Crandall, cut by Calgary, and Greene shared the duties, neither one having much success.

Although Shivers had given Barrett a two-year contract extension after the 2004 season, the natives were restless. It seemed the Riders were stuck in neutral. The fans wanted nothing to do with Barrett or Nealon Greene and were fed up with Shivers' tiresome lectures, accusing them of being fair-weather fans. Former player Jim Hopson took over as president and CEO, promising change. A pivotal year for the team came in 2006.

Chapter Thirteen

From Mediocrity to Grey Cup Glory

The Ottawa Renegades folded after the 2005 season. To get the first pick in the dispersal draft, Roy Shivers traded Corey Holmes and safety Scott Gordon to Hamilton and chose quarterback Kerry Joseph. Nealon Greene was traded to Montréal. In the 2006 college draft, Saskatchewan selected Western Ontario receiver Andy Fantuz, as well as Simon Fraser place-kicker Luca Congi to replace Paul McCallum.

Another change was that the executive sold naming rights for $4 million to a potash company, and Taylor Field became Mosaic Stadium.

The Riders with Kerry Joseph at quarterback played well throughout the summer. On August 19, they beat Hamilton in Regina 43–15 before a poor crowd of 22, 820. Their record was 4–5. The next day Roy Shivers was fired.

The general feeling was that the executive wanted Shivers to fire Barrett, and he refused. That made no sense because the board could have fired Barrett at the same time as they axed Shivers.

Shivers, a "my-way-or-the-highway" guy, was in conflict with the executive on three fronts. The behaviour of some players, such as Kenton Keith and Trevis Smith, was a real sore spot in Regina. When black players got into trouble with the law and the executive suggested a code of conduct, Shivers rejected the idea and implied that racism was involved.

Shivers had expensive tastes, reflected in huge expense accounts and in overpaying a number of players. Thirteen Riders would be free agents at the end of the year with over two dozen heading into their option year, totals that indicated Shivers wasn't doing his job. The team was barely solvent. They were concerned that Shivers would break the bank signing a group that had never finished higher than third.

Finally, the team had a president and CEO Jim Hopson who reported to the executive board and GM Shivers, who also reported to the board but not to Hopson. Two weeks before Shivers was fired, the board decided that Shivers would be under the direction of Hopson come 2007. Shivers was quoted as saying, "I can't work for him because I don't like him and I don't trust him."

Roy Shivers had to go.

The best adjective to describe his regime was mediocre.

Shivers was replaced by 49-year-old Mississippi native Eric Tillman who had managed the Ottawa Renegades and had won two Grey Cups as general manager of the Lions and Argos. Rather than fire Danny Barrett, he decided to observe him in action the second half of the season and evaluate the talent on the field. In a sense, Tillman gave Barrett enough rope to hang himself. Totally loyal to Shivers and full of rage at his dismissal, Barrett did exactly that.

As had been the case the previous four years, the team was average the rest of the way, finishing at 9–9. Kenton Keith scored two touchdowns, Dominguez one, as they upset the Stampeders in Calgary in the semifinal, 30–21.

Appearing in their third Western final in four years, the Roughriders lost to BC 45–18.

The Riders hadn't finished first for an incredible 30 years and hadn't hosted a playoff game since 1988.

The wunderkind Tillman was about to change all that.

His choice for head coach was the man Rider fans loved to hate, Kent Austin who worked with Tillman in Ottawa as the quarterback coach in 2003, his student being one Kerry Joseph. The following year, Austin had signed on as Toronto's offensive coordinator, helping them win the Grey Cup. When the Argos stumbled out of the gate in 2006, he became the scapegoat and was fired.

A hallmark of the Barrett years was undisciplined behaviour and a litany of excuses when opportunities were missed. Asked if he was going to be tough in demanding accountability from his players, Austin replied, "Of course. This is professional football. We expect it to mean something to be a professional athlete and wear this uniform. Guys need to care about what they are doing, both in the small things and the big things. It needs to matter to them to be a good person and a great player."

So there would be no more excuses? "We're not here to make excuses. We're going to have players that believe the same thing and who will buy into that philosophy. It is really that simple. You play to be a champion and to be the best," said Austin.

It is no coincidence that the two times the Riders won the Grey Cup they had outstanding quarterbacks, Ron Lancaster and Kent Austin. A big question mark going into 2007 was whether Austin had the field general who could get the job done.

"We will find out," he said. "If we don't, then we're going to go find one. Without a quarterback who is an elite player, you can't win championships in this league."

There were four quarterbacks in camp, veterans Kerry Joseph and Marcus Crandall, and rookies Darian Durant and Drew Tate. Kenton Keith was gone to the NFL. He was replaced by Wes Cates, traded by Calgary to the Riders for offensive lineman Rob Lazeo. D.J. Flick gave the receiving corps a boost, and trades for Wayne Smith and Mike Abou-Mechrek bolstered the offensive line.

Defensively, Austin had to replace Nate Davis, Jackie Mitchell, Omarr Morgan and Davin Bush. He did so with John Chick, James Johnson, Airbin Justin and Maurice Lloyd.

Saskatchewan opened the 2007 season in Montréal, traditionally a graveyard for Rider hopes. They won 16–7 when the defence intercepted three Anthony

Calvillo passes and sacked him eight times. The victory was followed by a 49–8 win in Calgary with Joseph throwing for four touchdown passes and Wes Cates running for two. The home opener against the Lions was a dreadful performance by Joseph and a 42–12 defeat.

Next up were back-to back games with the hated Eskimos, the first a 21–20 loss in the Igloo and a 54–4 thumping of the visitors at Mosaic Stadium. The Riders then avenged their loss to the Lions, 21–9, and beat Toronto 24–13 and Edmonton 39–32. They beat the Bombers on the Labour Day weekend to move into first place with a record of 7–2.

Along the way, Tillman got Corey Holmes back from Hamilton. Return guy Jason Armstead's father-in-law said if Jason wasn't used more, he wanted out. Although Armstead meant at the end of the season, Austin didn't want a player who didn't want to be on the team and got rid of him immediately, getting Holmes in return.

The following week, Matt Dominguez sustained a season-ending knee injury on September 9. Tillman brought in 15-year veteran Yo Murphy. The Riders then dropped three in a row to Winnipeg, Calgary and BC. Health care facilities in Saskatchewan were stretched to the limit treating the broken ankles of fans who jumped off the Roughrider bandwagon.

Said Kent Austin, "We don't have the level of maturity we need because we don't have leadership throughout the team. We need to mature as a team, we need players to quit looking around and looking for someone else to make a play."

The team responded by running the table, including the last five regular-season games and three post-season contests. Finishing second at 12–6, they hosted their first playoff game in 19 seasons. Henry Burris and his Calgary Stampeders rode into town and almost rustled up a win.

It looked like a mismatch on paper. Calgary's record was 7–10–1. The Stamps hadn't won a single game outside of Alberta. But Burris was a competitor, and his teammates knew coach Tom Higgins would be fired and didn't want him to go out on a losing note. They came to play.

The Riders led Calgary 13–0 after 15 minutes and 19–7 at the half. Going into the final frame, the good guys were up 22–17. The Stamps got a touchdown in the last minute of the game. Saskatchewan 26, Calgary 24. It was the Riders' first home playoff win in 31 years.

Next up was a visit to the Lions' den for the Western final. Saskatchewan was never behind, winning 26–17 and the right to meet the Winnipeg Blue Bombers in the 95th Grey Cup in Toronto, Kent Austin returning to the scene of his greatest triumph.

His team had to overcome several obstacles to get there.

The Riders lost receiver Matt Dominguez on September 9. His replacement Mike Washington went down with injuries in October. D.J. Flick played the Western final with a pulled groin. Wes Cates was playing on a broken foot. Fullback Chris Szarka played with a layer of gauze on his fingertips that were sewn back on after a run-in with a table saw.

No matter that they led the league in injuries, Austin and his players, unlike the Barrett regime, refused to accept any excuses. Austin demanded accountability. When he didn't get it, he sat a player out. By handling Andy Fantuz that way, he turned him into an all-star. Austin stressed what a privilege it was to wear the green and white. He told them they would also be judged according to their behaviour off the field. As one cynic commented earlier, "It's Labour Day, we're 7–2 in first place and nobody's been arrested."

Player for player, the Riders weren't the best team in the league, but their whole was much greater than the sum of their parts. No group was better as a team. Kent Austin was named Coach of the Year, and Kerry Joseph won the Most Outstanding Player Award, beating out Winnipeg's quarterback Kevin Glenn. Unfortunately for the Blue Bombers, Glenn broke his hand in the Eastern final. He was replaced by sophomore Ryan Dinwiddie, making his first pro start.

Canada's largest city hadn't hosted the big game in 125 years, and officials were worried about how Torontonians would respond. The natives embraced the classic, and a huge contingent of Roughrider fans stood staid old Hogtown on its ear. The festivities turned out to be more entertaining than the game.

The Rider offence struggled the entire contest with a pumped-up Joseph overthrowing receivers or receivers dropping catchable balls. The Bomber front-four manhandled the Roughrider offensive line and smashed Joseph to the ground at every opportunity.

Winnipeg opened the scoring with a Westwood field goal following a 61-yard, seven-play drive. The Riders conceded two safeties in the second quarter as the Bomber defence stopped everything thrown at them. Late in the half, James Johnson picked off Dinwiddie and returned 30 yards for a touchdown. Luca Congi added a field goal at the end of the quarter. Saskatchewan went to the dressing room leading 10–7.

On the second play of the third quarter, John Chick forced a Dinwiddie fumble, recovered by Scott Schultz on the Bomber 10. The Riders settled for a 17-yard Congi field goal, Saskatchewan 13, Winnipeg 7.

The Bombers replied on their next possession, a 60-yard pass and run to Derick Armstrong for a touchdown, giving the Eastern champions a one-point lead. Congi put the Riders back in front with a field goal, set up by Johnson's second interception.

Soon after, Joseph marched his team 78 yards in six plays for a touchdown, putting them ahead to stay, 23–14. Winnipeg added a safety and a field goal. The 23–19 victory was preserved when a last-minute drive was snuffed out by James Johnson's third interception. He was the Grey Cup MVP, Andy Fantuz copping the Canadian award.

After the game, Kent Austin met the media. "I'm ecstatic," he said. "To work as hard as we did, for our staff and players to work as hard as they did from training camp all the way forward, culminating in the championship, wow, that's why we play.

"Our guys believed they could do it all year. They went through a lot of turmoil like all teams do, and they bonded closer together as a result. That's what won the day for us. The turnover battle went our way and that was the difference in the ball game."

Asked if he realistically believed he could win the Cup in his first year, he replied, "You have to believe that or what is the point in playing? Belief requires action. If you believe you are going to win, you walk differently, talk differently, you do what it takes to back up your belief and win.

"This isn't about me. I didn't play a down this year. The guys in the locker room did it. It's not about me. It's about the players, my staff, Eric Tillman, Jim Hopson, everyone in the organization. It's not about Kent Austin.

"I know what it takes to win a Grey Cup in Saskatch-ewan. I guess I'm just meant to win the Grey Cup as a Roughrider.

"One of the reasons I wanted to come back is because there is no greater place in the CFL to win a champion-ship than Saskatchewan."

And then Austin was gone.

Early in 2008, he accepted an assistant's position at his alma mater, Ole Miss. Considering what happened to every successful coach and quarterback in Saskatche-wan, except Eagle Keys, it was probably a wise decision.

Austin's replacement was his 66-year-old elderly offensive coordinator, Ken Miller, a match for Danny Barrett in defending an incompetent quarterback.

No, not Kerry Joseph. Tillman traded him to Toronto in a salary-cap move and basically got nothing in return. He traded all-star defensive end Fred Perry to Edmonton for quarterback Steven Jyles who would compete with Drew Tate, Marcus Crandall and Darian Durant for the starter's job.

The 2008 Riders got off to a 6–0 start, going undefeated with three different quarterbacks, Crandall, Jyles and Durant, all of whom got hurt during that stretch. Crandall pulled a hamstring, and Durant cracked some ribs. The team lost 19 players to injury, including broken legs suffered by D.J. Flick, Andy Fantuz, O-lineman Belton Johnson, running back Neal Hughes and DB Leron Mitchell. Matt Dominguez's career ended with torn knee ligaments. After Labour Day week, the Riders were 8–2, in first place, four points up on Edmonton and Calgary. They were 4–4 the rest of the way, finishing second at 12–6.

While Eric Tillman made all the right moves the year earlier, he seemed to lose his touch in 2008. He brought in QB Michael Bishop from Toronto and cut Marcus Crandall. Although it was obvious to everyone except Ken Miller, young Durant was the better quarterback. But Miller stuck with Bishop who turned the ball over with dreary regularity, undoing the work of a magnificent defence and depriving his team of their first first-place finish in 32 years.

Home to BC in the semifinal, Bishop threw three interceptions, one returned for a major, and fumbled twice before Miller made a change in the fourth quarter. The Lions won 33–12, all Rider points scored by kicker Luca Congi. Receiver Weston Dressler won the Most Outstanding Rookie Award.

An angry Rider nation demanded Bishop be banished from their midst forever. He was.

A Turbulent Year

The team got off to a horrible start on February 9, 2009, when Eric Tillman was charged with sexual assault against a 16-year-old baby-sitter. He was eventually given a conditional discharge, but his career was effectively over in Saskatchewan. The season ended with the third worst day in Saskatchewan sports history.

With the salary cap system, teams become victims of their success. The Roughriders weren't immune, losing all-star linebackers Maurice Lloyd and Anton Mackenzie to Edmonton and BC. Safety Scott Gordon also signed with the Eskimos. James Johnson, 2007 Grey Cup MVP, went to Winnipeg. Still, at the beginning of the season, CEO Jim Hopson proclaimed, "The roster is the best I've seen in my memory, especially Canadian talent." Added Miller, "We are going to be strong in all areas."

They were right.

With Durant at the controls, the Riders battled the defending champion Stampeders all season long for first place. In the end, both teams were tied at 10–7–1 with Saskatchewan taking the top spot by beating Calgary twice, even without their injured star Weston Dressler. The other game was a 44–44 thriller between the teams. For the first time in 33 years, Saskatchewan would host the final.

Darian Durant was third in passing behind Ricky Ray and Henry Burris. Although he was the only

Rider quarterback to get the team to first place since Ron Lancaster, when asked about the most difficult thing for him to adjust to, Durant replied, "Dealing with the scrutiny around here. It's pretty tough. You hear everything that comes out because the media will let you know how the fans feel. There was a time this year I got kind of comfortable and felt I was getting settled in, and then we lose a game and they want to run me out of town."

The Roughriders continued their dominance of the Stampeders in the final, winning 27–17. Durant was good on 18 of 25 passes for 204 yards and three touchdowns. The victory was sweeter because the Riders had deprived the Stampeders of the opportunity to defend their 2008 title at home.

Saskatchewan's opponent at McMahon was the Montréal Alouettes who had beat Saskatchewan twice during the season. The Als dominated the East with a record of 15–3. This was their seventh Grey Cup appearance during the decade, all losses but one.

The dynamic duo of quarterback Anthony Calvillo and receiver Ben Cahoon were at the top of their game. Statistically, Les Larks led the league in both offence and defence. Four of the six league awards went to the Alouettes, including Most Outstanding Player, won by Calvillo. John Chick won for defence. Montréal was the prohibitive favourite to win the 96th Grey Cup before a crowd that was over 90 percent cheering for Saskatchewan.

Confounding the experts, the Roughriders didn't let them down, marching to Montréal's 35- and 33-yard lines on their first possessions. Congi missed the first field goal and made the second.

The teams exchanged punts. Montréal scrimmaged at their 25 when Marcus Adams forced Calvillo to fumble. It was returned 11 yards by Keith Shologan. First-and-goal at the eight, Durant found Andy Fantuz in the end zone for a touchdown. At the end of the first 15 minutes, it was Saskatchewan 10, Montréal 0.

The Alouettes opened second-quarter scoring with a 28-yard field goal. They drove deep into Rider territory soon after. Calvillo found Kerry Carter at the Rider 17, but middle linebacker Renauld Williams knocked the ball loose, recovered by Chris McKenzie.

Near the end of the half, Damon Duval shanked a seven-yard punt out of bounds at his 44. Three plays later, Congi kicked a 45-yard field goal and then scored a single on the kickoff. Saskatchewan got the ball back with 1:01 on the clock at their own 46. It was Cates for five, Durant to Fantuz for 10 and Gerran Walker for eight. Durant ran for 11. Fantuz made an acrobatic catch at the Montréal two. With two seconds left, Congi nailed a nine-yard field goal. Halftime score, Saskatchewan 17, Montréal 3.

The Als began their comeback with a nine-play, 74-yard drive culminating in a Calvillo to Jamal Richardson touchdown at 7:01 of the third quarter. Six minutes later, Durant was intercepted deep in Als territory by Billy Parker. The defence forced Montréal to punt from their own end zone. The Riders took advantage to record a 23-yard field goal. At the end of 45 minutes, Saskatchewan led 20–10.

Montréal recorded a single when Duval missed a 51-yard field goal early in the final quarter. Starting at his 35, Durant threw to Fantuz for 11. Cates picked up 17 yards. Gerran Walker ran for 18, Cates for 19, bringing the ball to the enemy 10, from where Durant ran into the end zone. With 10 minutes and 52 seconds left, Saskatchewan was in control, leading 27–11.

The never-say-die Alouettes roared back with a six-play 71-yard drive for a TD scored by Avon Cobourne. The two-point conversion was good.

On second down at his 33-yard line, Durant threw an interception. Montréal went 85 yards in eight plays for another Richardson touchdown.

Saskatchewan went three and out on their last possession. Starting at their 34, Montréal moved to the Rider 36-yard line. With no time left, Duval attempted a 43-yard field goal. It was wide. But wait! Saskatchewan was penalized for having too many men on the field. Ten yards closer, Duval lined up again. As the ball sailed through the uprights, all the wind was sucked out of the stadium and there was an eerie silence. More than 40,000 Roughrider fans sat stunned in their seats, and then seconds later, they quietly filed out to the parking lots.

Montréal 28, Saskatchewan 27.

Except for muffled sobs and a few players throwing up, the Roughrider dressing room was like a morgue. Coach Ken Miller wandered out into the night in a daze beside the clubhouse door. A few minutes later, he said, "We had 13 men on the field. We had a lack of communication. We had what we call a beef block go on the field. One of the men who should have run off, stayed on.

"We made a critical error and permitted them to win. I'm just so disappointed by the loss. It will affect each one of us as long as we're on the planet. We should have won the football game."

The following spring, Miller said, "There isn't a man who was part of that team who would ever want to experience that day after again. Coming back here, walking across the field to greet our fans empty-handed after such a terrible loss. For those of us who were involved, it compares to losing a job or you've had a relationship that failed, something like that. When you think about it, it's always with you."

Special teams coach Kavis Reed took responsibility for the error and accepted that his coaching days in Saskatchewan were over. But it wasn't his fault. Nobody owned up to the error, letting a fine man and coach take the fall. But there seems little doubt that the culprit was linebacker Sean Lucas. It doesn't really matter.

The fact is, Saskatchewan blew a 16-point lead in 10 minutes. If Duval had made the first attempt, the game would have been remembered as an epic comeback engineered by a great quarterback.

Compared to other gridiron disasters, Saskatchewan fans got over the 13th man rather quickly and looked forward to the upcoming season.

In 2010, during the 100th birthday of the storied franchise, every game was a sell-out. With Durant and the Canadian air force of Andy Fantuz, Chris Getzlaf and Rob Bagg, and North Dakotan Weston Dressler, the Roughriders were entertaining and competitive, even though they lost John Chick, Stevie Baggs and Renauld Williams to the NFL. Three-time All-Canadian Eddie Davis retired.

Six-time division and CFL all-star Barrin Simpson and All-Canadian O-lineman Dan Goodspeed came over from Winnipeg. Also joining the team from the Bombers was Doug Berry as offensive coordinator.

There were plenty of fireworks at Mosaic Stadium on Canada Day when Saskatchewan defeated Montréal 54–51 in overtime. Fantuz and Dressler caught TD passes in OT. Durant threw for 478 yards and five majors.

The Green and White followed that up with wins over BC and Edmonton before dropping a 40–20 decision in Calgary. At the halfway mark, they were 6–3, in second place, four points behind Calgary. Darian Durant led the league in passing.

From then on, Calgary was 5–4, Saskatchewan 4–5, losses in four of their last five games. BC came to Regina for the semifinal on a roll. To make matters worse, Luca Congi was injured during the October 17 loss to the Stampeders.

It was a shoot-out with the teams matching score for score. After regulation time, they were tied at 27.

First Cates tallied a touchdown in overtime, then BC quarterback Travis Lulay. In the second overtime period, Paul McCallum put the Lions in front with a field goal. Darian Durant responded with a pass to former Leo Jason Clermont in the end zone for the winning score. Saskatchewan 41, BC 38.

Although Calgary won the season series with the Riders, the Green and White always felt comfortable playing in Calgary, which they considered their home away from home. They also knew Henry Burris had never won a playoff game against them. The Western final was no different.

Usually, Calgary–Saskatchewan games were shoot-outs. Not this time. Calgary jumped into an 11–0 lead at the end of the opening quarter. Durant responded with TD passes to Chris Getzlaf and Cary Koch.

Calgary moved ahead in the third quarter on a single and field goal. Then Saskatchewan engineered a 75-yard drive for a major scored on a four-yard run by Wes Gates. The 11-play drive took nearly 10 minutes off the clock. The Stamps picked up a single, making the final score, Saskatchewan 20, Calgary 16.

The Roughriders were in their third Grey Cup in four years, this time in Edmonton.

The Alouettes once again dominated the East, finishing first at 12–6 and demolishing Toronto 48–17 in the division final. They didn't win any awards. Andy Fantuz was honoured as Outstanding Canadian. Calgary's Henry Burris beat out Anthony Calvillo for the Most Outstanding Player Award and the All-Canadian quarterback position.

The 2010 Grey Cup was a plodding affair on a cold day. Montréal scrimmaged on the Rider 38 on their second possession because of a no-yards penalty.

Calvillo surprised everyone by running for eight yards. Avon Cobourne carried for 13, and Jamal Richardson took a 15-yard pass to the two. Cobourne scored, Montréal 7, Saskatchewan 0. Wes Cates concluded an eight-play, 75-yard drive with a one-yard plunge for the TD. Montréal got a single and led 8–7 at the end of the first quarter. The Riders added a field goal in the second stanza, giving them an 11–8 lead at the half.

After the break, the often-gambling Ken Miller retreated into a conservative shell while the usually conservative Alouette coach Marc Trestman gambled. In addition, the great Calvillo staged a quarterbacking clinic, relieving the pass rush pressure with short stuff.

Saskatchewan took the kickoff to start the second half and moved to the Als 38. They punted, rather than letting rookie Warren Kean try a field goal. Starting at the 12, the Als picked up a first down to the 33 and eight yards more. On third and two, Trestman called for a fake and blocker Eric Deslauriers ran for a first down at the 51. When the drive stalled at the Saskatchewan 15, Damon Duval tied the game with a field goal.

Montréal went ahead with another three pointer at 1:37 of the final frame before adding a Cobourne touchdown to lead 21–11 halfway through the fourth quarter. Four minutes later, Saskatchewan benefitted from a no-yards call and started their drive at the Montréal 32. Durant threw to Fantuz at the one. He then found right guard/tight end Marc Parenteau in the end zone for the score. With three minutes left, Saskatchewan trailed 21–18.

Calvillo took his team from his 40-yard line to the Rider 33, where Duval missed a 40-yard field-goal try, and Weston Dressler ran it out. But that was it. Durant threw a desperation pass at his 25 that was intercepted. The final, Montréal 21, Saskatchewan 18.

Four times the Riders had a yard or two for a first down and elected to punt. Twice they punted rather than have their punter Eddie Johnson try a field goal. During the regular season, Dressler had picked up 323 receiving yards against Montréal. In the Grey Cup, he was two for 11 yards, and they never called his number in the second half. Darian Durant was the leading quarterback rusher in the league yet he ran but once for eight yards.

Although the Alouettes were the better team, once again the Rider Nation believed they lost a Grey Cup they should have won. They placed the blame on offensive coordinator Doug Berry. During the offseason, Berry was fired.

Ken Miller became vice-president of football operations and hired veteran defensive coach Greg Marshall to succeed him. Andy Fantuz left for the NFL, Omarr Morgan retired, and receiver Rob Bagg and defensive end Brent Hawkins were lost for the year with injuries in preseason.

After Stumbling out of the starting gate in 2011, when the team was 1–7, Marshall was fired and replaced by Miller. They won four more games, finishing last, 12 points out of third place. Soon after, Miller announced his retirement.

Once again, lightning hit the outhouse.

On December 15, 2011, Saskatchewan general manager Brendan Taman announced that 34-year-old Cory Chamblin would be the Roughriders 29th head coach. Chamblin, a native of Birmingham, Alabama, came to the CFL in 2007 as a defensive backs coach for the Winnipeg Blue Bombers who lost the Grey Cup that year to the Roughriders. In 2008, Chamblin won the Grey Cup as the defensive backs coach of the Calgary Stampeders. He spent the 2010 and 2011 seasons as the defensive coordinator of the Hamilton Tiger-Cats. Chamblin is one of the new breed of bright young coaches in the CFL, including Kavis Reed in Edmonton, Paul LaPolice in Winnipeg and Scott Milanovich with the Argos.

Coach Chamblin wasn't exactly inheriting the *Titanic*. The 2011 Roughriders were much better than their 5–13 record indicated. Needing to rebuild the offensive line after the retirement of 17-year veteran Gene Makowsky, Rider general manager Brendan Taman signed Weyburn native and former Winnipeg All-Canadian free-agent guard Brendon Labatte and Noel Picard, formerly with the Argos. Several players were signed to replace defecting receivers Corey Koch and Andy Fantuz. Quarterback Darian Durant is an outstanding quarterback. The defence will be tough. With hard work, a little luck and a prayer, Chamblin should be able to bring the Saskatchewan Roughriders back to the Promised Land.

Notes on Sources

Canadian Football Hall of Fame. www.cfhof.ca

Canadian Football League: Facts, Figures and Records. Canadian Football League Publication, 2011.

Kelly, Graham. *The Grey Cup: A History.* Calgary: Johnson Gorman, 1999.

Kelly, Graham. *Green Grit: The Story of the Saskatchewan Roughriders.* Toronto: HarperCollins, 2001.

Kelly, Graham. *Grey Cup Glory.* Calgary: Johnson Gorman, 2003.

Kelly, Graham. *Greatest Grey Cups: The Best of Canadian Football.* Canmore: Altitude Publishing, 2005.

Kelly, Graham. *Go Stamps Go: The Story of the Calgary Stampeders.* Calgary: Panorama Press, 2010.

Regina Leader-Post, various editions, 1909–2011.

Saskatchewan Roughrider Media Guide, 1976–2011.

Saskatchewan Sports Hall of Fame. www.sshfm.com

Walker, Gordon. *Grey Cup Tradition.* Toronto: ESP Marketing and Communication, 1987.

Graham Kelly

GRAHAM KELLY has covered 37 Grey Cups in a career that landed him in the Canadian Football Hall of Fame's media section. The author of *The Grey Cup History* and *Greatest Grey Cups*, Graham was the Roughrider waterboy in 1956–57. He covered the Riders for United Press International from 1963 to 1968 and has covered the CFL for the *Medicine Hat News* since 1972.